NORTH OF SAN FRANCISCO
is the creation of more than fifty Northern California
writers, artists, and photographers,
who were inspired to produce this book by the beauty
of the natural environment, which sets the pace of life
in the Redwood Empire.

We want to share these things with you:
the sound of a moody blue ocean crashing onto the
jagged cliffs of our coastline,
the tranquil vineyards,
and the majestic redwoods.

*To my parents, Carl and Florence, my sister Jane,
and my brothers Charles, Deane, and Jimmy; and
to their families. On this page we are all one.*
    *And to the forests, wildlife, and rural farmland
of Michigan. Long walks through these areas laid
the foundation for this book many years ago.*

NOTE: Pages 6-17, 23-29, 35-47, 51-55, 60-67, 75-79, 88-100
106-107, 114-124, 134-144, 146-161, 173-185, 198-211, and
215-217 are paid features. Before qualifying for these sections
the individual restaurants and lodging facilities must pass the
stringent criteria laid down by the author Robert W. Matson.
Quality always comes before personal profit; in that way the
consumer is assured of a top notch guide book to the finest
restaurants and lodging facilities North of San Francisco.

All listings in the various sections of this book were triple cross-checked for
accuracy; however, the Publishers cannot guarantee the compliers' correctness
of the information furnished them, or the absence of errors. Prices mentioned
in the writeups are subject to change due to fluctuations in the economy and
management. Operating hours are also subject to change, especially on a
seasonal basis in rural areas.

"To everything there is a season
and a time to every purpose under
the heaven . . . "

Ecclesiastes 3:1

This Cross can be seen on Mount Saint Helena
just off Lake County Highway where it overlooks
the beautiful Napa Valley.

North of San Francisco Foreword

It was not an easy task for the first Pioneers to break trail for the thousands that would follow. Scout, trapper, explorer, priest, often out of fear or hunger, forced themselves to the tops of the distant ridgelines. It was the natural beauty and abundance they found in the Pacific Northwest that made their journey worthwhile.

Imagine Captain John Fremont and his men marching through the Napa Valley in the 1800's, when the grizzly and cougar were abundant and great plumes of steam from The Geysers and mineral baths could be seen for miles around. And imagine one evening, topping the craggy peaks surrounding the Valley of the Moon, and by full moonlight, viewing a huge ocean of wild oats standing higher than a man, waving in the breeze, where Santa Rosa now lies. Moving Westward these Pioneers came face to face with the giant redwoods, trees larger than imagination, silently guarding the coast. "Ambassadors from the past," as John Steinbeck called them. Herds of elk numbering in the thousands raced up the hills, and the distant roar of the Pacific Ocean, "peaceful waters," as the native Indians called it, echoed in the air. Fremont and his men must have had a look in their eyes the day they first saw the Western sky meet the Pacific and felt the salt air and mist against their weathered faces. They had crossed the continent. Memories of two thousand miles were etched in their minds. Their buckskin clothes were as full of patches as their bodies were with scars. These unsung heroes had become as wild and rugged as the land they stood on. It would be some of these same men who would stage the Bear Flag Revolt in July of 1846, poising California on the threshold of a new era. Where do such men as these come from? What they had accomplished and what they had seen will remain forever out of our grasp. There are no new wilderness frontiers in this country — theirs was among the last. But what they discovered is now ours to love, cherish and learn from.

Fortunately, a few landmarks that were built by these Pioneers have been preserved. Mission San Francisco Solano, California's most northerly mission; General Vallejo's home, as well as the Old Adobe Rancho that he built near Petaluma; the Fort Ross Chapel, where a Russian Princess once lived; the Old Bale Mill, north of Saint Helena;

MOUNTAIN MAN

The North Coast is a wild coast.

Silverek

Colonel Haraszthy's Buena Vista Winery; Washoe House, the oldest roadhouse in the state; and the more contemporary landmarks such as the ruins of Jack London's Wolf House at Glen Ellen; and Luther Burbank's home in Santa Rosa.

Not all of the history is as clearly labeled as Fort Ross or General Vallejo's Old Adobe, but fog-wreathed souvenirs of the past can be spotted all the way to the Oregon border, from the red brick houses of Cloverdale to the gingerbread-embellished Carson Mansion in Eureka. Much of the town of Mendocino is now a living museum and Anderson Valley still appears to be held together with split rail fences.

You'll spot occasional hop kilns (although the industry that spawned them has gone), old barns (including an occasional round one) and redwood stumps so huge it's hard to imagine how the trees that topped them were ever felled with primitive saws and dragged out of the forests with the help of teams of oxen.

There are local museums such as the Mendocino County Museum in Willits, with its year-round schedule of such special events as quilt shows and a growing permanent collection.

Floods and fires have left their marks on the land North of San Francisco. Along the Navarro, on Highway 128, for instance, a sign marks where the high waters came in the winter of 1964. Second growth covers scars of natural disasters and over-zealous lumber cuts. In skyscraping groves of redwoods, though, it's easy to feel that nothing has changed since before the time of Christ.

There is much natural beauty here. In the winter you can see the storm surf and feel the driving gale at Bodega Head or Point Reyes, or stand amid giant

California has a great historical treasure in its barns. Enter an old barn, like this one near Windsor, Sonoma County, and California's rural past fills your being

Striking, controversial and temporal — Cristo's Fence.

Redwoods as the cool Pacific fog rolls in and blocks out the sun. Drive to the top of a rise and see how beautifully this portion of the earth was sculptured by the wind and rain. Reach down and touch the land Burbank referred to as "the chosen spot of all the earth as far as nature is concerned." The land where *Treasure Island* author, Robert Louis Stevenson, "first waded deep into the waters of life..." It was here that the newsboy, oyster pirate, hobo, and Klondike adventurer, Jack London, wrote and bridged the gap in American Literature between Mark Twain and Hemingway. And it is here that you'll find one of the most beautiful shows on Earth.

Our maps point out the more popular roads and then some. If you are a serious camper or hiker, may we suggest automobile clubs, Chambers of Commerce, or back packing stores as sources for more detailed maps of the area. For the explorer who wants to escape all — there are no maps, but watch out for Bigfoot, the legendary half man, half beast of the Pacific Northwest.

In his book, *The Backroads of California*, Earl Thollander states, "I rediscovered the pleasure of driving. It had nothing to do with haste, and everything to do with taking time to perceive, with full consciousness, the earth's everchanging colors, designs, and patterns. The most satisfying roads and byways followed the contour of the land."

You'll find one of the richest histories in the Pacific Northwest. But there is another kind of history where every individual becomes important. Ray Raphael writes about it in his book, *An Everyday History of Somewhere*, which focuses on the past and present life in the coastal region of Northern California. The point of Mr. Raphael's books is "to show how anyone can add new dimensions to their awareness of their immediate world by finding out its everyday history. The method is simple; talk with old-timers nearby; find out how the Pioneers and Indians used to live off the land," (you'll also find out how much horse-sense saved time and money in those days), "look through old newspapers and as you begin to get the picture of how other folks and other living beings have related to your home environment, you'll probably feel your own life in a new perspective. Each of us is another small chapter in the everyday history of the world...

It can be exciting when you find out what happened in your own backyard a hundred years ago; or while walking an old creek bed and stumbling across an arrowhead or old bottle. But there are more than arrowheads and old bottles in these hills. It is rumored that Black Bart's booty lies near Calistoga, a wealth of old coins is buried near Yountville, and a fortune in Spanish Gold was lost at Point Reyes.

More important is the God-given-treasure to be found in the natural environment North of San Francisco. Occasionally you'll be lucky enough to see a flash of unbearable beauty. It is after these experiences that our hearts become a little wilder and our souls a little stronger. The wilderness can bring out our better qualities — if we let it.

Remember . . . adventure is not in the guide book and beauty is not on the map . . . it lies within us . . . especially when we reach out and touch those we love amid nature's splendor.

Robert W. Matson

At one with nature, he soars with the gulls.

Silverek

Drawing by John Wielan

Table Of Contents

DIRECTIONS ON HOW TO FIND YOUR FAVORITE RESTAURANT, LODGING FACILITY, OR WINERY ARE ON PAGE 244.

Come as you are— HUNGRY!

Dining out affords one of lifes more rewarding experiences and the memory of a special dining experience lingers long indeed . . . .

One of the most vivid pleasures of dining out in the Redwood Empire is that whereever you eat, no matter how fine the food, you can depend on an atmosphere of casualness. There are no city flares; no big bright neon signs, and no elevators to the 54th floor for a "breathtaking view of the city."

On the pages of North of San Francisco you will find the best restaurants that exist in each particular region from Point Reyes to the Oregon Border. I review each restaurant anonymously to screen the food and service. If I think I have been recognized then I merely send someone else in to find out what I need to know. If the food is above average I begin my inspections. Each restaurant or country inn has been screened for the following:

1st. Quality and imaginativeness of the food the chef and staff prepare.

2nd. Freshness of produce (vegetables, fruits, herbs and seasonings), cuts of meat and freshness of fish.

3rd. Cleanliness of the kitchen. I personally inspect the cookware, ovens, walk-ins, and storage areas of each kitchen - if I am not allowed to do so then the restaurant is automatically excluded from major coverage in North of San Francisco (this has only happened twice so far). Ironically, I have found that the best food in Northern California does not come from the most immaculate kitchens.

4th. Table setting. Are the glasses and silverware spotless? Are the plates, serving dishes, napkins, placemats, and table cloths clean? Is the table set with candles and fresh flowers?

5th. The wine list and quality of the well drinks.

6th. Service. I personally will not tolerate arrogance or snobbish service. I feel anyone who patronizes a restaurant should receive friendly and supportive service. Let me say, however, that dining out in even the most modest of restaurants should be accompanied by courtesy and "bon vivance." Please let the proprietor, maitre d' hotel, captain, waitress or waitor and even the bus boy know that you are glad to be in their restaurant and that you are counting on them to deliver just one thing - an enjoyable dining experience. If you had a divine dinner and really want to make a hit, then send the chef a note telling he or she how much you enjoyed your meal. With a smile and a few comments of understanding; praise when due, you will be be almost certain to inspire superlative performance from those who are already anxious to serve you. And leave at least a 15% tip.

7th. Decor. Did they build a cement slab or thoughtfully restore an old Victorian? Is there a no smoking section that keeps the smoke out? Can you hear those obnoxious bar dice cracking against the counter? Are antiques, stained glass windows, plants, and comfortable sofas used or are the furnishings reincarnated flex-flab plastic tables and chairs? Originality and respect for the land and natural environment are a top priority in my book.

The Blue Heron Inn is one of those special little restaurants where a lot of people and a lot of love got together to create gourmet cooking in a rustic setting. This photograph was taken by Point Reyes photographer Art Rogers, who in the tradition of Edward S. Curtis, who documented the disappearance of the American Indaan from 1900 to 1930, is documenting the dissappearance of the family owned ranch. According to Art, four generations were often raised in the same ranch house. Like the native American Indian, when the ranching families are displaced and the ranch house disappears - thats it! The American cowboy, small farmer, independent trucker, and yes, even the small winery and small family owned restaurant are on the American Lifestyle Endangered Species List and will vanish unless something is done to prevent it. Art Rogers's sensitive portraits have been published natinnally. If you'd like to find out more about the "Dissappearing Family Owned Ranch," you can write Art Rogers at: The Old Western Building, Main Street, Point Reyes, California, 94956.

Rather than write something nit-picky about a restaurant not up to my standards and devistate them, I choose to ignore them totally. Consequently all restaurants listed in the index have been carefully screened and serve above average food for the given geographical area they are located in. I do not pretend to be a "Gourmet God." I make my share of mistakes, but if I feel a restaurant owner or manager or employee is playing games with my palate or pocketbook - they are going to know about it. Either that, or they will receive no coverage or minimal coverage in this book. Competition is keen as new restaurants open and more experienced chefs enter the Northern California arena, consequently the lists will change each year. Change is the rule rather than the exception in Northern California.

The food served in this region is largely inspired by the rich farmland, vineyards, and abundance the Pacific Ocean has to offer. The Northern California legends, rugged mountains, crashing surf, and mist shrouded redwoods tend to heighten the appetite.

I have attempted to let the reader know what to expect from each of the restaurants herein as for location, type of food, credit, points of interest or historicla preservation, and prices and hours, which off course are subject to change due to fluctuations in the economy and management. Operating hours are also subject to change on a seasonal basis especially in rural areas. I welcome your feedback. You can write me at North of San Francisco, Box G, Santa Rosa, California 95402. I have confidence that this book will make your dining experience more enjoyable and I sincereiy hope you have that special experience in Northern California that you are looking for!

". . .I firmly believe from all that I have seen that this is the chosen spot of all the Earth as far as nature is concerned. The climate is perfect...the air is so sweet that it is a pleasure to drink it in...the sunshine is pure and soft; the mountains which gird the Valley are lovely. The Valley is covered with majestic oaks placed as no human hand could arrange them for beauty...great rose-trees climb over the houses, loaded with every color of blossoms...I almost have to cry for joy when I look at the lovely panorama from the hillside..."

Luther Burbank, 1875

Burbank and Edison

Santa Rosa - the Chosen Spot?

by Harvey Hansen

Santa Rosa, at first glance, appears to be a typical California city which grew from a Spanish Rancho to an expanding American metropolis. In this fabled scenic valley a unique historical identity was carved out by names like the Fort Ross Russians, General Mariano Vallejo, the Bear Flaggers, Luther Burbank, the Fountain Grove Utopians, pianist Paderewski, to the contemporary comic strip "Peanuts" by artist Charles Schulz. The first town fathers stole the county seat from neighboring Sonoma and Santa Rosa started a history that is both romantic and rugged.

Santa Rosa developed in the center of a broad valley that stretches from San Francisco Bay to the Russian River. With the Russians settling on the north coast in 1812 this valley became the crossroads of a strategic frontier. To prevent the threat of further Russian expansion the Spanish

extended their chain of missions northward, and in 1833 the Mexican Government sent General Mariano Vallejo to Sonoma County for purposes of colonization. Senora Carillo, his mother-in-law, founded Rancho Cabeza de Santa Rosa, the first permanent settlement in the area.

The arrival of American settlers in the area, and the ensuing Bear Flag Revolt of 1846, turned Santa Rosa into an American trading post which became a surveyed village seven years later. The town fathers maneuvered a special election in 1854 which moved the county seat from Sonoma. Legend tells of a midnight ride with a galloping team that successfully stole court records from Sonoma and delivered them to Santa Rosa, a move intended to block any legal objections from Sonoma. Santa Rosans celebrated with a two day barbecue and fiesta.

Demolished in seconds, Santa Rosa begins rebuilding within the hour.

On a dark and stormy night in 1854, Old Peg Leg Menefee stole the court house records from Sonoma and delivered them to the town fathers of Santa Rosa. This made Santa Rosa the new county seat and started a rugged and romantic history.

This home is typical of the many built in the late 1800's in Santa Rosa. Some still may be seen along MacDonald Avenue, Cherry Street, and Mendocino Avenue.

Luther Burbank arrived in 1875 and for more than 50 years he publicized the resources of the region. In his experimental gardens the "Plant Wisard" produced major variations on some three hundred and eighty-five plants. People like Henry Ford, Helen Keller, the King of Belgium, pianist Paderewski, and Thomas Alva Edison came to Santa Rosa to meet Burbank. By 1900 he was Sonoma County's most celebrated citizen. The local school children staged annual pageants honoring Burbank. Rose parades brought tourists to see the land of flowers and sunshine! Charles Schulz, the cartoonist, is today the most famous Santa Rosa resident.

Santa Rosa suffered severely from the great earthquake of 1906. Nevertheless, the town rebuilt and flourished as an agriculturally oriented town and county seat. With the opening of the Golden Gate Bridge in 1937 modern transportation linked the area more closely to San Francisco. During the second World War the entire area underwent another population boom, doubling in size between 1940 and 1960.

Today, with a population near seventy thousand, Santa Rosa is the largest California city north of San Francisco. It is the gateway to the Redwood Empire, the center of the North Bay Region. A famous wine country is adjacent, and the surrounding orchards show that agriculture is still a mainstay of the communities. Suburban dwellers and retirement settlers have also shown much enthusiasm for the Santa Rosa Valley. Many sites of historical interest can

Greg Gessaman

Winter rains produce this subtle beauty in Annadel State Park east of Santa Rosa.

be found in the Santa Rosa area. The old Carillo adobe is a crumbling, unmarked remnant. The Luther Burbank Gardens and the Church Built From One Tree, which now houses the Robert "Believe it or Not" Ripley Museum, are situated close to the downtown area. The chief historical attractions, however, are the beautiful old homes. MacDonald Avenue suggests an unparalleled example of nineteenth century architectural design. So beautiful is this avenue with its splendid homes that it has been used as a filming location in several motion pictures.

Just to the north of town is the site of Santa Rosa's utopian "love" colony, 1875-1934, on Fountain Grove Ranch, ...now shared with Hewlett Packard's

modern electronics plant. Local parks like Spring Lake, Annadel Farm, and Sugar Loaf State Park suggest today the spectacular, unspoiled beauty of the Santa Rosa area.

Santa Rosa, then, is a vest pocket history of the forces that have shaped the land called California. The City of Roses, today, is at a crossroads. Santa Rosa faces a different problem — population growth. It has been described as the fastest growing area in the San Francisco Bay Region. Though this crucial problem has not yet been resolved, more and more area residents are concerning themselves in the effort to retain the beauty and unique historical identity which belongs to Santa Rosa.

ROSIE'S

On a sunny day, in the morning, when you walk in the front door of Rosie's, your eyes catch the spectrum of colors that dance against the beamed ceilings as the morning sun turns the huge stained glass window into fire.

This Rosie's, like Rosie's Cantina in Cotati, is usually packed. Three young owners (Rick Martin, Glenn Stocki, & Mathew Freeman) and a dedicated family of employee's have turned Rosie's into a delightful success story. The prices are right, the portions generous, and the Mexican food very good. The same basic menu is used at both locations (see page 66), except here an additoonal selection of Comida Especiales is offered. You can choose between Camarones Picado (prawns sauteed in a traditional Mexican Picado sauce, served with green salad & a flour tortilla), Steak Picado, or the Hacienda Dinner (a 7oz top sirloin steak and your choice of a taco, chile relleno, or enchilada). Your entree includes Mexican rice & refried beans ($7.95 - $8.95). Delicious drinks, appetizers, & desserts are served as well as California wines. At both locations beautiful murals created by Santa Rosa artist John Boskovich grace the walls. The wooden pillars, beamed ceilings, hanging ivy, weavings, and iron work blend with the charming staff to create a total dining experience.

ROSIE'S   610 3rd Street on Cinema
Mexican   Square, Santa Rosa, Ca.
(See page 66 for hours)

Full Bar, Beer & Wine. AE, CB,
MC, Visa (707) 523-2110
Entertainment on weekends.

JOE FROGGER

Joe Frogger Restaurant and Bar consistently offers fresh country food, attentive service, a charming atmosphere and a complete assortment of mixed drinks. To top that all off, its the only restaurant in Northern California where you can hear live Bluegrass Music nightly.

The restaurant is named after Joe Frogger, a legendary humanitarian who used to live in Cape Cod. Special luncheons and dinners are created each day from farm fresh produce, daily caught fresh catch, local mushrooms, Sonoma raised escargot, stock pot soups, Bay Shrimp and always fresh cheeses and fruits. Luncheons are $1.75 - $5.25 with dinners between $6.50 & $11.75. The well drinks are blended from fresh juices; rich dairy cream is whipped for Irish Coffee and according to owner Chet van Borst, "the Lizzie Lee Party Bowl does it all."

If you're aiming to be pleased, set your sights on Joe Frogger.

JOE FROGGER
Farm Fresh Dinners
527 4th Street, Santa Rosa
Lunch: 11am - 2:30pm Mon-Sat

Dinner: 5pm - 10pm Mon-Sat
Full Bar & Wine List and live
Bluegrass Music nightly.
AE, MC, Visa (707) 526-0539 Res.

LA FONTANA

Tony and Angelina Prendusi own and operate the La Fontana restaurant along with their two children Leonard and Teresa. Tony came to the U.S. from Italy in 1959. Their beautiful Italian restaurant is located amidst the Old Courthouse Square in Santa Rosa. The restaurant first opened 16 years ago and has consistently kept pace with the growth of Santa Rosa. In 1979 the La Fontana was completely remodled. Today you can dine surrounded by beautiful oil & acrylic murals in the plush confines of the main dining room or during Summer in the glassed in Garden Court amid a jungle of flowers & plants & the fountain.

The English translation of La Fontana is "the fountain". Tony has named his restaurant after the unique white marble fountain which is an important part of the decor at his restaurant. It was made in Florence and was originally located on the famous Plaza Vekio.

The La Fontana is open everyday and offers a complete menu of authentic Italian food including 10 Veal entrees such as Veal Picatta, Saltimbocca a la Romana, Saltimbocca a La Fontana (in a Brandy Sauce), 15 Pastas such as homemade Canneloni & Lasgna, 6 Chicken dishes & 5 selections from the sea. In addition Prime Rib (Sat & Sun), Filet Mignon, New York Steak, and Chateaubriand (for two) is served. Complete dinners include soup or salad, sourdough bread, and start from $6.50. Luncheons are also served Monday - Friday. You can also enjoy the Caesar Salad, Crab Louie, Shrimp Louie or Flaming Desserts (Cherries Jubilee & Peach Flambe) which Tony takes pride in serving at your table.

California & Imported wines are available as well as soft drinks, coffee expresso, cappucino and mixed drinks from the classy Italian lounge. After dinner you can listen or dance to live music. A visit to La Fontana and you'll understand why celebrities and noted political figures choose this peaceful setting to dine in.

LA FONTANA
Italian Cuisine
19 Old Courthouse Square, Santa Rosa
Lunch - Mon - Fri 11:30am - 2:30pm

Dinner - Wk Days 5 - 10pm, Saturday
from 5 - 11pm & Sunday 4 - 10pm.
Full Bar & Wine List.   MC, Visa
(707) 545-4797 Reservations advised

MARSHALL HOUSE

"When our country was two hundred years old - the Marshall House was one hundred years old," stated Harriet Watson the gracious owner of this elegant Victorian mansion which she operates as a restaurant. The house was built in 1876 by James Marshall, a Californian pioneer. Throughout the late 19th and early 20th centuries the home was noted as a gathering place of prominent Santa Rosans. The Marshall House was maintained by the family until it was purchased by Harriet in 1963. And since Mrs. Watson purchased it directly from the family - all the original fixtures still remain in the house, providing quite a rare and exciting visual treat. It is an interior decorator's delight with ceramic fireplaces, stained glass, crystal chandeliers, embossed paneling from France, parquet floors, and numerous other unique furniture items.

The first floor now serves as a dining area where delicious luncheons are served. Meals include a souffle casserole style entree, salad, home made biscuits with apple-butter jam, and are topped off by a choice from seven scrumptious desserts. All the food is made fresh daily (including the desserts), from recipes not found elsewhere. The restaurant also caters for weddings and receptions.

Upstairs the rooms are filled with shops containing unique gift items such as: paintings by local artists, handmade dolls, antiques, and other craft items.

Without a luncheon at the Marshall House — a visit to Santa Rosa just isn't complete!

MARSHALL HOUSE
Luncheons
835 - 2nd Street, Santa Rosa
M-Sat. 11:30am-2:30pm
Wines
(707) 542-5305 Reservations advised

La PROVINCE

Located near the corner of College and Mendocino is a charming French restaurant called La Province. It used to be the popular Painted House, but when two successful French restaurateurs took it over, they renovated the old home, painted over the murals, and started serving excellent French cuisine - the best in Santa Rosa.

Dinner entrees start at $9.00.   Friendly waiters guide you expertly through dinner entrees like Aiguillette de Saumon (grilled salmon) $7.50, Crevettes Royales Farcies (stuffed prawns) $7.50, or Selle d'Agneau au Poivre - Vert (boneless saddle of lamb cooked in a crust with green pepper sauce) for two only, and other entree's.   The wine list features California wines and is nothing less than superb. I heartily recommend La Province for French dining pleasure.

LA PROVINCE
French Cuisine
521 College Ave., Santa Rosa

D - 5:30pm-10pm Mon - Sat
Wine
MC, Visa
(707) 526-6233 Reservations advised

MANDALA CAFE

The unique Mandala offers an array of gourmet natural food dinners. Oriental style booths and low tables beckon one to relax and enjoy the company of good friends.

Order a complete dinner and treat yourself to a choice of soups accompanied by home-baked french bread, a colorful salad, and your selection from the list of eleven entrees including: French quiche, Japanese tempura, Indian curry, plus nightly crepes and specials.

Luncheon fare includes omlettes, sandwiches, a variety of salads, home-made soups, and fresh juices. Exceptional desserts and Vienese coffee have won a reputation of their own. Featured on the wine list are selections from France and Germany as well as many Napa and Sonoma County offerings.

MANDALA CAFE
Natural & Seafood
620 - 5th Street, Santa Rosa

L - M-F 11:30am - 3pm
D nightly 5pm - 9:30pm
Beer & Wine
(707) 527-9797

ENGLISH ROSE PUB

During the famous Scotish Games, that take place annually in Santa Rosa, kilted bag pipers and their lassies come to drink good English brew and play their "bonnie tunes" at the English Rose Pub.

Owners, Don & Betty Carpenter, have made their pub, the English Rose, as authentic as possible. Hearty dishes of steak & kidney pie, London curry, cottage pie, fish & chips (normally served in a newspaper, but for your delight on a plate) and specials like roast beef & Yorkshire pudding, are served nightly. Dinners ($4.25 - $6.25) include choice of delicious homemade soup or a crisp salad. Homemade desserts like mincemeat tart and old English sherry trifle add to the pleasure of dining here. The low ceilings of a century old English Pub and thick London fog are abscent, but the English food, hearty libations, and good cheer more than make up.

ENGLISH ROSE PUB
Authentic English dinners
2074 Armory Drive, Santa Rosa
One block off Hwy 101 at the

Steele Lane/Coddingtown Exit
Dinners: 5pm-10pm Tues-Fri,
Sat 12pm-10pm
Excellent selection of English beer.
MC, Visa. (707) 544-7673

BREAD BOARD

You are traveling the main artery in Coastal Northern California - Hwy 101. Your culinary values dictate wholesome gourmet or vegetarian food, but that usually means a long wait. However, there is a place in Santa Rosa where you can enjoy a nutritional meal and be on your way within a ½ hour of being seated. It is called the Bread Board and is located scarcely a block west of busy Hwy 101 in the Coddingtown Shopping Center (take the Steele Lane Exit).

The low-key restaurant/cafeteria contains a long serving counter, salad bar, jucie bar, and coffee table. For breakfast its old fashioned buttermilk - egg waffles, poached eggs, rolls and cereals served with accompaniments. For lunch you may choose from delicious sandwiches (reg $.85 to $4.25) served with choice cuts of meat or vegetarian style, 2 - 3 homemade soups (hot & cold), and the salad bar. Homemade deserts, a variety of coffee's, tea, beer & wine as well as smoothies & fresh squeezed juices are available. Innovative changes are planned for the future, but most important of all- at the Bread Board you can have your cake and eat it too.

BREAD BOARD
Continental & Vegetarian
344 Coddingtown Shopping Center,
Santa Rosa - Hwy 101 & Steele Ln.

B - 7:30am-11am M-F, 8am-noon Sat & Sun
L - 10am - 9pm M-F, 10am-7pm Sat, 11am-5pm
on Sunday. Call for dinner hrs. Orders to go.
MC & Visa & (707) 545-6237

VILLA

The Villa rests upon a beautiful and secluded knoll overlooking Bennett Valley. It was recently redecorated by its five new owners, Mario Peric, Michele Chieffo, Bernardo Gaspare, Gianni Giacri, and Tino Tochetto; who by the way all work at the restaurant and have international expertise in restaurant service. The restaurant is a virtual showplace with lofty ceilings, natural wood archways, hanging plants, and huge glass windows which afford visitors a fantastic view of the city below - and the view of the full moon rising over the distant Valley of the Moon is breathtaking. According to Michele, "La Luna che sorgie nei colli della valle della Luna lascia meravigliati; E' stupefatti!"

Although the building is impressive it maintains a warmth rarely achieved by large restaurants; this is because of the bright plum and burnt orange decor, comfortable furnishings, and the friendliness of the waiters. Visitors are expertly served in the European style of dining.

The food is excellent. Popular dishes served at Lunch are: Deep Fried Calamari - $ 3.25, Fettucini Alfredo - $3.95, and Filet of Sole All'agro - $3.50; and at Dinner: Saltimbocca - $6.95, Lazy Man Cioppino - $8.25, Steamed Clams Bordelaise - $6.75, and Veal & Scampi All'agro - $9.25. Surprisingly, for a restaurant as elegant as the Villa, the menu's list a whopping 110 items priced from $3.25 - $5.50 (for lunch) and $5.00 - $13.50 (for dinner). All dinners include fresh vegetables and rice.

The Villa offers a wide selection of premium California wines as well as imported wines from France and the owners' native country of Italy. There is a complete bar with the makings for really fine drinks and live entertainment is offered Wednesday thru Saturday starting at 9:00pm. There is a beautiful dance floor too. Banquet facilities are also available for up to 80.

In the future an outdoor deck will be added that will jut out into the open air above Santa Rosa. It will be an ideal setting for Sunday Brunch or elegant evenings under the stars. With its expert service, cuisine, setting, and entertainment the Villa offers a thoroughly relaxing Brunch, Luncheon, or Dinner.

THE VILLA
Italian and Seafood
3901 Montgomery Drive, Santa Rosa

L - Tues-Fri 11:30am-3:00pm
D - Mon-Sun from 5:00pm
Sun Brunch: 11:00am-3:00pm

Full Bar, Live Entertainment, Dancing
AE, BA, MC
(707) 528,7755

CATTLEMEN'S

Enjoy the finest in steak dinners amidst the casual old West atmosphere of Cattlemens' restaurants. A variety of delicious steaks and seafoods are served at both Sonoma county locations. Dinners range in price from $4.95 to $11.95, complete with salad, hot sourdough French bread, and ranch style beans. When dining in Santa Rosa, be sure to ask your waiter about the Saddle and Sirloin special steak dinner which includes: baked potato, coffee, salad, and a glass of house wine, for only $5.95. Both Cattlemens' serve generous portions of lamb and barbecued ribs, as well as the huge Cattlemens' T-bone steak.

Banquet facilities are available for small or large affairs. The Petaluma Cattlemen's features entertainment Wednesday through Sunday in tis spacious and comfortable cocktail lounge.

If you are in the Sacramento area, be sure to visit the Dixon Cattlemens' at Hwy 80 and Currey Road, or the Roseville Cattlemens' on Hwy 80 at the Rocklin exit, and the new Cattlemens' on Hwy 395 between Reno and Carson City. There's plenty of free parking at all four Cattlemens' restaurants.

CATTLEMEN'S RESTAURANTS
Petaluma
Steak & Lobster
5012 Petaluma Blvd North
D from 5pm-10pm M-Th, Fri-Sat 5pm-11pm
Sun from 4pm - 10pm. Full Bar
(707) 763-4114 Res.

Santa Rosa
Steak & Lobster
2400 Midway Dr.
D from 5pm-10pm M-Th, Fri-Sat 5pm-11p
Sun 4pm-10pm. Full Bar
(707) 546-1446 Res advised wk ends.

FLAMINGO HOTEL AND RESORT

At the base of Montecito Heights in Santa Rosa; where the business district ends and the Sonoma Highway prepares itself for the slow and scenic wine country of the Valley of the Moon, lies the semi-tropical setting of the Flamingo Resort Hotel.

Since 1956 the Flamingo has been a favorite location for receptions, banquets, sales meetings, formal balls, and thousands of travelors from all over the country. There are banquet facilities for 10 to 600 guests and lodging in 140 newly remodeled units.

The culinary delights served in the Palm Room are just as tasteful as the gardens outside the glass walls that surround the dining area. Breakfast, lunch, and dinner isl leisurely served seven days a week, or if you prefer room service - just pick up the telephone in your room and dial.

A standard breakfast is served, but with fresh squeezed juices, fresh fruit, omelettes and grain cereals. Lunch is more interesting with items like cold poached salmon (in season), Boeuf bourguignon (classic French stew), Trout, grenabloise and Hungarian Gulash on the menu. In addition a large assortment of appetizer's, salads, potages, omelettes and a selection of international sandwiches are served. Luncheons are $3.95 - $5.95. For dinner there is a fine selection of seafood, fowl, beef, and veal entrees ($7.95 - $24.95 for two). You can compliment your dinner with a wide array of appetizer's, pasta, vegetables, salads, potages, and sauces. Entrees such as Steak Diane (with madeira sauce), Canard "Maxime" (Roast duck with peach and cognac sauce), Prime Rib, Tournados Rossini (beef filets topped with pate au fois gras), and Escalope de veau Oskar (Veal Oscar) are served. The wine list is excellent.

The Flamingo Resort Hotel means overall convenience to the businessman or or tourist. In the past entertainers like Burt Reynolds have performed there and major motion picture companies hang their hats there when filming Sonoma Counties beautiful scenery. With remodeling completed in 1979 you will find an exciting dance floor, 6 new tennis courts, a solar heated Olympic pool, shuffle boards, ping pong tables, and luxurious rooms and suites. Room rates are from $35.00 to $70.00 (suites). Call or stop in for information and reservations - the Flamingo Resort Hotel is a good place for you to "hang your hat too."

FLAMINGO RESORT HOTEL
International Cuisine
4th & Farmers Lane, Santa Rosa
(707) 545-8530 Reservations advised
AE, BA, CB, DC, MC, Visa

Dining Room Open:
Breakfast - 7:00am - 11:30am daily
Lunch - 11:30am - 3:00pm daily
Dinner - 5:30pm - 10:00pm daily
140 units, Banquet facilities, full bar.

3rd STREET STATION

If you are looking for a German Beer Garden then look no farther than 3rd Street Station in Santa Rosa's historic Railroad Square. Music from the Old Country plays in the background while hearty patrons drink ice cold glasses of Becks, Spaten, Dartmunder, and Dinkel Acker as well as other imported beers from around the world.

For lunch, sandwiches such as the ¼ lb Station Burger with German potato salad, Bratwurst or Knackwurst on a roll with grilled onions & kraut or German potato salad, Vegetarian Quiche, and delicious ¼ lb jumbo frankfurters marinated in beer are served ($1.50 - $3.50). Occassionally specials such as Sauerbraten (marinated pot roast of beef), Special German Meatloaf with Suppen (soup) and fresh vegetable, or German sausages with Bavarian Style Sauerkraut and pumpernickel are served ($3.50 - $5.00). Besides dessert specials and homemade pies baked on the premises, Gluhivein (Glow wine served hot) is offered at the descretion of the chef. If you are planning a special get-together or party the owners of 3rd Street Station will let you take over their restaurant on any Saturday or Sunday (10am-6pm) and serve you a delicious brunch or lunch to boot. (minimum 20 - two weeks advance notice. Objects d Art such as elegant brass & glass lamps and original art (which are for sale) add much color to the cozy interior of 3rd Street Station.

3RD STREET STATION   *L - Mon - Fri 11am - 3pm*
German & American   *German Brunch Sat & Sun 11am - 5pm*
200 Wilson at corner of 3rd Street, Santa Rosa   *Imported Beer and Wine, MC & Visa*
(707) 526-4089

SOURDOUGH REBO'S

Despite the owners. Pete Eierman's & Bob Rebo s, cornball sense of humor (I refer to their newspaper menu) Sourdough Rebo's cannot fail. Pete & Bob have spared nothing to create a rugged Klondike Gold Rush type atmosphere which heightens your appetite and reduces your pocketbook, but not by much, for they are "smart" and have vowed to turn "gold into fish".

At $6.95 an entree, which includes home-cooked sourdough bread, fruit or vegetable garnish (seasonal), Sourdough Rebo's special clam chowder (Rebo sez he'll serve "spinach salad to those greenhorns who don't like clam chowder") and brown rice pilaf, it's hard to go wrong. Dinner entrees include Pegleg Pete's Prawns, Poacher Pacific Red Snapper, Skoakum Jim Shrimp Scatter, Klondyke Kate Kebob, and Fugelsangs Fry. Luncheons are $3.95 - $4.50 including a beverage. No one has found a gold nugget in any of Sourdough Rebo's chow yet, but for $1.50 you can get a slice of mud pie or some bonanza. You can also come frolic with the Malmute Can Can dancers.

SOURDOUGH REBO'S   *D - 5pm - 10pm daily*
Seafood   *Full bar and banquet facilities (26)*
24 Fourth St., Santa Rosa   *AE, BA, MC, Visa*
L - 11:15am - 3pm Mon - Fri   *(707) 526-6400 Reservations advised*

OMELETTE EXPRESS

In Old Town Santa Rosa where main street (4th Street) empties into Railroad Square you'll find a cozy restaurant called the Omelette Express. You'll see Santa Rosan's and visitors constantly filing in and out daily from 7am - 8pm for (you guessed it) some of the greatest omelettes in Sonoma County and certainly the largest variety (over 300 combinations are possible).

Here is what you can expect: No. 5 sausage, zucchini, green chilies and jack cheese, No. 14 shrimp, cream cheese, avocado and sprouts, No. B jack, swiss, cheddar, american, and fontina cheeses and No. CC fresh fruit with sour cream and brown sugar. Omelette prices range from $1.85 - $4.15 In addition there are 1/3 lb. beef burgers ($1.75-$3.50) served 12 different ways, hot roast beef sandwiches, turkey, shrimp, Alaskan King Crab, ham and others ($1.89 - $3.50). Garden specialties from avocado to crab - the most popular being the garden salad cold plate (roast beef, turkey, ham, salami, cheese & tomatoes). Homemade soups, potato or bean salad, "side tracked" breakfast specials and desserts are also served. There is a large selection of beverages as well as domestic and imported beer and wine.

The interior of the restaurant has been carefully rennovated. Antique tables and chairs amid countless plants provide the atmosphere and a large hand painted mural tells the story of Railroad Square "way back when". Guitarists like local favorite John Brandenburg entertain Monday - Friday from 5pm - 8pm.

Now ya know why all those people are flocking to Old Town Santa Rosa? So "all aboard" the Omelette Express where the food and the prices are just right!

OMELETTE EXPRESS
Omelettes & Specialties
112 Fourth St., Santa Rosa
B - 7am-11am/Omelettes

L - 11am-8pm/Omelettes & Sandwiches
Beer and Wine
(707) 525-1690

GOLD COIN

The seven Wong brothers first entered into the restaurant business in 1958 when they began operating a small catering service in Berkeley. They are now the proud owners of two elegant Chinese restaurants which feature Cantonese style cooking. Guests may choose from over one hundred Chinese dishes. The food is a delicate blend of select ingredients and spices, many of which are unknown in the Western world, and are imported from distant lands, such as, Birds' Nest from Borneo, shark's fins from India and Mexico, black Mushrooms and cultivated seaweed from Japan, bamboo shoots, and fine teas from the jungles and plantations of Formosa, beche-de-mer from the waters of the Malay Penninsula.

Popular dinners served are: Peking Duck Dinner $8.50, Special Vegetarian Dinner $4.50, The Szechuan $4.25, Gold Coin House Dinner $7.25. The Gold Coin also features two Chinese Wines: "WuFu" which is made from a white grape, and has a pleasant taste which is not too sweet or dry but just right. This wine is made in Mainland China, shipped to France and then imported to New York. The other wine featured is "Shui Hing" the Chinese Rice wine. The restaurants also offer a complete list of Polynesian drinks to enjoy with your meal, for example: The Scorpion, a classic Hawiian drink which consists of a special blend of brandy and rum, complete with a floating gardenia, or try a Bo-Lo which is a mixture of rare Rums and exotic nectars served in a fresh pineapple.

Each dish at the Gold Coin Restaurants is individually prepared in the manner of an Occidental a la carte order, a method which preserves the high standards of Chinese culinary art. And in the unlikely event that something you would like is not on the menu the Chef will be glad to cook it for you. The Gold Coin Restaurants serve their delightful and delicious foods daily. While there ask about their "Take Out Menu", Chinese Luncheon Smorgette, and their special club card.

GOLD COIN RESTAURANT
Chinese Mandarin & American
2400 Mendocino Ave., Santa Rosa
L & D Sun-Thurs 11:30am-10pm, Fri & Sat
'till 11:30pm
Full Bar, Banquets, Catering, Ample Parking
AE, BA, MC
(707) 544-2622 Reservations advised

GOLD COIN RESTAURANT
Chinese Mandarin & American
7311 College View Dr., Rohnert Park
Thurs-Tues 4pm-midnight
Full Bar, Banquets, Catering,
Ample Parking
AE, BA, MC
(707) 795-7331 Reservations advised

BLACK FOREST INN

The Black Forest Inn is owned and operated by two families   highly experienced in the restaurant business. Klaus Scheftner, formerly Exec. Chef at the St. Francis Hotel before buying the Black Forest Inn, functions as host, while his partner, Rolf Rheinschmidt, formerly Exec. Chef of the S/S President Roosevelt is responsible for the cooking.

The quality of their food is superb and there is a meal for everyone's budget - choose from a special gourmet dinner to the thrifty and delicious Black Forest Special, only $4.95. Specialties of the house finished at table side include Roast Rack of Lamb, $10.95, or Steak Diane , $11.00.

Next time you wish to experience a gourmet German, American, or Continental meal, visit the Black Forest Restaurant & Cocktail Lounge. Catering and banquet facilities are also available.

BLACK FOREST INN　　　　*L M-F 11:30am-3pm, D Mon-*
American-German-Continental　*Sat from 5pm, Sun from 4pm*
138 Calistoga Rd., Santa Rosa　*AE, MC, Visa (707) 539-4334 Res.*

Don't be fooled by the commercial exterior, for inside the Garden of Eatin' you will be greeted by a warm smile, and delicious aromas intermingling through a small forest of plants. Morning sunshine through the sky lights and cordial service add to the pleasure of dining here.

Capable owner Tom Patterson opened the restaurant in 1979. His innovative ideas include adding picnic baskets full of gourmet goodies, premium wine and maps to local attractions for tourists destined to explore this part of the Redwood Empire. By Spring of 1980 he hopes to add an interesting selection of original dinner entrees accompanied by the relaxing music of a guitarist.

GARDEN OF EATIN

For breakfast expect fresh squeezed orange juice, fluffy omelettes, eggs served any style (with cottage fries, garden baked muffins, and fresh fruit garnish) and dig - a bottomless cup of coffee. Luncheon selections include a variety of hamburgers "made with the best beef money can buy", salads, homemade soup, and sandwiches. Eve's temptations include homemade seasonal desserts. To arrive take the Hwy 101 Bicentennial Exit and drive west down Piner Road. In no time at all you'll be seated in the Garden of Eatin.

GARDEN OF EATIN '　　*L - 11am - 3pm Mon - Fri*
Breakfast & Lunch　　*Open Sat 7am-4pm, Sun 9am-4pm*
1770 Piner Road, Santa Rosa.　*Beer & Wine, MC & Visa*
B - 6am - 3pm Mon - Fri　　*(707) 528-9878*

From the Geysers to the San Sebastian

CLOVERDALE

by Joseph H. Wherry

Early Photo of the Geysers.

Hansen Collection

Two hundred years ago the only inhabitants of the northern part of Sonoma County were the Pomo, the Yuki, and the Lassik Indian tribes. The most numerous were the Pomo whose hunting and gathering culture was shared by their neighbors.

Their pleasant redwood-forested homeland was rich with a variety of flora and fauna which helped make their lives rather leisurely. The women of the Pomo villages excelled in basket making, and today their baskets are highly prized by collectors and museums. Warfare was a rarity among the Indians of what is now Sonoma County; their quarrels generally were resolved without undue bloodshed.

When the American settlers arrived on the scene the pastoral life of the natives would never again be the same. One of the first was William Bill Elliott, a former Bear Flagger who settled in what later became Cloverdale. In 1847, while engaged in the pursuit of a grizzly bear, he found himself some seventeen miles over the hills to the southeast in a frightening place of great mystery.

Elliott was the first American settler to gaze upon The Geysers. Some accounts have him rushing into the Healdsburg area, while others say he ran into Cloverdale with the news that he had found "the gates of Hades." Cloverdale was rapidly becoming a wide place in the wilderness trail.

Just eight years later, in 1856, R.B. Markle and W.J. Miller bought eight hundred and fifty acres in Cloverdale township, and Levi Rosenberg organized the first store in the area. The same year F.G. Hahman and J.H. Hartman established a trading post on the Markle's land which lay astride the trail between Santa Rosa and Mendocino.

When the railroad was pushed northward the population influx began, and in 1872 Cloverdale was incorporated. The town's first trustees, according to J.P. Munro-Fraser in his *History of Sonoma County, California,* were Harry Kier, Amasa Morse, John Field, W.E. Crigler, and Theodore Harper.

Newspaper publishing began in 1872 with W.J. Bowman's *Review* which, before the decade was finished, was joined by the *Bee* and the *News.* The famous *Reveille* came along in 1879 under W.S. Walker, and outlived its competing forerunners. Churches were soon established, with the Catholics, Congregationals, and Methodists being among the first. The Masonic Order and the Odd Fellows were already lively fraternities and, in 1878, the United Workmen organized Lodge No. 32. The several scores of families were served by a public school built by J.A. Kleiser, and the water works were established in the same year that the town was officially founded.

Because of the township's importance as a stopover point on the stage route the Cloverdale Hotel and the United States Hotel were established in 1858 and '59 respectively. By 1875, the latter was a handsome, sprawling two story structure that was probably one of the finest hostelries north of San Francisco. After all, forty thousand genuine U.S. of A. dollars got a lot in those halcyon days, including a whopping thirty-eight by thirty-nine foot kitchen, a barber shop, and a leather-lined saloon with a big mirror over the polished hardwood bar.

Timber was the basis of the region's prosperity, supplemented by the raising of livestock. The woods were full of lumberjacks, and the redwood forests echoed with the snorts and whistles of the steam-powered donkey engines which powered the sawmills.

Meanwhile, over the hills—in fact, even before Cloverdale was organized —a gentleman named Godwin and his partner had caught the vision reflected in the condensing steam vapors above old Bill Elliott's "gates of Hades". The pungent fragrance of the fumarees and solfatares and a couple of the bubbling hot springs were developed into Northern California's first spa near the upward reaches of Big Sulfur Creek. Europe had spas, why shouldn't the Bear Flag State have 'em! By 1860, sightseers from Baghdad-by-the-Bay were puffing up Petaluma Creek aboard a tiny steamer, the Ranger, and thence were carried overland by coach and horseback to soak their horses and enjoy the delights of the Geysers Hotel.

If someone had told the folks of Sonoma County that Cloverdale would one day grow oranges and host an annual Citrus Fair, or that The Geysers would be the site of the world's largest geo-thermal electric power plant complex and play host to four hundred and eighty scientists meeting in the United Nations Symposium on the Development and Utilization of Geothermal Energy, the prophet would probably have been ridden out of town on a rail.

Why, even Ulysses S. Grant, Luther Burbank, and a host of the nation's elite who visited The Geysers would have hardly believed such nonsense. Everyone then, just as now, knew that citrus growing and natural steam fields in Northern California were just curiosities. Even so, the pioneers and the native Americans who preceded them knew a good thing or two when they saw them.

The End

U.S. Hotel — 1880.

HEALDSBURG

by Ed Langhart

The meandering Russian River, known as the San Sebastian by the Spanish and the Slavianka by the Russians, wound through several Mexican land grants, the largest being Rancho Sotoyome. Cyrus Alexander arrived here in 1841 as custodian of Rancho Sotoyome for Captain Henry D. Fitch. After his agreement with Fitch expired in 1845 he turned the management over to Moses Carson, a half-brother of the well-known Kit Carson. The next American to take up residence in the area was William March who, by written agreement with Captain Fitch, was to erect a mill to provide lumber for ranch improvements.

These few pioneers, the native Cainamero Indians, and a few Mexican families were the only inhabitants of the area when the first settlers began to arrive in 1848. Among these early settlers were the John Williams family, A.J. Gordon and his family, George Storey, Louis Legendre, W.T. Morrow, and Lindsay Carson.

Harmon Heald and his brothers, Tom and Samuel, were among those who arrived in 1849, and after a short season in the gold fields returned to the Russian River country to settle.

Tom and Samuel were employed by William March at the mill, while Harmon built a cabin on the site of the present-day plaza. In 1851 he added a lean-to which he stocked with goods procured from Sonoma and San Francisco. This enterprise proved so successful that the following year he built larger quarters which became the first general store and post office, known simply as "Heald's Store".

Other early pioneers included Harrison Barnes who opened a trading post on Eastside Road in 1851, and in later years became president of The Farmers and Mechanics Bank in Healdsburg. Another was Cornelius Bice who settled in 1853 on what is now the Lewis M. Norton property on Grove Street. It was here that his home and all his belongings were burned during the Squatters War in 1862. H.M. "Squire" Willson came to Healdsburg in 1853 and engaged in merchandising with Harmon Heald, and for eight years served as Justice of the Peace. Both men were county supervisors, with Heald going on to become an assemblyman from this district before he died in 1858. Captain Lewis A. Norton was the pioneer attorney of Healdsburg, settling in this

WORK GANG NEAR HEALDSBURG IN THE 1800'S.

Healdsburg Archives

The Healdsburg Plaza in 1892

Healdsburg Archives

Healdsburg Archives

Harmon Heald (left)

Cyrus Alexander (right)

area in 1857. He was instrumental in resolving the Squatters War, and became the town's first mayor in 1867. Colonel Rod Matheson was responsible for the first schoolhouse in the city before he went east to join the fighting and was killed in the Civil War in 1863.

Harmon Heald was one of the first purchasers at a public auction in 1856 of the grant known as Rancho Sotoyome. The widow Fitch could no longer handle its many problems and the land was sold for as little as two dollars an acre. It was on this land that Healdsburg was laid out and developed in the following years.

The sale of town lots, going at first for fifteen dollars each, provided undisputed title to property and quickly established the little community near the river. Prior to 1857, when Heald filed his subdivision map, the community had been known as Sotoyome, Heald's Store, Stringtown, and Russian River.

Until 1870 access to the town from the south was by ferryboat, crossing the river close to the present site of the railroad bridge. Meanwhile, Healdsburg prospered as a center for farming and lumber operations, and during the Civil War grew to the limits that were its boundaries for seventy-five years.

Today we look out onto our valleys of varietal vineyards and some remaining prune orchards little realizing that for more than thirty years the principal agricultural crop of the land was wheat and grain.

The Healdsburg countryside has always attracted vacationers and sportsmen as well as those seeking the benefits offered by the early watering places. The first and most popular of these was the Geysers Hot Springs which opened in the early 1850's. Skagg's Spring, at the head of Dry Creek Valley, became popular in the 1860's, and in 1875 Captain W.H. Litton built a hotel and resort about three miles north of town known as Litton Springs.

The Russian River and Fitc Mountain, to the east, are synony mous with Healdsburg. Camp Hale Camp Rose, and Fitch Mountai Tavern were located on the south sid and were the first resorts around th mountain. Villa Chanticleer, on th north side, opened in 1910. In 192 the road was completed around th mountain, and a family resort area o individual cottages and summe homes began to flourish. It is also th river and the mountain that wi define the extent of Healdsburg' growth in the future, but, para doxically, it is these same feature that will continue to attract peopl to this fair city.

The End

The Healdsburg Wheelers — 1800's

MAMA NINA'S

Inside a spotless, white-walled kitchen, chefs at Mama Nina's knead, roll, and cut homemade pastas to serve with hearty Italian dinners. The classic minestrone soup, sauces, and desserts are also homemade. The menu offers a variety of entrees including: scampi, large shrimp sauteed in butter, olive oil, garlic, and wine; veal scallopini, and a number of steaks. Prices range from $3.95 to $13.50 for a complete meal.

Amidst a wooded setting with an outdoor tree shaded terrace, this restaurant has been completely remodeled by its present owners Lee Klein and George Willson, who also operate Mama Nina's in Yountville, two blocks north of Vintage 1870.

MAMA NINA'S
Northern Italian
Hwy 101, one mile N. of Cloverdale
Summer Hrs. Wed-Sun. 5-10pm, Winter W., Th. Sun. 5-9pm

Fri. & Sat. 5-10pm
Full bar, Extensive wine list
AE, BA, MC

(707) 894-2609 Reservations advised

CATELLI'S THE REX

Geyserville, California. Population 800, one school; one store; one barber shop and home of one of the finest Italian Restaurants on your journey north through the wine country of Sonoma County.

After coming to the area over 60 years ago, Santi and Virginia Catelli opened the restaurant in 1936 and have kept it a family owned establishment. Since then Richard Catelli, the son, has become the chief Chef assisted by his beautiful daughter, Domenica and son, Nicholas.

Dinners include a choice of poultry, steak, veal or pasta and include soup, salad and coffee from $3.50-$9.25, add $2.25 for a deluxe dinner which includes pasta, relish plate and dessert. Popular lunches are priced from $2.75 - $5.75. We heartily recommend one of Richard's delicious gourmet specialties ($5.75-$6.75): the Scampi, Leg of Lamb (Sat. or Sun), Cannelloni, Linguine with Clams (red or white sauce). For dessert be sure to try the zuccotto, it's great.

The dining room or bar is the ideal place to begin or end an afternoon visiting wineries amid the scenic beauty of the Redwoods and Russian River that surrounds Geyserville.

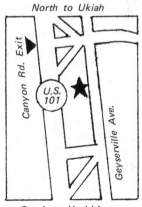

CATELLI'S THE REX
Italian
Old Redwood Hwy, Geyserville
L ll:30am-l:45pm D 5pm-8:30pm M-Th
Fri & Sat till 9:15pm, Sun lpm-9pm
full bar
BA,MC
(707) 857-9904 reservations required
for groups of 5 or more

TAMAULIPECO

A young and creative couple have won the approval of Healdsburg residents with their excellent Mexican dinners. Jose and Celia Ramirez' food became so popular that they built a brand new restaurant and moved from 309A Healdsburg Avenue to their new location at 25 Adeline Way.

The food served at the restaurant is native to the state of Tamaulipeco, located on the northeast coast of Mexico, where Jose Luis was raised. The daily dinner selection includes: Bistec Asado ($6.00); Chile Verde (carne de res, $3.95); Mole Verde (carne de puerco de pollo, $3.95); Chile Colorado (carne de res, $3.95); Chuletas de Puerco ($5.00); and Pollo Frito (fried chicken, $4.00). Dinners include beans, rice, soup or salad, and excellent handmade flour tortillas. A good selection of Mexican and American beer is served, as well as wine. For dessert you may choose between flan, sopapilla ($.65), or ice cream ($.65).

Single items include Tacos ($1.00); Tostadas ($1.50); Guacamole ($1.95); Enchiladas (cheese, chicken, or beef, $1.00); Burritos (beans $1.00, pork $1.75, or beef $1.95); Chile beans ($1.65); Caldo de Pollo (chicken soup, $2.50); and on Saturday & Sunday Menudo (tripe soup, $2.25).

Jose Luis is also an artist. The above illustration is his own. Several of his originals hang in the restaurant. Talent runs in the family; they designed and built a float that won the sweepstakes and 1st prize in the 1974 FFA parade. Who knows what other creative endeavors they will be involved in?

TAMAULIPECO RESTAURANT
Mexican
25 Adeline Way, Healdsburg
Tues-Sun 11am-10pm
Beer and wine
Watch for entertainment on weekends
(707) 433-5202 Reservations advised

WINE COUNTRY

   In addition to being new, Wine Country is one of the most carefully
planned and accomodating restaurants in Northern California. There
seems to be a dining or entertainment experience to suit everyone.
   Besides varying nightly entertainment, you will find distinctively
different dining environments. There is the cozy Bottle Room with
its cushioned wine barrels, the plant filled River Room with its
waterfall clinging to the bare cement walls, the plushly furnished
Conversation Room, and the lively long bar.
Luncheons include a choice of sandwiches, omellettes, salads, light
eater specials, South of the Border specials, as well as the unique
30 minute luncheon menu.
   A la carte dinners ($5.95-$14.95) include soup or salad, garnish,
vegetable and entree. Dinners of steak, poultry and seafood
($6.95-$15.95) include bread, soup and salad, rice or baked potato,
vegetable and entree. On Sundays you can enjoy the Sonoma
County Champagne brunch and from 5pm-7pm, Monday through
Thursday the Sundowner dinner - a choice of 3 entrees for $5.50
each.
   Over 100 varieties of wine compliment the wine list: Most from
Sonoma County wineries and for a dollar corkerage charge you
may bring your favorite vintage to dinner with you.
   The Wine Country experience was put together by a group of
seasoned professionals who have successfully mixed several new
ingredients with "Sonoma County's Rural Mystic". You are
cordially invited to partake of the thoughtful faire of Wine
Country.

WINE COUNTRY   Sunday Brunch 10:00-2pm
Steaks, poultry & seafood   Banquest Facilities for 80 plus
 106 Matheson St, Healdsburg   Full Bar, Entertainment
L ll:30-3pm M-F   (707) 433-7203 Res. Advised
D 5:00-l0pm M-F 5:00-llpm S&Sun   (Not accepted F or Sat)

HOFFMAN HOUSE

Hoffman House is a charming old Ranch House that has been converted into a delightful roadside restaurant, north of Geyserville in the heart of the Russian River wine country.

Hoffman House fills a need that has long existed for the traveler on 101 by offering delightful respite-lovely surroundings and easy freeway access. It's a perfect stopping point between Mendocino and San Francisco or points further north, and the proximity to fourteen local wineries makes it a natural place to lunch between winery stops.

The menu consists of homemade soups, Quiche Lorraine, salads and house specialties. Luncheons are served from 11:00am-3:00pm daily, and range in price from $2.50-$4.25. On Saturday evenings you may enjoy a five course dinner, by reservation only - Please!

Local wines are featured (priced at a minimum mark-up) to enjoy with your meal or to take home. There is also a large selection of imported beers. Outdoor or indoor dining and a super friendly atmosphere!

HOFFMAN HOUSE
Gourmet
Canyon Rd, Off Ramp 101, Geyserville
L 11:30-3pm daily, D Sat. Closed M-Tues   Winter Mos.
Complete wine and imported beer
Outdoor patio dining
BA,MC
(707) 857-3818 Res. for Dinner only

Cricklewood . . . an eating and drinking place . . . Walk through the frosted glass doors and share a before dinner cocktail or a selected Sonoma County wine with good friends in the intimate fireplace lounge.

Daily lunch features a full salad bar and many delicious entrees. But Cricklewood doesn't let the show or service stop there. The personally chosen staff will show you to a natural wood, tiffany lighted dining booth. The dinner selection of Prime Rib, New York or Top Sirloin steaks are cuts of carefully aged Colorado beef. The menu also presents broiled salmon steaks and mouth watering Bar-B-Que Beef Ribs. Dinners range from $5.25 to $12.00 and lunches from $2.50 to $6.50.

And there is more . . . . a lovely patio for lunch or private parties; a relaxing bar and contemporary background music makes Cricklewood a popular retreat for residents and visitors to Sonoma County.

CRICKLEWOOD
American
4618 Old Redwood Hwy, Santa Rosa
Brunch 11am-2:30pm Sun
L 11:30am-2:30pm M-F

D 5:30pm-10pm M-Thur
5:00pm-11pm F & Sat
5:00pm-10pm Sun
Full Bar & Banquet Fac.
(707) 527-7768 Res.

GIORGIO'S

Many Bay Area restaurant critics have endorsed Giorgio's Restaurant and two out of six in the Chronicle's Question man column responded "Giorgios"! when asked "Wheres the best Pizza in San Francisco"?

"The city was nice, " states George Anastasio the former owner of Giorgios (of San Francisco), "my new Sonoma County location is a different environment to contend with, but the tradition is the same".

In 1978 George placed an already well established restaurant located 70 miles to the north along Hwy 101 (formerly Healdsburg House) under the fine Giorgio's tradition. Here daily entrees of pasta, veal, poultry, fish and beef are laboriously prepared and served. New lunch and dinner items are hand written daily on the backs of envelopes. Dinner includes antipasto, soup, salad, beverage and dessert. Prices range from $4.50 - $13.50.

George plans to serve the famous Giorgio's Pizza so many San Franciscans hold dear to their palates, except this time the view from the kitchen windows is the rambling vineyards and orchards of Sonoma County - much like his former home on the island of Ischia in his native Italy.

GIORGIOS
Italian Cuisine & Pizza
25 Grant Ave., Healdsburg
Lunch: Mon - Fri 11:30am - 2:30pm
Dinner: everyday from 4:30pm

Sonoma County Wines and a Full Bar
Banquet facilities for 60, Russian River
Canoeing and Wine Tasting nearby
BA, MC, Visa
(707) 433-1106 Reservations advised

MARK WEST LODGE

On March 28, 1979, the Mark West Lodge burned to the ground. Only the arbor and 180 year old grapevines, reported by Ripley to be the oldest in the world, were saved. Many past guests who remember the elegant dinners hosted by Rene' Pavel and his maitre'd, Mark Bauer, were heart broken.

A former stage coast stop between San Francisco and the Northwest, Mark West Lodge was the oldest existing restaurant in California. The site the Lodge sat on was originally part of a huge Spanish land grant of 6,663 acres deeded to Marcus West, in the 1830's. Mr. West, a man of varied background, came to this area in 1833 and married a young woman of Mexican extraction, Guadalupe Vasquez.

There is good news. Rene' & Mark have reopened their restaurant in the Belvedere, a huge Santa Rosa Victorian that rivals Mark West Lodge for dining prominence. The same basic menu is followed. Guests can enjoy Canard a'la Mark West (Roast Duckling with prune sauce-Flambe au Cognac), Le Coq au Faison (Rooster - marinated in fine spices, wine and Pate de Foie, Gourmandise de Veau (Medallion of Veal, champagne sauce), and Carre' d.' Agneau a' la Rene' (for two - Roast rack of lamb, Flambe au Cognac). Prices range from $9.95 - $18.50, and dinners include salad, fresh vegetable, and sourdough bread. A variety of appetizers and desserts including Mark West Lodge's exquisite Souffle Grand Marnier (for two - $8.00) are also available. Drinks from the full bar or premium wines compliment your dinner perfectly.

CHEZ RENE'
AT THE BELVEDERE

There is more good news. Once again guests will be able to sit on the front porch among the ancient grapevines on those warm starlite summer nights and sip premium wine as the breeze drifts through the alder & pine and beams of light from the full moon come to dance among the clusters of grapes hanging overhead. Yes, Mark West Lodge will be rebuilt soon!

CHEZ RENE'
French Cuisine
7272 Mendocino Ave., Santa Rosa
(707) 542-1890 Res. advised
Lunch and Dinner - Champagne Brunch on Sunday

MARK WEST LODGE
(to be rebuilt by 1981)
2520 Mark West Springs Rd., Mark West
(Call operator for new phone number)

Wandering Through Western Sonoma County

by John Schubert

Monte Rio Highway along the Russian River

Phil Bray

If you are traveling on Highway One in Sonoma County, then you are on the westernmost boundary of one of the most historical areas in California. No doubt you will pass through the town of Bodega Bay, site for the filming of Alfred Hitchcock's thriller "The Birds." Almost two hundred years before the coming of Hitchcock, this bay, which was inhabited by Miwok Indians, was discovered by the Spanish navigator Lt. Juan Francisco de La Bodega y Cuadra, in 1775.

Some thirty-five years later the Russians, searching for land to support their Alaskan colonies, selected Bodega Bay as the shipping point for their farming settlements at Freestone, Salmon Creek, Jenner, and their most significant colony, Fort Ross. No other buildings from the Russian occupation stand. The last, a warehouse, fell down at Bodega in 1930.

Route One closely follows the contour of the coastline north of Bodega

Bay. Once you cross the Russian River at Bridgehaven turn left to Jenner. As you enter Jenner, look to your left and you'll see where the Russian River empties itself into the Pacific. Then head north to Fort Ross

Fort Ross was the site of the first church established north of San Francisco Bay and caused the Spaniards to extend their mission chain into the North Bay Area in order to protect their claims there. Although the Fort is completely reconstructed, it is extremely accurate in detail to the original.

Driving north from Fort Ross the traveler will drive across small points jutting into the sea and enter canyons that widen into coves. It was along here that lumber schooners, anchored in these sheltered areas, would fill their holds with redwood lumber. The mill sites that dotted the coast

Original Russian Orthodox Church at Fort Ross; leveled in the 1906 earthquake; now reconstructed and open to the public. A Russian Princess once lived here.

rom 1860 to 1910 were chosen so that lumber could be loaded from suspended cables and chutes. Today, ne may still see large rusty rings for nchoring imbedded in the rocks and liffs of what the sailors called "dog oles". Some of the names, Salt Point, imber Cove, Stillwater Cove, and isk's Mill Cove, still survive.

Returning south and passing Jenner, hile driving along the Russian River t Bridgehaven, the traveler will notice campground in a gulch on the west ide. It was here that the Duncans, lexander and his son Samuel, re-cated their mill from Salt Point in 860. After the timber was cut from ie surrounding countryside, the uncans, in 1877, again moved the ill, this time up the Russian River a broad flat protected from ocean inds. Here they remained permanen-y, as did the settlements name, uncans Mills.

Following the Duncans' trail from the oint just north of Bridgehaven east-ard along what is now Highway 116,

the traveler follows part of the old narrow guage railroad right-of-way to the permanent site of the mill. Duncans Mills, at the height of its development, was second only to Santa Rosa as a railroad center.

Duncans Mills still retains a few relics from the past. The most obvious is the refurnished train depot. The rails reached here in 1877 and the last train pulled out in 1935. Across the highway, to the north, you can see the last of the worksheds, still with the original yellow and brown paint of forty years ago. Northwest of the shed, standing by itself in a vacant field, is the one-room school-house, last used as such in 1945 and now serving as a storage shed.

The de Carly Store, in the center of town, is a large red building with white trim, known throughout the area as the Duncan Mills general store. Built in 1880, it was the only business rebuilt after the 1906 earthquake. It is one of several "Living" museums in the county, with old stock from

Austin Ranch Main Barn

Phil Bray

Sebastopol Apple Show, 1910.

seventy years ago still standing on its shelves.

If the traveler crosses the bridge, taking Moscow Road, he will leave Highway 116 and still be following the old railroad bed. The current bridge was built in 1966, the old one having been a one-way affair originally constructed as a railroad bridge. The annual floods finally weakened it so much that it developed a bow and had to be replaced.

Continuing in an easterly direction the traveler passes Villa Grande, formerly Mesa Grande. Along here the road is still just the width of a train. Passing Villa Grande the traveler will come to Monte Rio where he will see a parking lot which was once the center of town that also included a now absent train depot. The road to the right, along Dutch Bill Creek, is where the narrow guage railroad descended from Occidental. The road to the left was standard guage from Guerneville. The narrow guage arrived here in 1876, built mostly by Chinese labor. With the arrival of the locomotive new timber mills sprang up along the road, including the Riley, the Madrone, the Tyrone, and the Moscow.

Around the turn of the twentieth century the name of this town was changed from Russian River Station

to Montrio, and in 1901 finally settle on Monte Rio. The year 1901 als saw the construction of the seve story Monte Rio Hotel, boasting th first elevator in Sonoma County

To the east of Monte Rio is th famous Bohemian Grove, a sma valley of giant redwoods acquired b the Bohemian Club of San Francisc in 1900. For two weeks every yea the famous and near-famous gathe at this exclusive club for rest an recreation.

Once again joining Highway 11 after crossing the Monte Rio Bridg the road to Guernewood Park an Guerneville was the last area to b logged and settled. The settlers cam either from the coast or from th Santa Rosa Valley, slowly filling th void in between. And finally, in th early 1860's a trail was opened betwee the coast and the valley.

Around 1900, after most of th timber was gone, the villages of Vil Grande, Monte Rio, Guernewood Par and a half a dozen others becam vacation centers. The lumber com panies had all the land but no woo so lots were sold to tourists an vacationers from the San Francisc Area. Between 1910 and 1920 the single-walled boxes sprang up alon the hills flanking the Russian Rive and with them came the names of th different sections: Northwood, Gree stone, Mont Sano, Camp Vacatio and Guernewood Heights.

"kid Road" — Logs across the road made it easier for the oxen to haul out the giant redwoods.

Just to the east of Guernewood Park the town of Guerneville. The first settlers arrived here in 1858 and lived perhaps the largest forest of giant redwoods in the world. Lumber mills were erected in the 1860's and 1870's and Guerneville became a famous lumber center. The lumber for the 'Church Built from One Tree' in Santa Rosa, verified by Santa Rosa's own Robert "Believe it or Not" Ripley, came from Guerneville. In addition, the tallest tree in the world grew in Guerneville near Fourth and Mill streets and is recorded in the Guinness Book of World Records.

Guerneville possibly may claim to have had the largest amount of vegetation growing on a measured acre. Just the redwood timber alone totaled over one million board feet to the acre. Eventually, all the lumber was cleared and the mills shut down, the last closing its doors in 1902. But the town was not about to die. A few shrewd people with plenty of capital had bought up enough of the cleared lots to invest in summer resorts, and Guerneville became a leading northern California resort area, featuring many of the big swing bands, popular during the 1920's.

A few old buildings remain in Guerneville proper, but only one dates prior to 1894. In that year the town was leveled by fire. Everybody lost, everybody that is except one. River Lane Resort, located at First and Church streets survived. The white house, with its huge porch, was built before 1872.

The first and only serious attempt to make the Russian River a navigable stream occurred in 1869. The Enterprise, a steam-driven stern wheeler built here, made two trips to the ocean. The only trip up-stream to Healdsburg, literally ground to a halt, four miles shy of its goal in sandy shallows.

PANORAMIC VIEW OF THE RUSSIAN RIVER FROM RIVER ROAD.

The next stop up-river from Guerneville is the world famous Korbel Champagne Cellars. This business originally started as a lumber mill, but as the land gradually was cleared the Korbel Brothers planted wine grapes. They built a winery in 1886 and expanded as the need arose. Finally, in 1912, the lumber mill shut down permanently. The Korbels gave their full attention to the production of fine champagnes. The oldest building here is not the railroad depot or any of the brick buildings, but the old Korbel home which sits on a knoll just we of the winery and dates back to 1875

And there it sits waiting for you The traveler who is aware of this early history is now ready to embar upon a more rewarding experienc in his wanderings through wester Sonoma County. Informed of the remaining historical sites and awar or the antecedents of the present day the traveler now possesses a mor intimate understanding of the are and can let his imagination roam wit more accuracy in his imagining of things as they once were. **The Er**

Korbel Home and Lumber Mill, 1876

VAST'S GARDEN DINING

It's easy to see why Fred & Silvie Vast, owners of Vast's Garden Dining, have received special attention from reviewers. Much of the ingredients for their homemade food comes from their farm making the entrees especially fresh and delicious. The wholesome taste of the food is attributed to making it the old-fashioned way.

The scarce quince fruit (which grows next to the water wheel) helps make the fresh baked goods a special treat. Freshly picked vegetables and herbs from their garden add to the freshness of the salads, soups and vegetable compliment. Several changes are planned regarding the selection of entree's available, but in the past the Vast's have served the best in poultry, fish, amd meats. Their home-smoked bacon, ham, turkey, and chicken were mouth watering to say the least. A variety of offerings are served in the deli. Just one visit to this quaint restaurant which is situated in the picturesque farm land of Sonoma County is enough to get you hooked.

VAST'S GARDEN DINING   *Hwy 116, between Cotati & Sebastopol*
American Farm   *(707) 823-1980 Call for hours & menu info.*

CHEZ PEYO

In the apple country of Sebastopol you will find Chez Peyo, the only country French restaurant in the area. "Peyo" is the Basque nickname for owner and host, Pierre Lagourgue. After 10 years as chef and owner at the well-known Chez Leon in San Francisco, Pierre Lagourgue brought his fine french cooking to Sonoma County.

Chez Peyo is just 10 minutes off Freeway 101 (take the Sebastopol/Rohnert Park Hwy 116 West Exit). Complete dinners starting at $5.25 include homemade soup, salad and shrimp hors d'oeuvre, salad served family style, followed by entree, choice of creamy cheesecake, chocolate mousse, or creme caramel, and beverage. At Chez Peyo the special child's plate at $4.25 includes all courses and a half-portion of an entree. For dinner choose from Roast Duckling ($6.75), Filet Mignon ($8.50), Prawns Brochette ($6.75), a light Quiche ($5.25) or the evening special. Week-day lunches of hamburgers to seafood crepes start at $2.15, Saturday and Sunday brunches from $3.95 boast complimentary champagne and freshly made croissants.

Pierre caters special gourmet meals on request for small groups. The food is excellent at Chez Peyo and for the price the country servings extremely generous.

CHEZ PEYO   *Early Sunday Dinner 3pm-9pm*
Country French   *Brunch - 11am-2pm Sat & Sun*
2295 GravensteinHwy S., Sebastopol   *Beer and Wine*
L - 11:30am-2:30pm Tues-Fri   *MC, Visa*
D - 5:00pm-10:00pm Tues-Sat   *(707) 823-1262 Res. advised*

DINUCCI'S

Neatly tucked away amid rolling hills in a paradise of open space on the coastline, Dinucci's is one discovery you won't soon forget. Gene, Betty, and family will make you feel right at home in the traditional flavored atmosphere they have created. If Betty, your hostess, tells you you'll have to wait to be served - remember - all the food is prepared to order by Gene. Betty states however, "Everybody comes out pleased and contented." For a complete dinner plan on paying between $3.65 and $7.50. Dinners are complete with soup, salad, ravioli or spagetti, and hors d'oeuvre and coffee. Dinucci's is the only restaurant on the west coast serving Mountain Oysters. A Family Restaurant by heart, Dinucci's is one of the most memorable escapes to a small town along the north coast. You'll find motel accomodations 5 miles away at Bodega Bay.

DINUCCI'S ITALIAN DINNERS
Italian
Hwy 1, Valley Ford
D - M-Thurs 4pm - 8:30pm, F- Sat 4pm-9:30pm,
Sunday 12:30pm - 8pm
Full Bar
BA, MC
(707) 876-3260 Reservations advised

Nearly 100 years after the old Potter School in Bodega was built in 1873, at a cost of $5,000.00, the stately, picturesque, landmark became world famous for its setting for the classic Alfred Hitchcock movie "The Birds", filmed there in 1962.

Now the old schoolhouse is the location of a unique art gallery, boutique, and gift shop, operated by Dan Blackwelder, as well as one of Sonoma County's most delightful new restaurants.

BODEGA ART GALLERY AND RESTAURANT

The restaurant with Chef Terry Allen, features outstanding lunches and dinners. Specialties include Malasian Chicken, Medallions of Port, Beef Stroganoff, Scampi, Beef Florentine, Sweetbreads, Quail, plus homemade French Onion Soup, Quiche, Crepes, Salads, Sandwiches and delicious homemade Ice Cream Pies and Chocolate Cheese Cake. Beer and wine are also featured. Prices for lunch from $2.50, dinner from $3.95, champagne brunch $4.75.

You'll find out why first time guests usually make repeat appearances at this delightful Bodega dining room and gift shop.

BODEGA ART GALLERY & RESTAURANT   Beer & Wine, MC & Visa
Gourmet Foods, 17125 Bodega Ln., Bodega   (707) 876-3257 Res. advised

CASA de JOANNA

Poised above the shoreline of the Russian River, amongst the redwoods, sits Casa de Joanna. Don't be fooled by the plain exterior, inside the restaurant is an environment of soft music, antiques, beamed ceilings and stained glass which has charmed many a visitor and prepared their appetites for the feast to follow.

Joanna and Bob Matthews philosophy is "to give our guests a total dining experience: fine atmosphere, good food in generous portions, fair prices and good service". Everything is fresh, prepared to order, and the huge portions dictate that you come hungry. Popular Mexican fare include Flautas Con Pallo, Crab Enchilada (with Joanna's special sauce) and Enchilada Rancho (green sauce). You can order the Papa Pancho which very few have been able to totally devour. Favorite continental entres are steak stuffed with oysters and Sweetbreads Grenbloise. A la Carte or five course dinners are $4.75 - $9.00.

The bar, which serves beer, wine, wine cocktails and delicious homemade sangria overlooks the meandering Russian River. One more thing - Joanna and Bob want their guests to remember - "Mi casa es su casa" (My house is your house).

CASA de JOANNA
Mexican & Continental
17500 Orchard Ave., Guerneville
D - 5pm-9pm Wk nites, 5pm-10pm
Wk ends, L-(call for hrs), MC & Visa
Beer & Wine (707) 869-3756 Res.

BURDON'S

Burdon's - small and intimate, with a quiet air of relaxation - that's where you go on the Russian River when you want an excellent French or American dinner.

Superb recipes, moderately priced, from a chef who has over two decades of experience in fine dinner houses, include Coquilles St. Jacques Mornay, Steak Au Povier Hotel Paris, Mahi Mahi Dore or Veal California. Just one of the features of the dinners is a spinach salad with special dressing.

Burdon's is seasonal now, but in 1980 will be open weekends all year. Lunches will be served on the outdoor patio on balmy Sonoma County days from March through November.

There is a full bar serving all variety of cocktails as well as Italian, French and California wines. A space to experience good cheer with a casual air. Overnight accomodations are readily available nearby. An evening at Burdon's is an evening well spent.

BURDON'S
French-American
15405 River Rd, Guerneville
BA MC
Full Bar
(707) 869-2615 Reservations advised

HEXAGON HOUSE RESTAURANT AND RESORT

Hexagon House is located two miles north of Guerneville at the entrance to Armstrong Woods State Park. This beautiful facility, now under new ownership, is being restored to high standards of dining and lodging excellence. The cuisine includes such items as fresh Salmon Oscar, fresh Pheasant braised with leeks in Pear Wine sauce, plus gourmet vegetarian entree's, including as a house specialty Spinach Caesar Salad Maximus. Dinners range from $6.95-$13.50. Sunday Champagne Brunch is served from 10:30am-2:00pm. The reasonably priced wine list features the finest selections of Sonoma County wines.

There are 21 rooms ($34-$38 with kitchens) plus 18 modern cabins ($35-$45 with kitchens and fireplaces) set amid giant redwoods, a meadow and a crystal clear creek. There are two swimming pools, tennis courts, and a coffee shop (open for breakfast and lunch).

The staff at the Hexagon House, selected from the finest resorts in the Western states, adheres to the premise: "Excellence is as difficult as it is rare".

HEXAGON HOUSE
Epicurean
16881 Armstrong Woods Rd, Guerneville
Champagne Brunch Sun 10am-2pm
D 6pm-10pm Daily in Summer

Seasonal March-December
Full Bar, Conference, Banquet &
Wedding Receptions
Call for reservations &lodging info
(707)869-3991   MC, Visa

Le CHALET

Gerard and Josiane Moser liked the looks of the Russian River area, decided to open a French Restaurant, and in 1977 they hung the family crest, which reflects a heritage of fine cuisine since the year 1460 at Le Chalet.

Gerard, who received training in France and Switzerland, was opening chef and manager at Ventana Resort in Big Sur, executive chef at Quail Lodge, and television chef on KOIN - TV in Portland, Oregon. His charming wife Josiane oversees the rustic dining room where entrees are served French Country style.

Gerard expertly prepares each dinner from the freshest of produce, seafood and top grade meats. Among the 13 entrees are Filet Mignon Chateau Figeac (beef tenderloin with shallots, herbs, and red wine), Steak au Poivre Vert (pepper steak with fine frandy and green peppercorns), Coq au Vin Rouge (spring chicken in burgundy sauce, mushrooms, and croutons), and Carard du Chef (duck marinated in Grand Mariner, served with orange-cherry sauce). Entrees include soup du jour, salad, fresh homebaked bread and fresh vegetables with Hollandaise ($5.95-$10.50).

There is a fine selection of Hors d oeuvres, desserts (including souffle au Grand Marinier for two), soups, and the wine list is excellent. Exciting specialties are prepared Tuesday thru Sunday. Le Chalet is located near the charming cottages of Ferngrove Resort just west of downtown Guerneville.

LE CHALET
Country French
16632 River Road, Guerneville

D - everyday but Mon. 5:30pm - 10pm
(March - Sept) for Winter hours call
Excellent Wine List and Beer

Banquets up to 80, Special Wedding Receptions
MC, Visa (707) 869-9908 Reservations advised

FIFE'S

At Fife's a pleasant environment has been created where both straight and gay adults can share a 14 acre resort in comfort and with mutual respect for each others space and life style. The owner and his staff are not only friendly and pleasant, but also are extremely resourceful. They have utilized the land and buildings in such a way as to give one the impression that Fife's is a small independent settlement within the town of Guerneville.

The grounds and cabins are will maintained. Two fresh water creeks (Fife Creek and Livereau Creek) cut across the property and there is swimming in the Russian River or in the heated pool. Guests can walk or jog through orchards, sprawling meadows, redwood groves, the lushly landscaped grounds or along the private river beach.

The chef uses fresh produce from Fife's large garden. Brunch includes fresh squeezed orange juice, various egg dishes served with fresh fruit (in season) and several items from the lunch menu. Seafood, chicken & veal, or vegetarian crepes as well as sandwiches & specials are served for lunch. Here are examples of the evenings offerings: Veal Tarragon, Veal Dijon, Chicken Veracruz, BBQ Chicken, Mushroom Stroganoff, Fettucini Alfredo, New York Steak (3 sizes), Sauteed Scallops Provincale, Salmon (grilled or poached - in season), Grilled Sea Bass (served with lime and herbs), and popular roasts such as Leg of Lamb or Roast Pork. Dinners include a choice of homemade soup or garden salad ($5.95 - $11.95). For dessert try Fife's famous Chocolate Decadence (with whipped cream & raspberry topping) or Courvoisier Cheese Cake. A good! selection of California wines are available as well as mixed drinks from the full bar. In summertime there is dining on decks overlooking the pool and outdoor stage.

Lodging facilities range from 25 campsites ($10 per person per night - includes locker & bath facilities, $5 for each additional up to 4 per site) to 49 cabins including a plush two bedroom cottage suite with fireplace, living room, wet bar, and sun—porch. Cozy one room cabins with bath (for 1 or 2 - $37.50), two room with bath, and two bedrooms or one bedroom with sitting room ($56.00 per day 2 - 4) are available. Room rates are subject to change seasonally so be sure to give a call (rates are reduced by 25% during the week).

Besides Fife's facilities there are numerous attractions nearby. Groups or seminars are encouraged (for up to 100) and three fabulous feasts are served annually on Thanksgiving, Christmas, and New Years Eve.

FIFE'S
Continental Cuisine
16467 River Road, Guerneville
Brunch: Sat & Sun 10am - 2pm
L - 11:30am - 2pm
D - from 6pm-winter, 6:30pm-summer

Nov 1 - Mar 31 rest. clsd. Wed & Thur
48 cabins & a cottage (some with fire-
places, 25 campsites, back-gammon
tournaments. No pets & no minors.
(707) 869-0656 Reservations advised

NORTHWOOD RESTAURANT

Nestled in a grove of redwoods on the Russian River near the famous Bohemian Grove is Northwood Restaurant. The adjoining golf course was built by Jack Neiville, who also built the Internationally famous Pebble Beach. Many greats visit Northwood to play golf along the redwood corridores and later dine at the restaurant.

Stocked daily with a large variety of fresh produce, the Northwood Salad Bar is one of the better ones to be found in Northern Callifornia. A variety of hot & cold sandwiches as well as three egg omelettes are served for lunch. Dinner includes homemade soup & salad bar (a meal in itself), fresh vegetable & rice pilaf or baked potato. A good selection of fresh seafood, steaks, and teriyake entrees as well as specialties like Butterfly Leg of Lanb and Chicken Queen Elizabeth ($5.50 - $10.45) are available. The Sunday Brunch includes a fresh fruit bar, champagne, fresh baked muffins and a good selection of Egg entrees to choose from.

After dinner the tempo of this peaceful setting picks up with live entertainment and dancing complimented by a large variety of well drinks and premium California wines.

NORTHWOOD RESTAURANT
Seafood & Steaks
19400 Hwy 116, Monte Rio
Seasonal hours:
Breakfast: Tues - Sat 8am - 11am
Lunch: Tues - Sat 11am - 2:30pm
Dinner: Tues - Thur 6pm - 9pm,
Fri & Sat 6pm - 10pm, Sun 5pm - 9pm
Sunday Brunch: 9am - 3pm
MC, Visa (707) 865-2454 Reservations

BLUE HERON INN

The Blue Heron Inn is one of those special little restaurants where a lot of people and a lot of love got together to create gourmet cooking in a rustic setting.

The kitchen and bar are "dedicated to your enjoyment and health." Predominantly vegetarian entrees include fresh fish, daily varying International and South of the Border Specials, Chicken Specials, served with soup or salad and hot whole grain roll for $5.00 to $7.00. Daily Specials might be Chinese Springrolls with Pinapple Ginger sauce, Chilaquiles with homemade mole' sauce, Cornish Pastries or Pimientos and Chiles Rellenos. The bar offers a wide selection of imported beer, wine and liquor as well as exotic drinks prepared with fresh juices. It's a delightful place built in redwood and pine and with herb and flower gardens. For a simple lunch or an elaborate dinner, the Blue Heron Inn Family is ready to make you welcome.

BLUE HERON INN
International & Vegetarian
1 Steelhead Boulevard, Duncans Mills
Brunch: Sunday 10am - 2pm
Lunch: 12-4pm Soup & Sandwiches

Dinner: 5:30-9:30pm
Full bar, fishing and camping on the
Russian River, Unique shops nearby.
Checks, MC & Visa
(707) 865-2269 Reservations for
parties of 6 or more.

VILLAGE INN

The fall leaves flicker golden in the late afternoon sun and a gentle breeze sweeps the Russian River causing an endless display of sparkling ripples. The calming panorama visible from the outdoor deck is complimented perfectly by the rustic Old English architecture of the three story Village Inn.

Delicious aromas waft from the kitchen where the chef and staff are meticulously preparing tonites fare. The Village Inn varies its menu daily around specials such as Cossack Pie (vegetarian), Chicken Madiera, Chicken Sonoma, and Irish Leg of Lamb. Thursday is community night with wholesome & complete Vegetarian dinners for only $3.50 per person. The Village Inn chefs will delight you with their European Cuisine. The freshest of seafood, rack of lamb, succulent steaks, and delicate poultry entrees are served. Dinners include homemade soup, or fresh garden salad, fresh vegetables and the chefs choice of rice or potato, or homemade pasta.($6.25 - $10.50). Fabulous desserts include Tropical Fruit Pie, Sweet Potato Pie, French Gateaux and Beehive Cake.

New owner Kurt Visser has rennovated the 25 rooms ($15.00 - $45.00 per night for two). The Village Inn rooms make ideal retreats for weary travelors or couples who want to escape the city. Each room has its own distinct theme. Flanked by century old redwoods and poised above the Russian River,the Village Inn is indeed a majestic environment   to escape to.

VILLAGE INN
International Gourmet
River Boulevard, Monte Rio
Lunch: varies seasonally
Dinner: Summertime - 5:30pm - 10pm daily
*   Wintertime - 5:00pm - 9:30pm daily*
Sunday Brunch: 10am - 2pm
Full Bar, Cozy fireplace lounge, 25 antique &
contemporary furnished rooms; some overlooking the Russian River.
MC, Visa (707) 865-1180 Restaurant
reservations, (707) 865-2738 Lodging

CAZANOMA LODGE

As you approach the lodge you can hear the waterfall that feeds the pond where live trout occassionally break the surface. As you inhale the fresh air and survey the majestic redwood shrouded canyon you can feel your taste buds come to life. Welcome! You are about to experience some of the best German Cuisine in Northern California.

When the Neuman family purchased the already famous Cazanoma Lodge in 1976, they wanted their dinner guests to be completely rejuvinated after the drive there. They had no idea one of the best German chefs in Northern California would be comming to help them. Family style German and American dinners as well as the nightly special include relishes, choice of salads, homemade soup, potato pancakes with applesauce or homemade noodles and red cabbage (German dinners) or choice of potato pancakes with applesauce or french fries and fresh vegetable (American dinners). American entrees ($7.00 - $12.75) of New York Steak, Barbecued Spare Ribs, and fresh Rainbow Trout that Chef Udo Ludkins and his staff prepare are good, but it is the German entrees ($7.50 - $8.75) that stand out — Rouladen (steak stuffed with onion, bacon, pickles, browned and served in rich brown gravy), Hasenpfeffer (rabbit marinated in wine browned, baked and served in sour cream sauce), Ente mit Kirschsosse (Roast duck with cherry sauce), and Sauerbraten (sweet and sour beef roast with gravy).

Part of the tradition at Cazanoma Lodge are the complimentary after dinner drinks Randy Neuman serves and the annual Thanksgiving dinner with all the trimmings. For Sunday Brunch you may select from German Specialties like Bauern Fruhstuck (fluffy omelette stuffed with fried potatos, onion, bacon, sausage, cheese, pickle, and seasonings), Eggs Benedict, and of course the fresh Pan Fried Trout with lemon and butter. Brunch also includes a choice of three drinks from the spacious full bar. In case you decide to stay over, there are two rustic cabins ($20 for 2, $30 for 4) and two rooms in the Lodge overlooking the waterfall (one with private bath across hall - $20 & one with bath in room for $30). Cazanoma Lodge is a rare retreat to culinary and environmental pleasures.

CAZANOMA LODGE
German and American
Box 37, Cazadero 95421
1000 Kidd Creek Road, Cazadero
May 15 - Sept 15, D Wed - Sat 5 - 10pm
Sun 4 - 9pm Sun Brunch 10am - 1:30pm
Mar 1 - May 15 & Sept 15 - Dec 1 open
for D Fri & Sat 5 - 10pm Sun 4 - 9pm
Sunday Brunch from 10am - 1:30pm
Closed December, January & February
Full Bar, Wines, Swimming & Lodging
MC, Visa (707) 632-5255 Res. advised

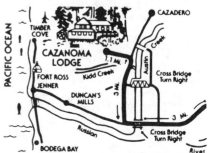

Diane Brown '79

Murphy's
JENNER by the SEA

California's Route 1 snakes its way 250 miles along rugged and breathtaking Pacific Coastline between San Francisco and Westport. Along this stretch there are few restaurants indeed that offer exceptional food and ambiance to restore the weary travelor. In Jenner at Murphy's Jenner by the Sea you will find a classic environment enriched with exceptional food, a panoramic seascape, soft music, and warm elegance.

A "living room" atmosphere prevails here with a crackling fireplace surrounded by cozy furniture and a nautical full bar with a beautiful view of the famous Russian River where it empties into the Pacific. Fresh catches of salmon, snapper, and sole from the nearby Bodega Harbor fishing fleet, are served up with fresh vegetables, homemade soup or salad, and a choice of brown rice or potatos. Delicious hot and cold appetizers, Cioppino (great for foggy coastal days), choice cuts of beef, delightful desserts, and Murphy's Sunday dinner - the succulent Roast of the day add to the pleasure of dining here. On Saturday and Sunday a Champagne Brunch is served. The Captain's Wine List of selected California Wines is excellent and the chef welcomes special requests provided the time and ingredients are available. In the future lodging facilities will be available.

Under the new direction of entrepreneur Richard Murphy, a Bostonian, the restaurant and for that matter the town of Jenner is going through a renaissance of creative change. Thoughtful spontaniety is the order of the day here. A quote from the menu gives you an idea of the environment you will find: "of a peaceful nature .....where the northern sun dances silver on a Pacific Sea. Welcome...... into communication of trust in the movement of life......be tranquil in beauty to the eye, the palate, and the spirit."

To arrive at sunset and dine by candlelight at a coastal retreat that offers the ambiance of Murphy's Jenner by the Sea is one of the fabulous experiences of life you owe yourself.

MURPHY'S JENNER BY THE SEA
Seafood Continental
Coast Hwy 1 at Jenner, where the Russian River joins the Sea.
Champagne Brunch: Sat & Sun 9am - 1pm
Lunch: 11am - 4pm daily Dinner: 4pm - 9pm daily
Nov 1st thru Mar 1st call for Winter hours.
Special Events, Private Parties, Banquets for 50 - 75
AE, MC, Visa (707) 865-2377 Reservations advised

RIVER'S END

Lying secluded in Jenner amidst the splendor of the north coast wilderness, Rivers End Restaurant offers a throughly relaxing dining experience. It is here where Herr Wolfgang, Frau Sybille and Fraulein Ina, with European hospitality, draw visitors and locals alike to experience gourmet dining complimented by the spectacular view of the Pacific Ocean and mouth of the Russian River.

Wolfgang, a master chef, introduces his patrons to such gourmet entrees as Coconut Fried Shrimps with orange rum sauce, Kedgerry (Oriental Seafood Curry with fried banana and chutney), Rum Roasted Loin of Pork for two or more ($11.00 per person), Crisped Duckling roasted with oranges and Grand Marnier, Seezungenrollchen (Filet of Doversole filled with crabmeat and mushroom), or Kalbsrouladen (tender veal cutlet rolled with beef, pork, and onions, braised in Marsala). Dinners range in price from $4.95 to $13.95.

Before ordering, a dish of crisp raw vegetables with dipping sauce is served to compliment your cocktails. Dinner includes an appetizer, bread and butter, mixed green salad, selected fresh vegetables and either homemade spatzle, parsley potato, or croquettes, with coffee or tea.

A selection of hot and cold appetizers (including Beluga Malossol Caviar and Crabmeat Crepes), soups, salad, and vegetables are available to complement your entree. For dessert try Rote Grutze, an enchanting raspberry pudding with roasted almonds and iced milk.

After dinner, you can enjoy an idyllic retreat in one of the three cabins ($26 - $30) or the newly built house ($53 per night). The cabins and house overlook the Russian River and Pacific Ocean. From their windows you can see the cabaret of common tern, blue heron, pelican, an occassional sea lion, or winter migrating whales.

Superb catered dinners can be arranged on the premises for up to 60 guests and off-premises unlimited. Those catered to include Nelson Rockefeller, Emperor Hiraheto, as well as numerous movie stars. The finest mixed drinks, wines, beers, and exotic cocktails such as the infamous "Point of no Return" are served at the bar. The Pacific sunset and full moon viewed from Rivers End is spectacular. So come and let Wolfgang's staff treat you to a unique dining experience and then retire to a rustic cabin perched on a cliff overlooking the Pacific.

RIVER'S END RESTAURANT
German and Gourmet Entree's
Hwy 1 just north of Jenner
Dinner: Fri & Sat 5pm - 10pm
Sun - Tues 5pm - 9:30pm

Brunch: Sat 11am - 4:30pm, Sun 10am - 4:30pm
Full Bar, Banquet facilities, Lodging in 3 cabins
and a house overlooking the Pacific Ocean
MC, Visa (707) 865-2484 or 869-3252
Reservations are necessary year-round

TIMBER COVE INN

Under the new ownership and direction of Richard & Carroll Hojohn, Timber Cove Inn is being restored to what it once was when so many chose it as their primary escape from the city. The massive - roughly hewy timbers, huge stone fireplace, beamed staircases and oriental island gardens blend perfectly with the natural environment. Here, San Francisco's best known sculptor, Benjamin Bufano, erected two of his famous works of art. The slow process that transpired from the time he first began to work on them till the day they were first set in place is a story in itself.

A fine chef has been hired to satisfy the culinary needs of the sophisticated travelor. The menu changes periodically to reflect the freshest of seasonal ingredients. Specialties include international variations of beef, poultry, fresh seafood and vegetables. Dinners include choice of homemade soup or garden salad, fresh vegetable du jour and rice pilaf ($5.95 - $15.95).

There are 47 rooms with rates ranging from $37 - $42 (double bed, tub & shower), $47 (queen size bed, fireplace, tile shower & view), $68 (king sized bed, fireplace, sunken shower & bath with cove view), or $200 for the luxurious honeymoon suite. On the 26 acres of coastline with bluffs & beaches for strolling you can renew your relationship with a loved ones or with life itself. The isolated natural setting , absent of artificial distractions, is very conducive to high intellectual output, making it ideal for conferences and seminars (150, conference equipment available). Also at the Inn is one of the finest gift shops on the coast. - the Timber Cove Craft Gallery.

Three miles north of Fort Ross, on a rugged promontary overlooking Pacific surf and rocky beaches, Timber Cove Inn awaits you in a setting beyond imagination.

TIMBER COVE INN
Seafood Continental
Breakfast: summertime - 8am - 11am daily
wintertime - 9am - 11am Sat & Sun with a
Continental Breakfast 8am-11am Mon- Fri.
L - 11am-2pm daily (summers), no lunch
during winter. Dinner: 6pm - 9:30pm daily
(summers), from 6pm daily (winter).
Full Bar, Wine List & fireplace lounge.
47 rooms, ocean views, fireplaces. Banquets
& Conferences for 150. AE, DC, MC, Visa.
(707) 847 - 3231 Reservations advised

SEA RANCH LODGE

The haunting beauty of isolation. . . .where can you find silence, where can you find peace to explore your own world? Framed by the dramatic Sonoma coastline cliffs, meadows and ocean, lies the Sea Ranch Lodge, a quiet, sophisticated response to your inner need for seclusion. Once the site of a coastal sheep ranch, this spectacular stretch of land from Gualala south to Stewart's Point on California's Coast Highway 1 offers you a wealth of natural experiences. Meandering trails through meadows and forests, rock and surf fishing, several beaches to explore, all provide a rich natural retreat for artists, photographers and nature lovers.

Aged redwood encases the twenty guest rooms, decorated with custom made furniture in natural woods. Your privacy is complete here, for no telephones, no televisions are included in the rooms. Dining is satisfying and relaxing in the Lodge dining room. Lofty, high ceilings, mellow cedar walls and oversize picture windows overlooking the Pacific Ocean make a refreshing backdrop for your meals. Complete dinners, served with generous salad, baked potato, brown rice or sliced tomatoes, fresh vegetable, home baked bread and coffee or tea, start at $6.25 for a hamburger steak with onions. Other entrees at various prices up to $9.95 include a vegetarian special, leg of lamb, Hungarian chicken with supreme sauce, pork chops with Robert sauce, fresh salmon or cod (in season), or a sirloin steak with choice of garnishes. Daily specials and delicious appetizers are featured, as are homemade soups and dressings. Friday and Saturday nights, a full prime rib dinner is served to your order. Delectable homemade desserts in large variety top off your dinner. Lunch is more of a salad-sandwich affair, although there are daily soups, quiches and other specials, and there is always excellent New England Clam chowder.

The Sea Ranch Lodge is a rare aesthetic treat. Built on the challenging Sonoma Coastline, it is a portrayal of man's wish to live with the beauty of his environment, and beyond it.

SEA RANCH LODGE
Continental & Seafood
Sea Walk Drive, The Sea Ranch
B - 8am-11am, L-noon-3pm

D - 6-9pm. Open daily except
Xmas, Hours subject to change.
Full Bar, Small Banquet Facilities
MC, Visa   (707) 785-2371 Res.

The cool coastal fog rolls in over the hills at Point Reyes.

Dennis Finn

Point Reyes - Land of Solemn Beauty

by Joan Diane Goode

Point Reyes is one of the most enchanting areas in northern California. The feeling that encompasses one while looking out across the ocean at the dots of tiny, bobbing fishing vessels is like taking a step into the past, to a time when the days were spent in easy harmony with nature. This is a land which has remained basically as it was one hundred years ago, as if it were by the land's own will. The population stays at a low level and most of the original buildings remain, some well preserved while others slowly deteriorate into the landscape. The feeling this writer has while experiencing Point Reyes is best described as being at peace with self and the world.

The first inhabitants of the Point Reyes area were Coast Miwok Indians, with an estimated one hundred and thirteen villages on the Peninsula. In fact, the National Park Service estimates more Indians lived at Point Reyes in 1500 A.D. than Caucasians in 1960. The Indians were a short but strongly

built race, known for their carefree, loving nature. It is believed that they relied on fish, acorns, fruits, and berries as their staple diet. When the ocean waters were calm they operated in crafts constructed of bundled rushes. Much has been learned of the Miwok culture by the shellmounds which they left behind. The Indians were removed to Mission San Rafael in 1817 to be educated by the priests, but with the break-up of the mission chain in 1834 they scattered, soon falling prey to the white man's vices and diseases.

Most modern scholars agree that Sir Francis Drake careened his Golden Hind into Drake's Bay, in 1579, to become the first Anglo Saxon on this continent. The second explorer to arrive at Drake's Bay was Sebastian Rodriguez Cermeno, a Portuguese trader, on November 6, 1595. Cermeno's ship, the San Augustin, was the first recorded shipwreck on Point Reyes. During a bad storm the ship was actually lifted into the air by gale force winds and thrown upon the shore,

Wreck of the Munleon off Point Reyes headlands in 1931.

losing twelve men and most of its supplies. On December 8, 1595, Cermeno and the remainder of his party left the bay in a small boat and returned safely to Acapulco.

In 1834 Mexican governors began granting land to private citizens. The first grantees on the Marin Coast were **James Richard Berry and Rafael** Garcia. Berry built a house in what is now Olema, while Garcia built his first residence at Bolinas.

James McMillan Shafter and his brother Oscar acquired Point Reyes in the 1860's, after Mexico's defeat in the short war of 1846. This put an end to the easy aristocratic lifestyle of the Spanish dons. Oscar died in 1873, and James went broke trying to keep the North Pacific Railroad alive. Meanwhile, he put the town of Inverness on the map, on the west shore of Tomales Bay, in a vain attempt to recoup his losses. He died on August 29, 1892, a man of dreams unrealized.

The dense fog over Point Reyes caused many shipwrecks. Dr. Horace

Byers has stated that Point Reyes has the second densest concentration of fog in the United States. A lighthouse built on Point Reyes headlands began operating in September of 1870, but the shipwrecks continued. Today, thanks to technological progress, compass locations can be flashed to ships, making wrecks a rarity.

The greatest earth movement of the 1906 earthquake occurred on what is now Sir Francis Drake Boulevard. The San Andreas Fault, which runs down the center of Tomales Bay, stranded a fisherman's boat on the mud when the waters receded. As the water surged back into the bay, he was overwhelmed by a tidal wave he estimated to be "100 feet high." Masses of reporters arrived, their stories stressing the perversities of nature. For example, Payne Shafter's cow was thrown head first into the crevice, only her tail protruding, while the dogs who witnessed the incident remained barking wildly at the place where she had disappeared.

Point Reyes saw active bootlegging during the Prohibition Era. Most of the liquor was brought down from Canada in ships and unloaded on the beaches. One nocturnal incident involved an excursion boat, the Queen. Agents forced the Queen into service, with hired help at the wheel, and were taken to the mouth of the bay, only to find that hijackers, with fake badges, had beaten them to the haul. Near the end of Prohibition many bootleggers became bolder, transporting their goods to San Francisco via a black hearse. What federal agent would ever suspect the somber-faced driver to be hauling contraband?

As long ago as 1935 the National Park Service recommended buying extensive portions of Point Reyes, concerned that the area would become another giant subdivision. The government finally purchased much of it as a National Seashore, and by 1970 the total amount paid for land there was fifty-seven million dollars.

The three men instrumental in legislating the bill to save the seashore were Congressman Miller, Senator Engle, and President Kennedy. Unfortunately all three of them died soon after passage of the legislation. Congressman Miller was the victim of a plane crash; his grave is located on half an acre of land overlooking Drake's Bay. On September 5, 1963, President Kennedy planned a ten state tour of conservation projects, which included Point Reyes, but last minute changes routed him, instead, to Dallas. Senator Engle died of cancer on July 3, 1964.

The population of Point Reyes has not increased significantly through the years. Every plan to turn it into another seaside resort has failed. For the most part the land remains in its natural state. At Point Reyes, it seems that man must take second place to nature, or have no place there at all. A visit to Point Reyes is a welcome change of pace, a place for relaxation, contemplation, and appreciation of the natural beauty with which this land has been blessed.   *The End*

An old railroad car stands amidst an open field; a remnant of an era that is past.

Dennis Finn

TOMALES HAS ITS OWN SMALL TOWN IDENTITY

Tomales hasn't changed much over the past few decades. This small coastal community has one general store, a bank, one restaurant, one bar, a guest house, 2 gas stations, a post office, a school and one church. It is quiet and peaceful here most of the time; although it does get hectic during tourist season. At Diekman's General Store tourists & residents stock up on picnic items, beer & wine, and groceries. You can gas up across the street or at the south end of the 4 block long main street (Route 1) at Rick's 76, which is owned by Rick Basso. The Diekman family run one of the most friendly general stores on the coast. That same degree of friendliness holds true for the Davis family who serve delicious meals at their restaurant, the Village Coffee House. Across the street is the William Tell Bar and up the hill, secluded by a tree line, is Byron Randall's Famous Tomales Guest House; one of the more unique country inns you can stay at in Northern California. Tomales is surrounded by the rolling green hills of dairy farms and ranches. To the south is Point Reyes National Seashore and to the north the rugged redwood covered Pacific coastline. Tomales fits nicely into this natural masterplan. Many of it's residents seem to care enough to want to keep it small and friendly. I guess thats why it has proven to be such a popular stop along the way for the many tourists who visit this portion of the Redwood Empire.

Marin Coast Restaurants

VILLAGE COFFEE HOUSE

The spotless interior of the Victorian building is decorated with old photos, antiques, hanging lamps, and well cared for plants. Its usually very peaceful in Tomales at the Village Coffee House.

The Davis family have created a dinning environment in harmony with this small coastal community. Ernie Davis meticulously rennovated the structure and his wife Adele is the hostess. Their two sons, Ron and Gary share the responsibility of running the restaurant; and are assisted by chef, Keith Peterson. A simple dinner menu of Trout, Ground Round, and choice cuts of Top Sirloin allows extra time to be put into each entree. Dinners are very good and include french bread, homemade soup & salad ($6.95 - $7.95). Occassionally a gourmet special is added to the evenings festivities. The house desserts are beet cake (delicious) or cheese cake ($1.15 - $1.25). Imported and California wines are served.

For breakfast or lunch you may choose from a variety of egg dishes, sandwiches, homemade soup and delicious salads served with a special buttermilk dressing. The fresh cut flowers, candlelight, soft background music, and Pacific fog blanket that silently drifts in mixes well to make a very cozy environment. The Village Coffee House is the perfect oasis from which to start the day or romantically wind down the evening.

VILLAGE COFFEE HOUSE
American
26950 State Hwy 1, Tomales

B - 10am - noon
L - 10am - 3pm
D - 6pm - 9pm
Closed Monday & Tuesday
Beer & Wine, MC & Visa
(707) 878-9996 Reservations wk ends

STATION HOUSE CAFE

The atmosphere is very peaceful in this small coastal town in Marin County. Point Reyes Station is known for nearby Point Reyes National Seashore, its dairy ranches, the Pultzer Prize Winning Newspaper, the Point Reyes Light and an abundance of natural beauty. Any community, especially one with these credentials and diversified population is fortunate indeed to have a restaurant that is capable of satisfying the appetites of locals and visitors.

There are three good reasons for this popularity - breakfast, lunch, and dinners are served, the menu is very diversified and excellent food is often prepared from local or organic farm produce. Fresh fish comes from the nearby fishing fleet, the oysters are right out of Tomales Bay and Drakes Estero. For breakfast; fresh squeezed orange juice, a wide variety of omelettes, pancakes, oatmeal, fresh fruit, and egg entrees served to your order with all the traditional meats. At lunch the corn bread and delicious country fries and hearty homemade soups are memorable. Fresh spinach salad with avacados, banannas, Mandarin oranges, paper thin onion rings, or tomato stuffed with Dungeness crab are two of many salads offered. Tuna melt, daily casseroles, excellent hamburgers served on whole wheat buns, fresh fish and chips are but part of the offerings. At dinner assorted appetizers: ham mousse, steamed clams or baby oysters and cheese delice are offered. Full dinners include soup, salads with two house dressings, a basket of popovers and cornbread, fresh vegetables and assorted starches served with everything from fresh bay scallops, boned breast of chicken, tempura, catch of the day, New York steaks, and the chefs daily special ($6.00 - $10.25). Light suppers: Spanikopita, crepes, quiche, and the soup & salad supper ($3.50 - $6.00) are also served. Homemade desserts vary daily but include fresh apple and seasonal fruit pies, mousses & cremes, and coffee cakes.

Owner, Pat Healy is very concerned about the safety of the whales as well as endangered species of wildlife around the world. Framed pictures of whales drawn by children line the walls. From the fine wine list you might select a fifth of Edmeade's Whale Wine, from which a portion of the cost is donated to the Whale Protection Fund.

Concentrating on the freshest of seafoods, fruits, and vegetables the Station House Cafe caters to the needs of its large local clientele and enjoys meeting and serving the visitors who come from all over the world.

STATION HOUSE CAFE
Fresh Seafood, Vegetarian
& Continental Cuisine
Hwy 1, Corner of A & 3rd Streets,
Point Reyes

B - 8am - 11am Wed - Mon
L - 11am - 5pm Wed - Mon
D - 5pm - 9pm Wed - Mon
Beer & Wine, MC & Visa
(415) 663-1515

NICK'S COVE

If you're in the mood for some good food at a reasonable price, served in a friendly atmosphere, then stop in at Nick's Cove. You will be greeted by the owners of the restaurant: Alfred and Ruth Gibson. Guests may dine on the patio or in the cozy dining room. Here everyone is treated to a view of the wide blue expanse that is Tomales Bay, and the fresh salt air.

The building, once a dance hall half a century ago, was moved from the opposite side of the bay to rest on its present location on Highway 1 in Marshall. Today it is the home of the annual Tomales Bay Shark Catching Festival. This year seventy-five sharks were caught, one of which was a great white weighing 1500 lbs.

Of his restaurant Alfred says, "We don't specialize in 'fancy foods' because we'd rather concentrate on serving foods that people can enjoy and afford." Most of the meals at Nick's Cove are prepared according to old family recipes, for example, their barbecued oysters. When Alfred and Ruth first introduced barbecued oysters to Tomales Bay, they sold approximately one hundred each weekend, now they serve over four thousand per weekend. The Dinner plates available are Fried Prawns $5.00, Fried Oysters $3.50, Fish and Chips $3.00, and the Combo Plate (oysters and prawns) $5.00, all come with fries, salad and bread. A retail wine cellar will be added in the future.

One word of warning. the Gibsons say that their barbecued oysters are habit forming — while there just ask one of the San Franciscans who keeps coming back for more.

NICK'S COVE
Seafood
3 miles north of Marshall on Hwy 1
noon to 8pm everyday except:

Summer closed on Monday
Winter closed on Wed & Thur
Full Bar (closing time varies)
(415) 663-1033

MARSHALL TAVERN

The Marshall Tavern was built by the Shields family in 1873, along with an adjoining hotel and railroad station. The Narrow Gauge Railroad came to the area in the 1930's. Originally the tavern was used as a General Store. During prohibition it was used as part of a bootlegging operation, complete with a handy trap door in the back. And during World War II it was used as a Navy billet. It has been operating as a restaurant/bar off and on for about 15 years. In November 1971 the hotel and railroad house burned down -- the tavern is now the only building remaining.

In 1972 John Vertigan bought the building and operated it as a restaurant/bar. Under Vertigan's direction you could get a real taste of the old west the way it was during the bootlegging era. Then in 1977, Al Reis bought the Marshall Tavern and kept it much the same. This rugged building was constructed so that it rests entirely over Tomales Bay. Pieces of history adorn the walls, old paintings and posters which once hung in the hotel - memories of a different era.

The Marshall Tavern specializes in seafood dinners ($3.95 - $6.95). The tavern has a complete bar which features Australian wines and beer. On weekends there is live music and dancing, featuring local musicians ranging from Folk to Rock, Blues to Jazz. A surprising number of good musicians like Jesse Colin Young live in the area.

The Marshall Tavern is conveniently located - only an hour's drive away from San Francisco. It is near the Point Reyes National Seashore, and only 600 yards away from the San Andreas Fault. Vertigan boasts of an 11-foot shark caught near the Tavern one summer. The Tavern provides a real change of atmosphere for those wishing to escape the monotony of everyday dining.

MARSHALL TAVERN
American and Fresh Seafood
Hwy 1 N of Pt. Reyes Station, Marshall
Thurs & Sun 6pm-10pm
Fri & Sat 6pm-11pm
Full bar open till 2am, live music
(415) 663-8141

Robert H. Morra '76

VLADIMIR'S

Are you looking for an escape from ordinary living? How about escaping to an unique restaurant in the romantic town of Inverness? Vladimir's, one of the few original Czechoslovakian restaurants in the United States, has served as a lovers retreat for those individuals who enjoy fine Czech cooking and a mellow, unusual atmosphere in which to relax.

Vladimir Nevl, owner of Vladimir's, came to the U.S. in 1958 from Czechoslovakia. He brought with him all of the richness of the culture of Moravia, the central lands in which he grew up, a land renowned for its folklore of music, dress, and fine food. Traditional designs from Vladimir's village of Valassko frame the entrance of the restaurant. Maps and pictures of traditional Czech costumes hang on the walls, and make an interesting backdrop for your dining.

With his wife, Alena, a trained dietician, Vladimir presents to you a rich composite of Czech dining. The Cabbage Roll ($3.50), stuffed with ground pork, veal, and champagne kraut, is quite popular, and the Moravian Duck ($6.50) is known for its excellence. During the summer, fresh vegetables are served to you from Vladimir's terraced garden. Other enticing dishes include Chicken Paprika ($3.50), Hungarian Goulash ($3.50), and Roast Loin of Pork ($6.50). There is also a full bar, and banquet facilities are available.

VLADIMIR'S
Czechoslovakian
Sir Francis Drake Blvd., Inverness
Sat., Sun. 12-10pm, Tu., W., F., L - 12-2pm, D 5-10pm
Closed Monday and Thursday
Full bar and banquet facilities
(415) 669-1021 Reservations advised

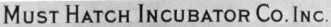

MUST HATCH INCUBATOR CO. INC.

ESTABLISHED 1898

LEO A. BOURKE
PRESIDENT

A CHICK IN THE HAND IS WORTH TWO IN THE SHELL

HATCHERS AND SHIPPERS OF
WHITE LEGHORN BABY CHICKS

PETALUMA, CALIFORNIA

December 1923

A Chick in the Hand is Worth Two in the Shell!

by Ed Manion

The first English-speaking settler in southern Sonoma County knew a good thing when he saw it. The region of the Kotatis, with an abundance of game in the valley and wood and water in the eastern foothills, looked like the garden spot of the world to John Thomas Reed who wasted little time planting fields in wheat and building a home along Crane Creek. Reed didn't stay long, however. The local Indians instituted their own version of a growth limitation ordinance in 1827 by burning him out and forcing him to flee to the safety of Marin County. Today, Rohnert Park's John Reed Elementary School commemorates his name.

Kotati, a coast Miwok village, has lent its name to the original land grant called Rancho Cotate, to a local high school, to the present city of Cotati, and to another spelling of the locale as soft-sounding Cotata. The diamond-shaped, 17,300 acre Mexican grant was first given to Juan Castaneda in 1844. Two years later the huge grant was deeded to Thomas O. Larkin who later sold most of the land to

Joseph S. Ruckel who transferred ownership to Dr. Thomas Stokes Page.

Was it Dr. Page who laid out the interesting six-sided plaza when downtown Cotati was planned? This possibility has been suggested many times, but it seems unlikely considering that he lived in Valparaiso, Chile most of his life, and spent little time in the area. It seems more likely that a son, Wilfred Page, who directed ranch operations for a number of years placed the names of his brothers—George, Arthur, Charles, Henry, Olaf, and William—on the streets surrounding the downtown hexagon. There are also Page and Valparaiso Streets in the city and a Wilfred Avenue to the north.

Cotati was incorporated in 1963, one year after neighboring Rohnert Park came into existence as the seventh city of Sonoma County. Paul Golis and Maurice Fredericks are credited as the founding fathers of Rohnert Park, having negotiated with Waldo Rohnert, and later his estate, for land said to have been among the most productive in the state, and once boasting a seed farm claimed to be the largest in the world.

Turn of the Century Chicken Ranch near Petaluma.

Penngrove, to the south of Cotati-Rohnert Park, is now more than a waystation on the Northwestern Pacific Railroad, owing to general growth trends and the advent of Sonoma State College, just two miles to the north. As early as 1852, David Wharff and his family homesteaded in the region because, as one account has it, a chicken coop fell off the Wharff wagon at that point and the occurrence was taken as a good omen. In the 1870's, William Woodworth owned the land where Penngrove proper is situated. He granted the right of way for what was then called the San Francisco and North Pacific Railway, and in return was allowed to name the station, calling it Penn's Grove for the oak trees near the spot and in memory of his native state of Pennsylvania.

Penngrove is situated on Petaluma Hill Road, one of two formerly heavy-trafficked transportation arteries between Petaluma and Santa Rosa, the other being Stony Point Road to the west. Newcomers to the area may assume that the central route up the valley (Highway 101) has always been used, but for many years, even into the twentieth century, much of the

Cotati-Rohnert Park region became a marsh during winter rains and even during the summer months travel was limited. The Washoe House, built in 1859 and located at Roblar and Stony Point Roads, is an active survivor of the time when buggies, wagons, and stagecoaches took the higher and drier ground along both sides of the valley floor.

Water, however, was not a problem for Petaluma's founding fathers who gained access to the future town site via Petaluma Creek. These men were members of a hunting party bent on supplying San Francisco with meat. They set up camp near old Cedar Grove Park in the fall of 1850. Members of this party included John (Tom) Lockwood, Thomas Baylis, David Flogdell, Charles Patton, Major Singley, and Linus and Wiatt. Deer, elk, and duck, among other things, made for a bountiful harvest, and if one of Mariano Vallejo's cows got in the way of a stray bullet the fact was not likely to be recorded. Vallejo's Petaluma Rancho, the present-day site of East Petaluma, was six years old in 1850 and his adobe headquarters were a going concern when Lockwood and his companions erected their wigwams on the west bank of the creek.

By 1851 a village was beginning to incubate, not an inappropriate word considering its future slogan as the "Egg Capitol of the World". One of the great natural advantages of the county's southland was the location of Petaluma as the head of navigation to a main estuary of San Francisco Bay. The "up country" toward Santa Rosa and Healdsburg, western communities including Point Reyes Station, Tomales, Bodega, Valley Ford, and Bloomfield, and Sonoma Valley to the east funneled a tremendous amount of commercial traffic through what was then called Petaluma Creek. On April 12, 1858, California's legislature gave it the incorporated status of a city.

An interesting sidelight is that rival villages and cities were not happy that Petaluma seemed to arrange boat schedules so that passengers had to stay overnight in the terminal city's many hotels. Several attempts were made to break the monopoly. Efforts were tried to start water service through Tomales Bay, the Russian River, and Sonoma Creek, but Petaluma continued smug and prosperous with its dependable tide water stream until the arrival of the railroads in the 1870's changed the situation. But the waterway continued to have considerable influence as rail rates in this section were among the lowest in the state. Trucks and the combustion engine, however, doomed most of the river traffic.

Two steamers named Gold are the most remembered of all the many paddlewheelers on the Petaluma-San Francisco run. Boat traffic started on a regular basis in 1852 and lasted

Penngrove Railroad Depot

Ed Manion Collection

Fred Wiseman flying first airmail flight in the world — February 17, 1911.

Ed Manion Collection

until 1950. The third steamer named Petaluma, built especially for the local route and called the "Egg Boat", made its last trip on August 24, 1950, ending paddlewheel freight commerce on the west coast.

Among the variety of vessels plying the river none was more unique or successful than the scow or "hay" schooner. Usually a scow was square on the ends, about sixty feet long, and with its flat bottom could rest on a slough without damage when the tide went out. It could operate with two or three men and, although slow, carried an enormous amount of bulk goods to and from the North Bay.

The "Egg Capitol of the World" still has plenty of chickens around but is more newsworthy these days for wrist-wrestling, a popular woman mayor who

was one of the state's first, the movie "American Graffitti", and its determination to control growth without paving over the entire countryside. An unusual city ordinance limiting subdivision housing to five hundred units a year is headed for the United States Supreme Court and will become a landmark case.

John Reed, chased out by the Kotati Indians so long ago, didn't get a chance to see his first harvest. Today's farmers and ranchers face an uncertain future too. With the State's population moving northward at such a rapid rate southern Sonoma County finds itself face to face with a growth problem while trying to sustain the area's rich agricultural tradition rather than have it become a historical statistic.

Waldo Rohnert's Horses

Ed Manion Collection

FARRELL HOUSE

All of Petaluma patiently waited for the doors of the Farrell House to once again open . . . . . .

Built in 1888 by city fire chief Frank Burns, it became the home for Frank's sister Irene Farrell and her husband Bill, who became one of Petaluma's more colorful mayors. In years - gone - by Bill and Irene hosted some of the more memorable political parties at their mansion. Youngsters used to refer to it as the Castle on the Corner.

In 1977 the home was threatened by the "wrecking ball of progress"; and restoration specialist Skip Sommer moved it to a grassy knoll overlooking the deep mooring water of the Petaluma River. That year Farrell House was declared a Petaluma Historic Landmark. The ground work had been laid for Joel Coopersmith and his associates to turn the century old Petaluma landmark into an elegant restaurant.

By spring of 1980 the doors of the Farrell House were opened to cheering Petaluman's and their guests. Now all can experience a taste of the party atmosphere Irene and Bill Farrell once hosted; except this time the view from the Victorian windows is yachts floating on the tranquil surface of the Petaluma River and shimmering lights at night. Inside you'll find two dining area's, a private dining room (16-20), a full bar, and dance floor. Proprietor Joel Coopersmith promises elegant waterfront dining with predominately seafood, beef, and veal entrees. Fresh Sonoma Duck (with sauce du jour), Trout Lafayette, Calamari Friti, Beef Wellington, Veal Picatta (milk fed white veal) are representative samplings from the menu; and in addition, gourmet specialties are offered nightly. All entrees are available a la Carte, with an impressive assortment of appetizers & pasta to compliment them, or as dinners with soup du jour or salad to start (from $7.50). Selected California & Imported wines as well as offerings from the full bar round out the festivities. Farnham Hogue, the starting chef at famed Scott's Seafood in San Francisco, graces the kitchen and the food is fabulous. There are docking facilities available should you decide to come by yacht and moonlight strolls along Petaluma's waterfront are in order.

Thanks to Skip Sommer and Joel Coopersmith, and their associates, the Burns-Farrell House was not destroyed and it's rebirth has generated an environment only a Grand Old Victorian River House can host.

FARRELL HOUSE
Seafood & Continental Cuisine   *Full Bar & Yacht docking facilities*
222 Weller Street, Petaluma   *(707) 778-6600 Reservations advised*
L - 11:30am - 2:30pm M- Sat
D - 5:30pm - 10:30pm daily
Sunday Brunch from 10am - 2pm

STEAMER GOLD LANDING

Looking for an adventureous dining experience - try the Steamer Gold Landing in Petaluma. Decked with history, rich decor (an incredible amount of work went into the restoration of this old building), inside and outside dining (weather permitting), upstairs bar and entertainment, and over 30 unique shops in the Great Petaluma Mill next door.

Entree's include a generous cut of Prime Rib ($10.50), Mahi Mahi ($6.95), Red Jacket Ribs (beef ribs baked in the Landing's barbecue sauce ($8.75), and when available Fresh Swordfish. There is a different homemade soup everyday and tasty desserts like the Landing's Original Mud Pie.

Situated on the Petaluma River, it's a 4½ hour trip by yacht from San Francisco's central city location and docking facilities are available. There is ample parking, the dress is casual, and the experience adventureous.

STEAMER GOLD LANDING
All American
No. 1 Water Street, Petaluma
Lunch - daily 11:30am - 2:30pm
Dinner - daily from 6:00pm
Brunch - Sun from 10:30am - 2:00pm
Full Bar with dancing and entertainment (Wed-Sun)
Reservations for 6 or more, Yacht docking facilities
available, overlooks Petaluma River.
AE, MC, Visa (707) 763-6876

****The owners of Steamer Gold Landing and the management of North of San Francisco will give complimentary dinners and a wine tasting to any Australian or New Zealander who sails their boat from his or her respective countries up the Petaluma River to the Steamer Gold Landing - docking facilities. One week advance notice required. Radio telephone your notice to (707) 527-0367 or (707) 763-6876. Have a safe journey.****

I was born on a forgotten day in 1859, during the middle period of roadside hostelries; when Californians enjoyed old fashioned pastimes, gold was freely

spent, and a rugged West was still in its formative years. Strong, skillful hands placed my hardy redwood beams and anchored them as if forever, with hand beaten square nails and wooden pegs. Not even the great quake of '06 could claim my soul. I've meant warmth and supplies for many a stage coach filled with weary travelers. These were the days when miners paid their keep with gold dust from the distant fields. I gave them room and board for a dollar a night. I used to listen to them tramp up my stairway with their high boots amid the laughter of elegant ladies. I remember a day when Petaluma Southerners and Santa Rosa Northerners converged at my doorstep, guns in hand, only to end the day drinking together at my bar. For more than a century my upstairs has been a favorite gathering place for social functions and private parties. General Ulysses S. Grant spoke from my balcony to a cheering crowd.

A handmade European piano made for the ears of kings and queens and brought to me from around the rugged Cape Horn made my dances the liveliest and merriest. Many a romance has budded within my walls. Many a pretty lady has graced my dance floor.

I'm firmly set on a rock foundation amid rolling hills and untouched pastureland. The air around me is scented by the Eucalyptus. In the evening a blanket of cool coastal fog rides a light wind over the hills. I've been seasoned and aged by a thousand sunrises and sunsets — and I'll come to know a thousand more. I'm known for my good food, drink, and company. I await you. I am Washoe House.

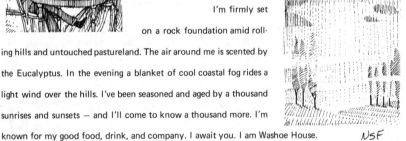

NSF

WASHOE HOUSE
American
Stony Point Rd & Roblar Rd, Petalum
L 11am-2pm, D 6pm-10pm daily
full bar and banquet facilities
BA, MC
(707) 795-4544

WASHOE HOUSE NSF

There is a California great escape waiting for you scarcely two miles off Highway 101 in the heart of rolling hills and eucalyptus. It's called the Washoe House.

Washoe House was founded in 1859. For over a century satisfying meals have been served there. Today the menu is limited, yet very adequate. Daily entrees are written on a chalk board at the end of the bar. They include a 16 oz. New York Steak ($8.00), Jumbo Prawns ($6.00), Chicken in the basket ($4.50), Fish and Chips ($4.50), and Prime Rib: served on Saturday and Sunday ($7.50). Dinners include French bread, tossed green salad, vegetables, hand cut French fries, and delicious home made biscuits (no soups are served). Special cut steaks are tender and juicy and always cooked to perfection. For dessert you have a choice between Champagne Sherbet or Vanilla Ice Cream, or Chocolate pudding. Washoe House hosts a large selection of local wines and imported bottles from Spain, Germany, and Portugal. The house wine is Inglenook Chablis or Burgundy and costs $.65 a glass. Vintage wines are available upon request and a nice selection is hidden away in the wine cellar.

Dining at the Washoe House means an historical education as well as a pleasure. Old photographs, oil paintings, original old-fashioned advertisements, lithographs, and a wide variety of rare antiques cover the walls. In the banquet room upstairs is a handmade European piano brought from around the horn. A huge Buffalo head silently watches the banquet room. If you desire a lively evening, you can dine at tables along the bar. There is an old-fashioned nickelodeon piano should you fancy old-fashioned music. There are two dining rooms; one that opens into the bar and a large back dining room where you can dine quietly by candlelight for those special occasions.

There is a large "country" parking lot and the dress is casual. Overnight accommodations are two miles away. Washoe House has a unique hardy atmosphere where all walks of life interact. After complete restoration, the Washoe House will become a refined historical monument. We can think of no other gathering place in Sonoma County that stands out more in our minds than Washoe House. Its people, its fine dinners, its colorful past, and its picturesque country setting give such life to the old building. Your visit will be a pleasurable one — your memory forever: of the oldest roadhouse in California.

PETALUMA CAFE

One of the nicest ways to create a restaurant is to preserve an old building, decorate the interior with rare and elegant furnishings, hire charming help, and most importantly serve interesting as well as fine cuisine.

The Petaluma Cafe, located on the first floor of the historic McNear Building is such a restaurant. Owner Gary Hill takes great pride in his creation. Most of his patrons are Petalumans who have discovered his restaurant suits them just fine. They come back daily to enjoy entrees like steaks & chops ($5.95-$8.50), broasted Petaluma chicken ($4.95), steamed clams ($4.95), as well as fresh garden salads ($1.50-$3.95), omelettes, homemade soups, breads, desserts, beer, wine, and a variety of other delicious libations.

Gary plans further additions to his already fine eating establishment - we politely suggest a visit to the Petaluma Cafe will prove very worthwhile.

PETALUMA CAFE
American
23 Petaluma Blvd. N., Petaluma
B - 9am-1pm weekends
Full menu 11am-10pm daily
Beer and wine
BA, MC Visa
(707) 763-9839

OLD CHICAGO

"Go West young man, go West" . . . and so he did. Bill Berliner left the "Windy City", but incorporated it's namesake in his restaurant, Old Chicago Pizza.

Bill, his managers; Larry Sinclair and Francie Feerick, and their friendly staff serve the legendary thick crusted pizza as well as assorted luncheon specials on the second floor of th historic Lan Mart Building in downtown Petaluma. The average large Chicago Pizza serves 5-6, measures 14" in diameter and weighs between 4 & 5 pounds. At Old Chicago the pizzas (well worth the price of $3.75-$7.25) are elegantly served on elevated trays with a candle beneath to warm the delicious slices. There are seven toppings to choose from (.50¢-$1.00 extra each), but be prepared for the 30 minute wait while your pizza is being expertly prepared.

The century old brick walls are decorated with lush plants, art

work, and a crystal chandelier hangs above the bar where you can order a variety of beer and wine. Old Chicago Pizza - one of the few eating establishments "out West" that still serves a legend.

OLD CHICAGO PIZZA
Chicago Pizza & Italian Dishes
41 Petaluma Blvd. N., Petaluma
L - 11:30am-2:30pm
D - 2:30pm-Midnight (pizza)
beer & wine - private room for 14
BA, MC, Visa
(707) 763-3897

THE EGGERY

Going to The Eggery is a unique "eggsperience," says Marv Dolowitz, owner and proprietor since 1949. Nestled in the rolling hills of west Petaluma, it is one of many original chicken ranches dotting this beautiful countryside. It is still a chicken ranch and much, much more.

Developed as a farm store in 1969, it wasn't until 1975 that a combination restaurant and art gallery were added: An interesting, large room, fashioned from old redwood, salvaged from chicken houses; the seats and tables made from chicken hoppers. Lush plants hang from the beamed ceilings, colorful paintings and interesting crafts adorn the walls, while through the tinted glass windows one may observe the colorful birds in the aviary, or watch the sheep peacefully grazing along the hillsides. Over all the strains of soft classical music, one feels totally in tune with the universe.

The Eggery was the first popular omelteet house in Northern California. Made at you table, your choice of ingredients, it's on your plate in one minute with a fresh fruit salad - Perfection! Dinners of Beef Burgundy, Shrimp Curry, and Broasted Boned Chicken are also available. Your entree includes a choice of soup or salad, with price's under $6.00. Farm fresh produce from the Farm Store and elegant Sunday Champagne Omelettes are also served.

On weekends, folk music, flamenco guitar, belly dancing or perhaps a poetry reading may be offered for your enjoyment. Marv has found his great escape, and he wants to share it with you.

THE EGGERY
Omelettes & Gourmet Dinners
4480 Bodega Ave., Petaluma
Farm Store 10-6pm (Closed M.)
L from 11:30am, D - Fri, Sat, Sun

from 5:30pm. Omelette Brunch
Sunday from 10:30am - call to
confirm hours & reservations.
MC & Visa. (707) 762-7228

Nowhere did we find more generous portions of good Mexican food than at Rosie's Cantina in Cotati. Most nights of the week you'll find Rosie's packed. So successful has the restaurant been that owners Glenn Stocki and Matthew Freeman have expanded the restaurant for the 3rd time in six years. A new bar and additional dining area, complete with handcrafted wooden booths and more art murals, plus the addition of another Rosie's which is located on Cinema Square in Santa Rosa and managed by owner Rick Martin.

The dinner selection is more than adequate with 40 combination dinners to choose from. Dinner costs between $3.80 and $6.65. There are also 14 a la carte items, imported Mexican beer, fine domestic wines, numerous beverages and side orders. The house specialty is Rosie's Special Soft Tostada: A plate-smothering meal for only $5.30 that consists of beans, rice, monterey jack cheese, lettuce, tomatoes, avacado, and a special sauce all rolled in a flour tortilla. Needless to say, this special is just another exciting change of pace that separates Rosie's from other Mexican restaurants. Another treat is the Cheese Enchilada Verde with sour cream: only $2.10 a la carte.

Tasteful woodwork, stained glass windows and murals decorate the interior. Friendly waitresses and a generous serving philosophy please all but the most finicky. On the menu, csstomers are told to "compliment their meal according to their own appetite." Rosie's Cantina is the only Mexican restaurant in Sonoma County where you can enjoy a satisfying dinner and then spend the rest of the evening in a comfortable atmosphere of tasteful and relaxing music.

ROSIE'S CANTINA
Mexican
570 E. Cotati Ave. Cotati
(707) 795-9211
(Also see page 6)

Mon-Thur 11:30am - 10pm
Sun 4:30 pm - 10pm
Fri & Sat open till 10:30pm
Beer and wine
AE, CB, MC, Visa

610 MAIN

Clay and Lois Thompson had a dream . . . . she loved to entertain and he loved to cook. They turned their old Victorian home, which has been in the family since 1918, into a restaurant. The result . . . 610 Main: the most pleasant and relaxing place to dine in Petaluma.

From the outside, you would never know the building is a restaurant, with its gardens, waterfall and gazebo. Once inside, you'll discover a very homey atmosphere with rooms full of antiques, palms and nostalgic memorabilia of past generations.

Luncheons feature an assortment of mouthwatering crepes, omelets, soups, salads, sandwiches and occasional specials at the whim of the chef. When the weather is nice, a few tables are set poolside in the shade of birch and oak trees, with a Hawaiian tiki guarding the guests.

Special private five course gourmet dinners are offered for groups of ten or more wishing to celebrate a birthday, anniversary, engagement or other special occasion in the privacy and elegance of the 610 Main parlor and dining rooms. A wide selection of dinners accompanied by their already famous gigantic hot popovers with jam is offered. Entrees have included Lobster Thermidor, Blue Lake Trout, Tournedoes Rossinni, and Veal Mozart. Prices are from $6.00-$10.00, and arrangements should be made well in advance. You may choose from a nice selection of wines from California and France to accompany the cuisine.

Thoughtful consideration by the Thompsons has gone into 610 Main, making it a very popular retreat as you will soon discover when you dine there.

610 MAIN
Mostly French
610 Petaluma Blvd., Petaluma
L - 11am-2:30pm M-Sat

D - by arrangement
Sunday brunch - by arrangement
wine and beer
(707) 762-6625 reservations advised

a few years later, Father Jose Altimir while exploring the area for a propose mission site, noted in his journa "We came to the plain of a place calle Sonoma by the Indians who in oth times dwelt there." So even then, 1823, the Sonoma Indians were litt more than a name remembered.

Years later, General Marian Vallejo wrote in his memoirs that tribe, while traversing the valley floo noted the moon rising above th craggy hilltops seven times. The called themselves "Sonoma", whic meant "Valley of the Moon". His so Dr. Platon Vallejo, later stated th actually Sonoma was the name of chief and that it meant "Big Nose This is a classic illustration of ho the sacred record of Sonoma's pa has been guarded. To some, histo may be myth agreed upon, but Sonomans, history is mainly myth argue about.

The first European to settle in t area was Father Jose Altimira; of t Mission San Francisco Solano California's 21st and last missio He was exploring the area for proposed mission site. His intenti was to remove the Indian conver from the contaminating influences commercialism springing up arou the Port of San Francisco. He fou

BEAR FLAG REVOLT   NSF

The Legendary Sonoma Valley

by Jim Alexander

Over a thousand years ago, roving members of the Miwok, Pomo, and Wappo Indian tribes stumbled upon the lush little inland valley. In their number was a small tribe who identified themselves as the "Sonoma". Since they had no idea that one day the valley, a city, and even a county would use their name, they made no effort to let anyone know just what "Sonoma" meant.

The first Spaniard to explore the valley was Captain Moraga. He must have left some record of this tribe, for

the Sonoma Valley an ideal spo because of its superior climate an soil, as well as for the potentia converts in the surrounding area

If Father Altimira thought that h valley was a peaceful haven he wa soon to learn otherwise, for in th third year the Indians rose in revol A few of the wood and thatch buil ings were burned, and Father Altimir was forced to flee for his life.

In 1827, he was succeeded at Sa Francisco Solano by the older, mor conservative Franciscan, Fathe

Buenaventura Fortuny. He was good news as far as the mission was concerned, having recently made the Mission San Jose one of the most prosperous in the entire California chain. Fortuny was determined that this stepchild of the system would become one of its proudest representatives, and in the six years of his administration the mission enjoyed its golden age.

Mexico opened up California's ports to the clamoring Yankee merchant ships, and in the period before the American conquest gave over eight hundred vast tracts of California land, much of which was formerly in custody of the missions. In addition to this difficult task, Governor Figueroa was still confronted with the Russians at Fort Ross. Looking for an administrator of suitable capabilities to assist him, he chose Lietuenant Mariano G. Vallejo.

At twenty-five years of age, this young officer had become Commandant of the San Francisco Presidio. Personable and politically astute, "Commondante - General" Vallejo was on his way to a brilliant future. By the end of the year he held the rank of Lieutenant Colonel and the title, "Commandant General in charge of the Northern Frontier".

Following Governor Figueroa's instructions, the young commandant founded the Pueblo de Sonoma in 1835 and laid out the plaza which was used as a parade ground for the garrison. By 1840, the three adobe buildings which comprised Sonoma's Casa Grande were nearing completion. It was here that the General and his lady extended their hospitality to dignitaries of the province, and to those emissaries sent by foreign powers to spy out this little-known land. It was from here, on June 14, 1846, that the General was escorted to Sutter's Fort on the Sacramento River as a prisoner of the Bear Flag Republic.

This group consisted of a band of recently arrived American immigrants

General Vallejo with his daughters.

who, fearing deportation, by Governor Castro, solicited the leadership of Captain John Fremont, a surveyor with the U.S. Army, and marched on the undefended Sonoma Pueblo. A group of them ran up a homemade flag in the plaza and declared California an independent Bear Flag Republic. Three weeks later, on the basis of the U.S. War with Mexico, Commodore Stockton ran the American flag up over the provincial capitol of Monterey, and declared California a territory of the United States. Captain Fremont was ordered back to Washington for a court martial, and the Bear Flag Republic came to an end.

In January, 1848, gold was found at Sutter's Mill, and shortly thereafter the stampede began. Until then, California could claim a population of not more than five or six thousand. Overnight, the population north of San Francisco had jumped to two hundred and fifty thousand. Even remote little Sonoma felt the explosion as families of the San Francisco merchants and occupation forces moved to Sonoma to escape the madhouse that the gold rush had made of San Francisco.

In 1850, Sonoma was incorporated, and a few months later became the county seat. There was nothing of any dramatic import for the next year or

Henry Beeson, last survivor of the famous Bear Flag Party, raising the Bear Flag in Sonoma on September 9, 1907.

Sonoma County Historical Society

so until one dark and stormy night the county clerk, "Old Peg Leg Menefee", bribed by some folks from that upstart town called Santa Rosa, made off in a spring wagon with all the records and the county seal in the direction of Santa Rosa. Thinking that Sonomans were in hot pursuit, he used his peg leg to spur the horse on. Later, by legal election, Santa Rosa became the county seat. In 1852 the U.S. Occupation Forces pulled out of "Camp Sonoma", taking with them the town's chief economy. From that day to this, Sonoma never did overcome the stigma of being considered a depressed area, a factor thought by many latter day residents to be a blessing in disguise, since there was no industry to destroy the pastoral charm of the region.

Supplanting this, General Vallejo, with an unshakeable faith in the agricultural potentials of the area, pioneered the wine making industry, in 1850. He started purchasing lands just west of the plaza, and by 1852 had acquired, piecemeal, five hundred acres for the purpose of cultivating the grapevine and citrus trees He called the place Lachryma Montis Latin for "tears of the mountain", after an artesian-fed reservoir on the hillside. Open for public viewing since 1933, this unit of the State Department of Parks and Recreation has been restored to appear as it did during the forty years of his occupancy.

He passed his remaining years here, constantly giving his increasingly limited resources toward the development of his beloved California. At the time of his death, at the age of eighty-three, in 1890, the lands that had once been his had been reduced from 175,000 acres to less than five.

His fabled Gothic Revival frame house, completely furnished with imported Victorian furnishings brought to California by sailing ships, lush Victorian-style gardens with trellis fences, cast iron fountains, and charming pavillions all testify to this great Californian's soul-hearted acceptance of the American lifestyle.

General Vallejo had been winning prizes on his mission grape wines when, in 1857, a Hungarian Count,

Agostin Haraszthy, established in the Sonoma Valley what would become the largest acreage given to viticulture in the world. His contributions to wine production in the United States earned him the title "The Father of Wine Making".

This was the age of the fourteen course dinner and, consequently, of the spa. Among Sonoma's other attributes were an infinite variety of underground mineral waters. Even the General wanted to get in on that bandwagon, for Lachryma Montis would have been ideal. He even went so far as to let James Donahue's railroad cut across the fields fronting his house. His plans for a resort, however, never materialized.

Cast Iron Fountains at the Vallejo Home, which is now a California State Historical Monument.

Sonoma Historical League

The story of General Vallejo's activities and the fortunes of the Sonoma Valley went hand in glove, and when the Sonoma Valley narrow gauge railroad chugged into Sonoma in 1875, the Vallejo family was there to greet it, make speeches, and throw garlands around the little engine's smokestack; and, of course, the little engine was called the "General Vallejo".

Railroads have never been great respectors of private rights, particularly in the day when communities felt that they could not survive without them. It's not easy to think of Sonoma's tree-shaded plaza with a round house in its northwest corner, a depot in the center, and a water tower nearby, but that's the way it was. The train rumbled up and down Spain Street in front of the crumbling old mission, finally forcing the parishioners to relocate their church on the west side of town.

Today, the names of El Verano, Boyes Springs, Kenwood, Glen Ellen, and Annadel, to name just a few, are reminders of the past, having served as railroad stop-offs where resorts and hamlets were established.

Obviously, the Sonoma Valley has played an important role in the development of California. The founding of the last mission in the California chain; the contributions of General Vallejo; the Bear Flag Revolt; which precipitated American annexation of California, and the world famous wine industry have helped to insure the valley's place in history. All of these events, however, have not altered greatly the physical beauty of the area. The lack of "big industry", save that of the wineries, has helped preserve its pastoral charm. Today's visitors are fortunate in being able to see for themselves what it was that attracted the Indians and, later, the first European settlers to the Valley of the Moon. **The End**

Silverek

A typical pastoral scene near Kenwood.

"I would rather be ashes than dust!
I would rather that my spark should
burn out in a brilliant blaze than it
should be stifled by dryrot.
I would rather be a superb meteor,
every atom of me in magnificent glow,
than a sleepy and permanent planet.
The proper function of man is to
live, not to exist.
I shall not waste my days in trying
to prolong them. I shall use my time."

Jack London

Jack London in his office at the ranch

Jack London: The Man Who Lived His Dreams

by Russ Kingman

Nestled below Sonoma Mountain, overlooking the Valley of the Moon, lie the nearly fourteen hundred acres known as the Jack London Ranch. Jack bought the first segment of the ranch in 1905, and in 1910 he purchased land that had previously been owned by one of the oldest wineries in the valley — Kobler and Frohling. The red volcanic earth provided one of the finest wine soils in the world and the four hundred tillable acres had never felt the bite of frost.

The "Beauty Ranch", as Jack called it, soon became the most advanced scientific ranch in California. Everything new was tried. Jack terraced the hill areas to prevent erosion, planted and plowed under soil-building crops, built what is now one of the most beautiful private lakes in the country for recreation and irrigation, purchased the first manure spreader in the area, constructed the first concrete silos in California, erected stone barns and water troughs to "last one thousand years," and stocked the farm with pedigreed Shire horses, Jersey cows, Duroc Jersey hogs and White Leghorn chickens. Luther Burbank and Jack London spent many hours studying their spineless cactus experiments at the ranch. Wine grapes were planted, and on July 17, 1914 the "Jack London Grape Juice Company" was formed. Jack's dream of "making two blades of grass grow where only one had grown before" gradually became a reality.

Success, unfortunately, was matched by heartaches. In 1910 Jack started construction on "The Wolf House". It was to be a big, unpretentious home in the redwoods. In 1913, just before the Londons were to move in, an arsonist burned it down. Jack planned to rebuild the Wolf House, and actually began to accumulate material, but he could never bring himself to begin; it was destined to be a magnificent memorial to a magnificent man.

The Jack London Ranch was never planned as an experiment in communal living or socialism. The fact that it moved in the direction of a self-sustaining colony grew out of the big heart of Jack London. It was to be a scientific farm and one of its main purposes was to help farmers in the area have better crops and a better life.

Jack's whole heart and soul went into its operation. He wanted the working men to have a better way of living. He planned to give each worker an acre of ground and a home of his own. A store, post office and a school were in the planning stages.

Jack was a "big" man and Charmian, his lovely wife, was just as "big" a woman. She was small of stature but large in deed and the best wife, companion and "mate" a man could ask for. She was Jack's companion at home and around the world and he loved her dearly all his life.

Education and fun walk hand in hand when you visit the Jack London State Park. For 1976 an added inducement will be periodic tours to the Ranch itself. At the park you can see the "House of Happy Walls" built by Charmian London in 1921. It now serves an the Jack London Museum. You can visit the museum, and then take a gorgeous nature walk down the trail, near Jack's gravesite, to the ruins of the Wolf House.

It was at the top of the hill and at the start of the trail to the Wolf House that Charmian built her own lair — a complement to Jack's Wolf House. It's as though she wanted to be sure that the Wolf House would be Jack's and his alone. A monument to the spirit that was within him. It is plain that her House of Happy Walls was designed as a future museum to Jack and her love for him.

As you leave the valley, look up and see why the Indians named it "the Valley of the Moon", and why Jack and Charmian came to make its name known in every country around the globe.

Russ Kingman

Jack and Charmian in their favorite transportation vehicle.

Eastern Sonoma County Restaurants

DEPOT 1870

In 1890, the owners of this historic building -- once owned by General Vallejo -- opened their living room as a bar. With passengers arriving daily by train from San Francisco, the bar did well and a dining room was added to the lower floor. Continuing this tradition, designer/owner Russell Brown has created an ingenious and impeccable interior as bright and refreshing as a greenhouse in spring. No Victorian cobwebs here.

Five-course dinners are available for $11.00 and the entrees are limited to two or three per night. The chef's whim and availability of fresh food dictate the menu. Depot 1870 is open Thursday-Sunday, 5:00-9:00pm, with brunch served the first Sunday of each month (no dinner that night.) Reservations are requested. Wine and cocktails.

DEPOT HOTEL 1870
Continental
241 First St. West, Sonoma
Brunch-1st Sun of month
*   from 10:30am-1:30pm*

L - Fri only 11:30am-2pm
D - 5-9pm Thur-Sun
Full bar
AE, BA, MC, Visa
(707) 938-2980 Reservations requested

CAPRI

Tucked away in the corner of a large stone building overlooking Sonoma's Historic Plaza is the Capri Restaurant. It was here that the Bear Flag Revolt of 1846 occurred - an event that eventually catapulted California into statehood. It is also here that the owners of the Capri, Joanne and Keith Filipello serve some of the finest cuisine in Northern California.

Dinners are served with Sonoma French Bread, appetizer, soup, and salad served before or after entree (a la carte entree deduct $1.00). You can enjoy entrees ($6.75 - $23.00 for two) like Escalope de veau saute (milk fed veal sauteed with wine), Carre d' agneau (succulent rack of lamb with special herbs & sauce - $22.00 for two; $12.00 for one), Quiche au fromage (cheese tart served with vegetables), Poisson de mer (fresh fish of the day), or Civet de lapin (rabbit sauteed in wine). The wine list has been carefully thought out and should satisfy most.

One reason why the cuisine is so excellent is the selection of produce. How many chefs care enough to leave once a week at 3:00am in the morning to personally select fresh fish from the warf and 1st grade choice cuts of meat from the finest butchers in San Francisco? Joanne has explored the countryside to find out which farmers raise the highest quality rabbit, duck, quail and pheasant. In addition, she is known for her fresh culinary herbs. Only the ripest vegetables and fruits are served. It is unusual when a fine Northern California chef prepares daily the imaginative cuisine he is truly capable of - Keith is such a chef. Therefore I endorse the Capri Restaurant as one of the finest resturants in Northern California.

CAPRI
Fresh Country Cuisine
101 East Napa Street, Sonoma
Dinner hours: Winter - Tues - Thur 5:30pm - 9:30pm
Fri & Sat & Sun 5:30pm - 10pm
Summer - Tues - Thur 6pm - 10pm
Fri & Sat & Sun 6pm - 11pm
All year a Sunday Brunch is served from 10am - 2pm
Beer and Excellent Wine List
MC, Visa (707) 996-3866 Reservations advised

GINO'S INN SONOMA

   Located on the famous Sonoma Plaza directly across from the
monument commemorating the Bear Flag Revolt of 1846 is Gino's Inn
Sonoma. This restaurant and lounge is a very popular luncheon and
drinking establishment for Sonomans. Pleasant help host the colorful
full bar and for lunch serve a selection of salads ($2.50-$3.75), delicious
sandwiches ($2.00-$3.50), and desserts. The atmosphere is very
comfortable with stained glass windows and lamps, monthly art shows,
and plants decorating the century old brick and stone walls. Owner
Jerry Rosenburg is very proud of his fine establishment and very proud
that he was asked to be the first to serve New Albion beer, which is
brewed and bottled in Sonoma at the smallest brewery in the United
States.

GINO'S INN SONOMA
American
420 1st Street East, Sonoma
Lunch 11am-2:30pm Mon-Fri
full bar
BA, MC, Visa
(707) 996-GINO

IL DESINARE

The Continental feeling prevails when one dines on food prepared by Chef David Serafini and his ample staff. Chef Serafini learned his craft from the Marche region of Italy and has expanded his culinary skills to include dishes from virtually all parts of the world. The people (Marchegiani) are known for their integrity, hospitality and distinctive cooking. Their dishes are simple, delicate, and extremely tasty.

IL DESINARE
Catering
20540 Broadway, Sonoma
(707) 938-3760

The entire staff of Il Desinare takes sincere pride in the quality of their service and food. Particular care is taken to authenticate regional dishes from every country.

Left to right: Phyllis Serafini — Executive Chef, Jane Blasi, Mary Zepponi, Mary Ellen Serafini, — Assistant Cooks.

Sommelier for Il Desinare is Gino Zepponi, well known lecturer on wine tasting, co-owner and wine-maker of ZD Wines, and wine consultant. Mr. Zepponi selects wines for dinners, tastings, and parties, with suggestions for proper serving. He also teaches courses in wine appreciation. Steven Serafini, left, wine steward and head of customer services.

SONOMA CHEESE FACTORY

There are few places in the wine country where one can dine in the manner the Sonoma Cheese Factory offers. There is the absence of many things a plush expensive restaurant requires - like the long wait to be served; the absence of waiters and cooks which makes your food less expensive, because for the most part you select and serve the food yourself.

The aroma of 101 varieties of cheese and 50 varieties of meat flavors the air. Sample the cheeses that three generations of family tradition have created - golden Sonoma Cheddar, Caraway Jack, Teleme, and the house specialty, Sonoma Jack made from a 40 year old family recipe. Browse through the shop. Shelves are lined with gourmet food, Mayacamas soups and spices, wholesome bread from the Sonoma French Bread Bakery, domestic and imported beer, and racks filled with the finest California wines; some from vineyards just outside Sonoma. You'll find one of the most appealing points is the wine selection. You may select a fine bottle of local or imported wine, open it, serve yourself and your guests on the pleasant outdoor patio.

In this age of freedom, independence, and the economy minded the Sonoma Cheese Factory certainly fits the bill. The outdoor patio is located in the heart of the wine country across from the park where the Bear Flag Revolt occurred in 1846, General Vallejo could have asked for no better. So declare your independence and enjoy a good meal to boot at the Sonoma Cheese Factory.

If you would like to order selected gift boxes from Sonoma Cheese Factory products, please request the Cheese Factory Gift Catalogue, P.O. Box 215, Sonoma, California.

SONOMA CHEESE FACTORY
Cheese & Gourmet Foods
2 West Spain St., Sonoma
Open 9am - 6pm Daily
Beer & Wine
(707) 996-2300

The lights of the Magnolia Hotel
on a warm summer evening in Yountville.

The Lilli Coit Suite in the elegant
Mount View Hotel in Calistoga is fu[r]n-
ished with $27,000 worth of antiqu[es]

HIGHWAY 29
THROUGH THE NAPA VALLEY

The Napa Valley is known as one of the best premium wine producing regions in the world. It is also a haven for a handful of elegant lodging facilities, antique shops, art galleries, gourmet restaurants, historic shopping centers, spas, unique bookstores and museums.

There are two main thorough fares into the Napa Valley from the south. From San Francisco take Hwy 101 north past San Rafael and head east on Hwy 37 just south of Novato. Stay on Hwy 37 through Sears Point until you reach Napa. From Oakland and Berkeley take Hwy 80 north, go over the bridge at Vallejo and keep going until you come to Hwy 37. Then turn west into Napa. If Napa is the first stop in a trip that will eventually take you through the wine country and north to the redwoods or Oregon Border; then you might pay a visit to the Book Cellar in Napa or Morning Sun Books in Calistoga. Though North of San Francisco has become the number one book of its kind on Northern California, there are other books and maps that cover smaller regions and specialized topics that may prove of value to you. For example at the Book Cellar Bookstore in Napa you can find numerous books devoted just to history or wine-making as well as

quality works for leisure reading along the way. The same is true for Morning Sun Books in Calistoga, except here free coffee is served and you can buy a pastry from next door to enjoy while purveying the titles. There are also weekly cultural events and a book rental library ($1.00 per book the 1st week or 25 cents per day).

If you want to sneak preview premium wines before tasting at the wineries then visit the wine cellar at Chick's House of Spirits on Trancas Avenue in Napa or the wine vault in the Bottle Shop on main Street of Saint Helena (open till 10 pm Mon - Fri). There are several good places to dine at in Napa. Among them - the Carriage House, La Gamelle, La Boucame, Olive Tree Inn, Olivers, Optimum Foods, The Penguins, and Rainbow Bridge. At the Witter Tea & Coffee Company on main street in Napa the aroma of fresh ground coffee beans wafts from the coffee bar. Over fifty varieties of coffees and teas are available as well as quality kitchenware and gift items.

Just northeast of Napa are the beautiful grounds of Silverado Country Club. Besides an excellent restaurant, there are luxurious rooms and suites for special seminars and conventions. Vacationers can enjoy a heated pool, tennis courts and two beautiful Robert Trent Golf Courses. A few miles north of Napa on Hwy 29 lies the historic community of Yountville. Thanks to the visions of a few people, Yountville acts as a buffer preventing destructive real estate and development interests from eating away at the precious southern Napa Valley farmlands & vineyards. In Yountville you can enjoy anything from buffalo stew at the Yountville Saloon or impeccable French Cuisine at Domaine Chandon or the French Laundry. Flanking the Historic Vintage 1870 shopping complex from all directions are other noteworthy restaurants including the Chutney Kitchen, the Diner, Grape Vine, Hooper Creek Inn (huge steaks), Magnolia Hotel Dining Room, Mama Nina's and the Washington Street Restaurant and Bar. Yes indeed, quite a selection of fine cuisine to choose from. Also you'll find several luxurious and intimate lodging facilities. Both the Magnolia Hotel and Burgundy House are treasure chests of antique furnished rooms immaculately tucked away inside the stone walls. On a quiet side street is Webber Place, a two story wooden home painted red and converted to a cozy country inn.. Just to the north is the spacious Best Western - Napa Valley Lodge with its outdoor tiled jacuzzi bordered by vineyards. Luxurious suites contain fireplaces and the best beds possible. Each room has a telephone and television.

In Yountville there are several botiques and antique shops, but of special note is Antique Fare, with showrooms of large oak & walnut antiques from France, Belgium, England, and Austria. Also large wardrobes, bedroom sets, brass beds, fixtures and lamps are sold. Twin Turrent Antiques displays a maze of antique crystal, china, glassware, blue willow, chandeliers. candle opera's and high quality antique furniture and collectors items.

North on Hwy 29 you'll come to the tiny roadstop of Oakville. Be sure to purvey the deli and gourmet foods sold at the old fashioned Oakville Grocery Co. Store. Next door is the Oakville Pub & Restaurant. In Rutherford, outdoor theater is offered under the starlite summer sky. Mary Tjilden Morton thoughtfully created Rutherford Square, a unique oasis with restaurant, bar,

downstairs lounge, and old fashioned parlor and giftshop.

A few miles south of Saint Helena near Franciscan Winery and on the left side of Hwy 29 is the Ink House, a large farm house that has been partially converted into a fine country inn. A few miles south of Saint Helena is the picturesque Chalet Bernensis Inn - the most elegant victorian inn in the Napa Valley. Chalet Bernensis offers nine antique furnished rooms in the main house and adjacent water tower. Next door solidly sits the stone & beamed suites of the Harvest Inn. Flanked by a 15 acre working vineyard, the Harvest Inn has been a successful experiment with modernized Old World elegance. In Saint Helena you can dine at Maggie Gins (excellent Chinese food), Lord Bruce, La Belle Helene, and the exquisite Miramonte, one of the finest restaurants in Northern California and also a first class lodging facility. A visit to the Saint Helena Craft Gallery (across from Maggie Gins) is well worth your time. Young proprietor David Tiedmann periodically displays exciting art & craft exhibits.

Between Saint Helena & Calistoga on the right of Hwy 29 is the Freemark Abbey Complex - a wine cellar, restaurant, candle factory, gourmet gift shop and Freemark Abbey Winery. Next door is Findings Unlimited, a antique store which is full of collectors items. Just down Lodi Lane is the elegant Wine Country Inn. Marge and Ned Smith carefully combined natural Napa Valley stone and redwood to create the 16 individually decorated rooms with balcony or patio view, fireplace, and poster beds covered with handmade quilts. Across the street from the Wine Country Inn is the Arbor Antique Shop.

Drive up Hwy 29 and turn right on Larkmead Lane for a tour of the Champagne Cellars of Hanns Kornell. Hanns arrived in America almost penniless from Germany in 1940; he was even forced to a few hours in jail in Calistoga. He good-naturedly dismissed the ignorant short-comings of the incident and went on to build a champagne empire. Even today it sometimes seems that the police of Calistoga and other small towns in Northern Cllifornia have nothing better to do than victimize curious visitors with petty traffic tickets.

Adjacent Hanns Kornell Champagne Cellars is the Larkmead Inn. The Victorian is gently flanked by a expanse of vineyards. The elegant rooms are named after varietals of wine.

In Calistoga are several good eating establishments and lodging facilities. Calistoga is also famous for its health spas. Among them is the family run Dr. Wildinson's Hot Springs where you can take mud baths, mineral baths, jacuzzi's and receive expert massage and treatments. Dr. Wilkinson is known as the Dean of the Hot Springs in the Napa Valley. His wife, Edy, runs a small gift shop adjacent their large air conditioned motel. You can also enjoy Pacheteau's Spa and the Roman Spa. The Calistoga Spa has 39 rooms (some recently remodeled), a large mineral pool, jacuzzi, small swimming pool and huge Roman Olympic Pool (summers only).

Just north of town and off Tubbs Lane is the famous Old Faithful Geyser of Calistoga. If you want to experience a spectacular site; then early some morning before the sunrise breaks up the fog layer over Old Faithful Geyser, drive a few miles up the hillside on Hwy 29 towards Mount Saint Helena, park your car and wait for the geyser to spout through the fog blanket -incredible! Another neat experience is to go for a ride in one of Jim Indrebo's gliders over Mount Saint Helena and the Upper Napa Valley. Most gliders can hold a pilot and two passengers so the flight can turn out to be a romantic adventure. At the Treasure-house of Worldly Wares on Tubbs Lane you can meet a very colorful Indian lady—Stevie Standing Bear Whitefeather. Her gift shop is like a museum. Indian artifacts displayed date back to Prehistoric times.

You can tour several shops in the historic Calistoga Depot (built 1868).

Seven interesting shops and a ice cream parlor await you. The Depot's Wine Shop is housed in a coach car that was present when the gold spike was set at Promontary Point in Utah.

A variety of cuisine can be enjoyed at the Calistoga Inn, El Faro, Silverado Restaurant and Tavern, Cinnabar, and the showplace of the Napa Valley - the Mount View Hotel. Not only is the food excellent, but the rooms of the Mount View Hotel are the best to be found in the Napa Valley. The Coit Suite alone is furnished with $20,000 worth of historic antiques. At the Calistoga Inn an imaginative selection of entrees is changed every month and at the Silverado Restaurant and Tavern you can wine taste by the glass. El Faro has been a popular Mexican restaurant in Calistoga for a decade. "Preparamos todo en neustra cosina con mucho amor especialmente para su deleite," proudly state owners Greg and Carmen Hernandez.

The Silverado Museum in Calistoga is a must. Curator, Ben Sharpstein was one of Walt Disneys first animation artist, with credits including "Lady and the Tramp." Don't forget Morning Sun Books.

There are many other places you can visit. There is Meadowood Golf Course where you can play golf, dine on gourmet dinners and stay at a very elegant suite on a hillside secluded by trees and vegetation. Over the mountains to the east is Pope Valley Airstrip. You can watch dare-devil parachutists, hot air ballonists, and hang glider pilots perform acrobatics high above you and then retire to the restaurant & bar to feast. At Angwin is the Adventist College and helicopter airstrip, there is Lake Berryessa and of course numerous wineries and tasting rooms scattered throughout the Napa Valley.

Thats it - not all of it, but some of the better parts of the Napa Valley to be explored and appreciated. I hope you enjoy your trip.

Richard Geyer proudly leans against the hand carved wooden sign at the entrance to his lodge- the Harvest Inn. The working vineyard in the background is part of the 23½ acre estate which is located just south of Saint Helena.

You can sleep on the mirrored bed of famous actress Carole Lombard, at the Mount View Hotel in Calistoga.

Feather River bed rock help cook as well as hold down the succulent 2" thick teaks on the griddle at Hooper Creek Inn n Yountville.

Good Grub! Thats what the pioneers who settled the Napa Valley feasted on at days end. At the Yountville Saloon you can feast on buffalo stew (no longer an endangered species) and listen & dance to Country Western & Blue Grass music.

The Age of Elegance

by Betty Dopson

History of the Upper Napa Valley

The first Europeans to set eyes on the Napa Valley were from the Sonoma Mission, which was founded in 1823 under the leadership of Father Jose Altimira. They came seeking a sheltered inland valley to pasture their horses and cattle. They also brought with them the grapevine (not the pedigreed European strains of today, but the Mission Grape), the olive, the fig, and the golden mustard that covers the valley in late winter and spring.

Altimira and his men also discovered Indians living in the Napa Valley who were enjoying a flourishing culture and civilization. Based upon religious experiences and a harmonious coexistence with nature, these Indians were leading satisfying and healthy lives when the first white settler, George Yount, came riding into the valley in 1831.

Yount, from South Carolina, came in search of new frontiers, and found them in the beautiful Napa Valley. He settled here and became a friend of General Mariano Vallejo, to whom he explained the merits of wood as a

building material rather than clay, and subsequently made the shakes for the general's Sonoma home for which he received land as payment. He was given a Mexican land grant which comprises the heart of the Napa Valley, 11,800 acres, upon which he built a two-story Kentucky-style block house.

One of Yount's many facets included an understanding and respect for the Indians who worked for him. Together they planted vineyards, raised sheep, horses, and cattle, maintained fruit orchards, and built a flour mill and a sawmill.

Yount, who was widely known for his hospitality, was honored at his death with the changing of the settlement's name from Sebastopol to Yountville.

Yount's death marked the end of the Mexican land grant era. Settlers interested in putting the land to crops began to pour into the valley. The soil was perfect for planting, and one of the first major crops was wheat, reaped with a rough sickle, dried a day or two, then threshed by driving

Lincoln Avenue in early Calistoga.

The Cougar, Indian and Grizzly were thick in the Napa Valley in the 1800's when George Yount first rode in.

horses over it as it was spread on a wooden floor. Flour mills were erected, among them the Bale Mill near St. Helena and the Chiles Mill in the Chiles Valley to the east. Sawmills were built for the lumber taken from the mountains and hillsides as the trees began to fall before the woodman's axe.

Cattle were raised for food, but more importantly for hides and tallow. Oak bark was plentiful, and cured hides became a valuable export. Wine was made by trampling grapes in a hide trough with bare feet, then fermenting in skin bags.

At the same time, many covered wagons were beginning to come through the Sierras. Many members of the Bidwell-Bartelson party bought land in the upper valley, as did settlers of the Grigsby-Ide party. Fenced land began chopping up the ranches. Squabbles over land, burnings, gunfights, and Indian battles marked the late 1840's. The Gold Rush of 1849 sent many of the settlers into the motherlode in search of instant wealth. However, finding the pickings slim and the work hard, many chose to return to their farms and make a profit from successful miners wintering in the valley. Prices soared, and anybody who had farm produce to sell could command his own price.

Commercial development of the vineyards began in the late 1800's after experimentation with crops of wheat, barley, and oats. A good market for wine was at the valley's door in San Francisco, fast becoming wealthy as well as cosmopolitan in its tastes. Less fertile land was found to be ideal for wines. Men came to the valley in the last decades of the century with wine on their minds, and the government lent a hand with research, commissions, and tax advantages.

Charles Krug was the first to make non-Mexican type wine in the county. In 1858, with his cider press and European winemaking knowledge, he proved a fine wine could be made from the valley grapes. Count Agostin Haraszthy introduced European varieties into the state in 1860. The first vinifera vineyard in the valley was planted from Haraszthy's European stock in 1861. There was no stopping the flood tide. By 1867 there were one thousand acres in vinifera grapes, and this was only the beginning. The largest vineyard, owned by Sam Brannan, was one hundred and twenty-five thousand acres near Calistoga.

Robert Lous Stevenson and his bride Fanny. They spent their honeymoon on the slopes of Mount Saint Helena in the year 1880, close to the site of the once bustling mining town of Silverado City which was abandoned in 1875 after the vein ran out.

Following the discovery of the wine-

Workmen build the arch and wall in front of Christian Brothers Winery

A history of the upper Napa Valley would not be complete without mentioning Sam Brannan. Brannan had a passion for doing things in the grand manner. He built the first spa at Calistoga, now Pacheteau's Spring Grounds, erecting a handsome hotel designed to attract the wealthy and prominent of San Francisco. He brought the first railroad up the valley, created the first fire department, and donated the costly and spectacular engine. His friends, among them Huntington and Leland Stanford, brought their horses to race on Sam's track near Calistoga.

Sam Brannan's Calistoga, nestled at the foot of five thousand foot Mount Saint Helena, also attracted the internationally famous English writer

making process and the growth of the industry, overplanting occurred. From 8,520 gallons of wine in 1860, 297,070 gallons were produced in 1870, and by 1880 wine production totaled over 4,000,000 gallons. The Depression of 1890 sent the price of grapes to eight dollars a ton, and this, coupled with phylloxera, an ineradicable root disease, threw the industry into a slump from which it took years to recover. Production took an upswing after a cure for phylloxera was discovered, but was knocked down again with the coming of Prohibition in 1919.

Despite the wine industry's hardships, a few men left their mark on the industry. Prominent among them is Charles Krug, California's first viticulture commissioner, a former newspaperman and neighbor of Haraszthy. He acquired a tract of land, built a store, and offered free lots to anyone who would build on them, thereby paving the way for the beginning of the town of St. Helena in 1853.

At Yountville, J. Groezinger, of San Francisco, bought land, planted a vineyard, and built a wine cellar. His handsome brick buildings now house Vintage 1870, a complex of unique shops in Yountville. The town of Rutherford, the home of Captain Niebaum and his Inglenook Winery, and Georges deLateur, with his Beau-lieu, was named for another important figure, T.F. Rutherford, an early settler and grape grower in the area.

These handsome wineries, and a few of the beautiful Victorian homes their owners built, still lend grace to the valley. The Schram estate, the Cap-tain Niebaum home, faithfully re-stored, are among them, as well as the Beringer home, the Rhine House, a valley landmark and the hospi-tality center for the Beringer Winery. The deLatour home, at the end of an avenue of flowering plum trees, brings back visions of the Napa Valley's Age of Elegance.

These men, with the courage and tenacity to build for the future, laid the foundation for the wine empire of today. Possessing visions of greatness for the valley's wine, they persevered through ruinous prices, disease, and decimated crops with an undaunted faith in the future of California wine.

They made great wine, and lived with a gusto that created a life style admired and emulated by those who followed. Theirs was, indeed, a legacy of color and romance that will last as long as grapes grow in the Napa Valley.

Some of the men who "dreamed their dreams on these warm hills." Wine-makers at Sutter Home Winery.

Bob Trinchero Collection

NapaCounty Restaurants

SILVERADO RESTAURANT, TAVERN, AND WINE SH

If you're into good wine, quality food and service only a family-operated establishment can offer, then visit the Dierkhising family (Drake, Alex, Mark, and their wives) at the Silverado.

Mark is the chef and his specialties include Abalone, Trout, Sole, Beef Ribs, Sirloins and Filets, ranging from $4.25 to $8.00, all served with fresh garden vegetables. Alex is the wine merchant, the Wine Sh providing the widest selection of wines in the valley, including many hard-to-get wines from small premium wineries. He's also in charge of the wine-tasting parties held Tuesday nights (RSVP.) Drake maintains the casual, comfortable, and affordable atmosphere of the Silverado (the dining room makes all wines available at only one dollar over reta

The Silverado is an excellent place to begin and end your next wine tasting tour.

SILVERADO RESTAURANT & TAVERN
Creative American
1374 Lincoln Ave., Calistoga
B & L 6:30am-3pm, D 5-10pm, Bar 10am - Midnight
Full Bar, Banquets, Catering, Music Weekends, Off Sale Wine
MC, Visa. (707) 942-6725 Reservations advised

MOUNT VIEW HOTEL

The ringed silouette of a leaping stag etched on glass doors marks the entrance to the Mount View Hotel. When you walk through these doors and into the spacious lobby, be prepared to step back 50 years. "It took us a year of our lives and a million dollars," remarks owner Carol Campbell Wenaas. She and her crew of associates worked tirelessly to turn the Mount View into a showplace commemorating the 1920's - 30's Art Deco Era. The hotel is under the thoughtful direction of Alain Gregoire, who has an excellent back-ground in managing some of the more elegant hotels and restaurants of Europe. The keys were turned and the doors opened to the public on the threshold of a new decade - January 12, 1980.

The suites and rooms are elegantly furnished. The Carole Lombard Suite is furnished with her peach mirrored bed and dressor's. In the Tom Mix suite the furniture and bed is accented with bull & steer horns. The elegant Coit Suite is furnished with $27,000.00 worth of antique furniture. The rooms and private baths are kept spotless. There is even a evening maid service. Room rates vary from $50 - $165 a night for two.

In the kitchen Classic French Cuisine is prepared under the watchful eye of an executive chef and his capable assistant & staff. The dinner menu is changed each day. To compliment your entree you can choose between homemade soup or garden fresh salad, a selection of appetizers (served a la carte) such as Pheasant Pate, Pork and Veal Terrine or Goujonnette of sole tartare, and desserts like homemade fruit tarts, cheese boards, or chocolate mousse torte. Each day a variety of fresh seafood, milk fed veal dishes, choice poultry, prime cuts of beef and seasonal vegetables are served in the Classic French tradition. Dinners range in price from $9.00 to $15.00. There is a outstanding wine list and mixed drinks are served from the full bar. Entertainment varies from a pianist to strolling musicians. There are pool parties with varying themes and outdoor BBQ's. I'm sure you'll find the large heated pool and tile jacuzzi to your liking. The Mount View Hotel is located on main street in Calistoga. "We wanted to create a lively social scene complimented by elegant lodging and Classic French Cuisine." states Carol. I don't think you'll be disappointed .

MOUNT VIEW HOTEL
Elegant lodging and Classic French Cuisine
in the Napa Valley Wine Country.
457 Lincoln Avenue, Calistoga
Breakfast: 7:30am - 12:30pm daily
Dinner: 6pm - 10pm daily during winter
6pm - 11pm daily during summer

Excellent Wine List & Full Bar, Large heated swimming pool, large tile jacuzzi and outdoor bar. 34 individually furnished rooms & suites. Room rates - $50 - $165. AE, MC, Visa. (707) 942-6877 Res. 24 hrs.

CALISTOGA INN

As you are traveling north on Highway 29, through the beautiful Napa Valley, and you come to Calistoga, turn right on Lincoln Avenue and go one block to the Calistoga Inn for delicious gourmet dinners and lodging.

The Calistoga Inn is an old-fashioned type place that has been in the same location for over seventy five years. Don't worry about dress because your casual traveling attire is compatible with the delightful decor of the Inn. The menu is changed weekly and includes a selection of appetizers, soups & salads, and usually six to eight Country Continental variations of fresh water fish, seafood, poultry, beef, veal, lamb, or vegetarian entrees. Dinners range in price from $5.75 to $12.50. The wine list features an excellent selection of wines from the California wine growing regions.

For six years various owners have quietly toiled at rennovating the upstairs into very comfortable lodging facilities. Rooms are priced at $18 (single) or $20 (double occupancy) per night and Continental Breakfast is included. There are no television sets in any of the currently available 10 rooms. More rooms and innovative changes are planned in the future. Poised at the northern gateway of the famed Napa Valley Wine Country, the Calistoga Inn offers a welcome all its own.

CALISTOGA INN
Restaurant and Inn
Country Continental
1250 Lincoln Ave., Calistoga

Open Tues - Sun, closed Mon.
Dinner is served from 5pm - 10pm
MC & Visa (707) 942-4101 Res.

EL FARO

Button

"We prepare everything in our kitchen with lots of love especially for your delight". Thats what it says in Spanish at the bottom of the El Faro Restaurant menu, and we must agree, Greg and Carmen Hernandez, the owners, certainly have.

The El Faro Restaurant, located in the heart of Calistoga on Lincoln Avenue, was opened by the Hernandez family in 1970. Greg and Carmen are very proficient at preparing the Northern Mexico Cuisine and have kept the prices reasonable - Combination Plates ($2.95-$3.95), Mexican style steak dinners ($5.25), and the "Acapulco Surprise" ($2.95); we won't tell you what it is other than we found it to be one of the best bargains on the menu. Mexican and American beer, wine, and soft drinks are served also.

On one wall of the restaurant are pictures of famous Mexican singers and movie stars - among them - Alicia and Jose Alfredro Jimenez, Gilberto Valenzuela, and America and Ziomara Martin, who Greg and Carmen know. In the near future they hope to build a new El Faro Restaurant at the east end of Calistoga and a little closer to beautiful Mont Saint Helena. The Hernandez family hope to create an atmosphere of fine Mexican entertainment for you to enjoy with the fine cuisine they already serve. World famous organist Karla Pandit has been known to drop in to dine at El Faro and later play the organ Greg and Carmen have in the dining area. Occasionally Greg or Carmen find time to entertain by playing the organ while El Faro dinner guests enjoy the delicious cuisine - and don't forget: "Preparamos todo en neustra cosina con mucho amor especialmente para su deleite".

EL FARO RESTAURANT
Mexican
1353 Lincoln Ave., Calistoga

D - M,W,&Thur: 5pm-9pm
     Fri, Sat & Sun: 11am-9pm
Beer and Wine
MC, Visa
(707) 942-4400 Reservations advised

ABBEY *

Framed by silent, firm stone walls protected by timeless oaks stands
the Abbey Restaurant, a quiet ode to the tradition of quality Napa
Valley dining. Within this cool monastery-type building, highlighted by
carved doors, stained glass windows, and colorful baskets of dried
flowers, a rich variety of wine, dinner, and warm friendly atmosphere
awaits you. Mr. & Mrs. John Pappas, formerly from the well-known
Ondine restaurant of Sausalito which won the Holiday Magazine award,
are the proprietors of this unusual dining experience. Their warm,
receptive attitude towards their patrons is expressed in their words
"a stranger is a friend we have not met." In fact, they have stated that
"every customer is a celebrity." The Pappas' special attitude of
warmth and respect for their diners' pleasure is reflected in their
impressive menu: Luncheons offer Breaded Veal Cutlet (2.90),
Cannelloni Supreme ("delicate crepes stuffed with pork, veal, chicken
and mushrooms" - $3.15), Beef Kabob ($3.60), New York Steak
($4.95), and a variety of fish entrees, sandwiches, and salads. Dinners
are equally appetizing: Scampi Provencale ("huge prawns sauteed in
butter" - $7.00), Roast Prime Rib of Beef au jus ("generous portion of
seiect beef" - $7.50), Breast of Chicken Vladimir ("classic Russian pre-
paration with a subtle sour cream sauce and a whisper of vodka" -
$5.75). Greek pastry, peach melba, mousse au chocolat e, polish the
dessert menu. Cocktails are served at the table, as well as a fine list of
wines from local wineries: Zinfandel, Pinot Noir, Cabernet Sauvignon,
Johannisberg Riesling, Pinot Chardonnay, all afford welcome accom-
paniment to your entrees. The patio addition to the Abbey affords a
peaceful view of the mountains.

The aim of the owners is to present to you quality food in a serene,
friendly atmosphere, so characteristic of the Napa Valley wine country.
Overindulgence, overly rich food is abhorred by the Pappas, "We
believe excessive smoking and drinking is indirect suicide." The
emphasis is placed on economy, integrity, and grace: your meal at the
Abbey is cooked to perfection and served with gentle dignity amidst a
charming background of classical music. Dining at the Abbey is truly a
superior experience!

THE ABBEY RESTAURANT
Continental Cuisine
3020 St. Helena Hwy No., St. Helena

L 12 noon-4pm, D 5-9pm
Lunch, Dinner, Banquets
BA, MC
(707) 963-2706, Reservations advised

·James Dowlen····

LA BELLE HELENE

LA BELLE HELENE . . . A renovated Napa-stone building situated near the train Depot in St. Helena, provides an "AFFAIRE D' AMOUR" with French cuisine and its Cafe Art Gallery.

Thick stone walls, candelight, and antique tapestries create an elegant atmosphere. The patron gives audience to the owner and chef, Gregory Lyon's, personal creations of the day. A recent evening's menu included cream of lettuce soup, duckling braised with green peppercorns, a saute' of veal with mushrooms, roast leg of lamb and trout stuffed with a shrimp mousse' and poached in butter. Dinner prices are 7.50 to 10.50. Extraordinary desserts are available a la' carte. A distinguished wine list offers the choicest hard-to-find Napa Valley vintages and select French wines.

Luncheon specialties include quiche, omelettes, patés, chicken dishes and the same desserts available at night. Luncheon reservations are not required. Upstairs from the restaurant, the Cafe Gallery offers a complete European coffee menu with espresso, cappuccino, cafe'au lait and other coffee and tea specialties served homemade ice creams, our pastries and desserts.

Petits DeJeuners: French brunch served Sunday from 9:00 am with croissants, fresh orange juice and coffee specialties. Champagne cocktail mimosa also available.

The Gallery offers a distinguished six week program of one artist's exhibits of paintings, photographs and sculpture. Artists and collections shown at La Belle Helene Gallery are of international importance and receive the attention of major art publications and reviews.

Next to the Gallery is La Belle Helene's small collection of French antiques, furniture, china, glass, brass, modern and antique jewelry and other items of special beauty and interest.

LA BELLE HELENE
French
1345 Railroad Ave., St. Helena
Lunch from 11:30am Wed.-Sun.
Dinner 5:30pm-10:00pm Wed.-Sun.
Brunch from 9:00am Sunday

Wine & Aperitifs
Banquet Facilities
(707) 963-9984
Dinner reservations advised

MIRAMONTE

On a quiet side street in Saint Helena is the Miramonte Restaurant and Country Inn. Saint Helena is located in the heartland of the Napa Valley and the Miramonte has become a culinary pillar in Northern California. The cuisnen served by chefs Udo Nechutny and Edouard Platel is already legendary. Both chefs have international credentials.

The casual bar theme is dedicated to the Napa Valley winemaker. Photographs of the winemakers line the walls of the bar and the wine cellar is stocked with premium bottlings from new and little-known wineries. Chandeliers of elk antlers hang in the main dining room and at one end a fireplace is stoked on chilly Napa Valley evenings. The atmosphere is both festive and elegant.

On the menu is printed a code of ethics: "all food produce is fresh and selected for its prime quality within its season and market availability. Our menu is planned in conformity with this precept. We prefer to be out of a particular dish temporarily rather than to compromise the fine quality of our food."

The menu is changed every 2 - 3 weeks. Usually three entrees are available each evening. A sample of one of the opening dinners included truffle soup, Scallop Mousse, Steak de Canard, Jerasulem artichokes and Chinese mushrooms. A variety of European dishes are prepared from salmon, crayfish, pike, sole, sea bass, duckling, milk fed veal, beef and lamb. Edouard boasts of the fresh trout pond near the restaurant. Full course gourmet dinners vary in price from $20 - $30.

There are two elegant suites upstairs ($45 - $55). with private bathrooms, and a delicious continental breakfast is served the following day. A fabulous dining adventure awaits you at the Miramonte Restaurant & Country Inn.

MIRAMONTE RESTAURANT & COUNTRY INN
French Cuisine
1327 Railroad Ave., Saint Helena
Dinner: 6:15pm - 9:00pm everyday
but Mon & Tues. Sun. Brunch 11:30am - 2:30pm
(707) 963-3970 Reservations necessary

MAGGIE GINS

Finally, the Upper Napa Valley has a 1st class Chinese Restaurant. Maggie Gins, named after none-other than Maggie Gin, author of six cookbooks, and bay area celebrity noted for her gourmet cooking exhibitions & classes.

Plates are heaped with delicious Chinese Cuisine. Serving is cafeteria style and everything is prepared fresh daily with the recipes coming right out of her cookbooks. Seasonal offerings include stir-fried crab, BBQ or sweet & sour pork, chicken chow mein, spare ribs, roast duck with plum sauce, cold Szechwan, hot & spicy salad, and fresh Napa Valley fruit and vegetarian plates. Usually 5-6 hot and 2-3 cold entrees are served each day for lunch & dinner.

MAGGIE GIN'S
Chinese Cuisine
1234 Main St., Saint Helena
Lunch & dinner served Tues-Sat

from 11:30am - 2:30pm, & 5pm - 9pm.
Seasonal on Sunday & Monday,
excellent Napa Valley wine list.
(707) 963-9764   MC & Visa.

OAKVILLE GROCERY

Often the old-fashioned country store was the social focal point of a small town. Visitors to the Napa Valley will be delighted to know one exists in the tiny town of Oakville. Not only does the Oakville Grocery Co. stock the freshest of produce, but its cases & shelves are lined with many gourmet items for the sophisticated travelor planning that special dinner party or wine country picnic.

For picnickers, beautiful wicker & bamboo baskets specially choosen to be used again & again ($15-$40)

can be filled with exotic meats & cheeses from the deli, whole-wheat or sourdough bread, chilled mineral water, Imported beers(50 brands from 12 countries) and bottles of premium Napa Valley wines. There are also ornate tins full of delicacies, cookies, crackers & candies. The gourmet chef of the house will delight in purveying the selection of fresh black or white truffles (when available), common & difficult to find herbs & spices, Wagner's flavorings & extracts (30 kinds), fruit & nuts from California & Australia, Olive oil, wine vinegar (30 varieties), mustard (50 varieties), coffee beans, and European jams & jellies. Special caterings can be arranged at the Oakville Grocery Co. Friendly help will assist you in making selections as well as answer questions about the unique selection of produce they carry.

OAKVILLE GROCERY CO.
Gourmet Grocery Store & Deli

Hwy 29 at Oakville (707) 944-8802
Special caterings arranged.

RUTHERFORD SQUARE

In the heart of beautiful Napa Valley is Rutherford Square: a unique cultural complex with a floral-arbored patio encircling an outdoor theater, a country bar and wine cellar, and a restored Victorian house, "The Cottage."

Rutherford Square Theater creates magic, music, dinner & dancing, under the stars Saturday or Sunday nights through August. The Square, created by Mary Tilden Morton, is a dream coming true, dedicated to all arts and artists, sculpture, music, theater, painting, wood carving, and the culinary arts. Within the Square you will find the country "Corner Bar" serving fine wine and spirits. Homemade garden-fresh soups, cheeses, fruits and specials are available indoors or out on the Square.

Stroll through the gardens to "The Cottage," featuring homemade ice cream by Old Uncle Gaylord, a gourmet deli, hot or cold food, and beer or wine...to go. Champagne breakfasts served 10am-2pm Saturday and Sunday. Upstairs, "The Attic" is a creative clothes and gift shop.

Gather your friends together to spend a weekend in the Napa Valley wine country. Come find the magic of Rutherford Square in our little town of Rutherford, on the St. Helena Highway, Napa Valley.

RUTHERFORD SQUARE
Homemade Soups and Specialties
Heart of the Napa Valley
Restaurant 11am-3pm daily
Bar 11am-7pm Sun-Thurs
11am-11pm Fri & Sat
The Cottage
11am-4:30pm Tues-Sun

Champagne Breakfasts
10am-2pm Sat & Sun
Cabaret Theater open July-Aug
weekends only. BA,MC
(707) 963-2317 Cottage
(707) 963-7744 Restaurant (lunch only)
(707) 963-2617 Outdoor Theater
Reservations advised

YOUNTVILLE RESTAURANT
and COFFEE SALOON

What's wild in the Wild West? For starters, authentic buffalo lassoed and cooked to perfection in unique Western dishes such as Miner's Meat Pie (buffalo meat in pie shell), Buffalo Stew, or Camp Meat & Beans (broiled buffalo, ranch beans, rice with mushroom butter.) The only place in Northern California where you can find this hearty western grub is at the Yountville Restaurant & Coffee Saloon.

The lively, old Western restaurant, complete with old-time music, was originally constructed in 1901 as a livery stable. Greg Cochran, the saloon's first owner, bought the dirt-floor building in 1973 and remodeled the interior. Each inside wall now has its own wood pattern, on which hangs a rich array of 1880's Western memorabilia. Beamed ceilings, fashioned scrollwork, railings made from old wine tank staves all add to the interesting 19th century Western feeling of the place (an interior photograph may be seen in *Sunset* Magazine, June 1976.)

New owners Mark Raus and Zephyr Hedgpeth have kept the Yountville Restaurant & Coffee Saloon the same, presenting an interesting early Western setting in which to enjoy the varied menu. In addition to the 100% Wyoming buffalo meat dishes, which taste like beef but have a more gamey flavor, you'll find hand-carved rib eye, T-bone steaks, and fresh fish when in season. Nightly specials vary from prime rib, leg of lamb, pork, and cioppino. Prices for the dinners range from less than $4.00 to $9.95. Special homemade pies and old-fashioned bread pudding, baked daily by Nannette Clanton, are mouth-watering and foot-stomping good.

For a uniquely Western experience, visit the Yountville Restaurant & Coffee Saloon - the buffalo meat alone will make you feel proud to be in the West.

YOUNTVILLE RESTAURANT & COFFEE SALOON
American
6480 Washington St., Yountville
D Wed-Sat from 5:30pm-9:30pm
*   Sunday from 5:00pm-9:00pm*
Beer and wine
BA, MC
(707) 944-2761

CHUTNEY KITCHEN

If you haven't been to Yountville's Vintage 1870, then you have missed an important part of Northern California's wine country. An old winery has been converted into a multitude of beautiful shops including; a gallery, plant shop, theater, wine shop, and two restaurants. Both eating places are primarily for luncheons, and both are run by the management of Vintage 1870. The Vintage Cafe, an old rail station, boasts marvelous hamburgers, an espresso machine, and an assortment of cold beer and wines. It has a much used open deck for summer days, and a wood burning stove for chilly ones.

In the main building there is a lovely open kitchen and a colorful dining room, called the Chutney Kitchen. The area is a bustle of activity. Chutney maker, Carol McConnell hand processes eight unique varieties of chutney. They are all available for tasting, and mail orders are promptly handled. For lunch each weekday there is a different special and soup to compliment a variety of excellent salads and sandwiches. The special might be Mustard Chicken ($3.75), stuffed Pork Chops with Chutney ($3.75), Quiche ($3.50), Greek Spinach Pie ($3.50), and assorted Curries ($3.50). The soups are a long standing favorite - and are prepared fresh by the Chutney Kitchen staff. Some of the more popular are green vegetable, potato & leek, black bean or cold avocado soup for sunny days on the outdoor patio. For dessert, fresh cheesecake and chutney pound cake are long standing favorites.

There is house wine and beer as well as a select group of premium wines. Open everyday except Monday. The Vintage Cafe serves from 10:00 a.m., the Chutney Kitchen from noon till 5:00.

THE CHUTNEY KITCHEN and the VINTAGE CAFE
American – Continental
Vintage 1870, Yountville
Napa Valley

Sunday Brunch
The Chutney Kitchen
10:00 – 12:00
944-2788 (707)

MAMA NINA'S

The popular Mama Nina's restaurant of Yountville (like its counterpart - Mama Nina's of Cloverdale) accents northern Italian cooking with a tempting variety of homemade pastas, plus meat and seafood entrees. The soups and desserts also are made in Mama Nina's kitchen. Nightly specialties include lasagne verde, cannelloni, and osso buco. Meals are priced from $3.95 to $13.50.

A wide-ranging selection of Napa Valley wines complements the dinners at reasonable prices. The setting is tastefully appointed adjoining rooms offers courtyard and vineyard views. An outdoor terrace has been added for fair weather dining. The handsome bar with tables by a large stone fireplace is a friendly place to begin or to end the evening.

MAMA NINA'S
Northern Italian
6772 Washington St., Yountville
Reservations: (707) 944-2112
Banquet facilities available

Open at 5pm
Thursday-Tuesday (closed Wed.)
Full bar; Extensive wine list
AE, BA, MC

OLIVER'S

Oliver's has only been in Napa for two and a half years now, but its reputation is rapidly spreading. In that time it has become the CRITIC'S CHOICE and a member of "INTERNATIONAL WORLD FAMOUS RESTAURANTS." Owner Ernie Andon and Chef Condido Paz, have, through years of experience, put together what they call one-of-a-kind cuisine. . . take a look at their menu and you will discover

Rack of Lamb Bouquetiere, and Entrecote Marchand De Vin among Oliver's gourmet specialties. As an additional treat, included in your dinner, Chef Paz, prepares a variety of Mousses. Other superb dinners include scampi provencale and Oliver's creation (a combination of scampi provencale and fish in a light champagne cream sauce). Dinners range from $7.95 to $10.95 . . . a reasonable price for "one-of-a-kind cuisine."

OLIVER'S
Classic International Cuisine
1700 Second Street, Napa
L - M-F 11:30am-2:30pm

D - M-Sat. 5:30pm-Approx. 10:00pm
Sun. 5:00pm-Approx. 10:00pm
AE, BA, MC
(707) 252-4555 Reservations advised

CARRIAGE HOUSE

Having trouble meeting a restaurant with the right personality? How about a warm dinner house where casual, relaxed dining is the keynote amidst the charming seventy year old building known as the Carriage House Restaurant. The Carriage House service is warm and responsive to you, "a friend comes to the table, and takes care of your needs."

Originally built in 1904-5 as the carriage house to the Noyes Mansion, it was rennovated in 1974 into a charming restaurant complete with crystal chandeliers and brass mirrors making a rich contrast to the all wood interior.

The dinner entrees are limited to six ($6.95-$9.50) with a daily special. Among the choices are beef bourguignon (in a red wine sauce with mushrooms and onions) or Crab Mornay (Dungeness crab sauteed with mushrooms, green onions and sherry baked in Mornay sauce and served with piped potatoes in a scallop shell). All entrees include soup du jour and a fresh salad.

Lunches ($2.50-$4.25) are served outside on the patio (summertime) as well as in the main dining room, and include hot sandwiches, salads, and daily specials. Homemade desserts are a must, especially Aunt Millie's Lovely. The distinctive black walnut bar offers a varied selection of liquors and you may select a bottle of wine from one of 18 wineries represented on the wine list. The owners have taken care to choose wine from local small wineries. Over half of the 41 wines on the wine list come from small Napa Valley Wineries. The Carriage House Restaurant is an excellent way to end a Napa Valley wine tour. A cozy atmosphere with fresh and imaginative cuisine awaits you.

CARRIAGE HOUSE RESTAURANT
modified continental
1775 Clay Street, at Jefferson, Napa
L - 11:30am-2:30pm M-F
D - 5-10pm Mon-Sat
full bar
AE, BA, DC, MC
(707) 255-4744 reservations advised

The rural farmland of Sonoma County meets the proud lady of the Napa Valley—
Mount Saint Helena.

The Coast Of Mendocino County

By Barbara Dorr Mullen

The town of Mendocino posed above the Pacific Ocean

Some say the coast of Mendocino County reminds them of Maine. Others insist it is more like Scotland, or perhaps Japan.

With or without a family resemblance to anyplace else in the world, this twisting rocky shore is a very beautiful part of California, extending a welcome to sensitive visitors.

By long custom, the coast divides into three parts — the south coast, the middle (including the best known town, Mendocino, as well as three state parks) and the somewhat mysterious northwest corner, beyond Rockport.

The south coast starts just north of The Sea Ranch (at the northern tip of the Sonoma County coast). This is the mildest section, sometimes known affectionately as the banana belt. There is a fine string of beaches, coves and cliffs, between and in the small towns of Gualala, Anchor Bay, Point Arena, Manchester and Elk. Along the south coast, Highway One sticks close to the ocean, except for a slight turn inward around Manchester.

There's a variety of motels and inns for travelers along the south coast but the total number of rooms available is not very large so reservations are advised, especially during such special events as the Art in the Redwoods show, sponsored each summer by Gualala Arts.

The best known section of the Mendocino Coast is the middle part, some 35 miles reaching from Navarro-by-the-Sea where Highway 128 comes out of the redwoods and meets the Pacific north through Albion, Littleriver, Mendocino, Caspar and Fort Bragg to Westport.

North of Westport, there's at least one notable beach and a well known inn, but signs of civilization decrease as Highway One nears Rockport, a once prosperous lumber town. There the highway turns east away from the ocean, joining U.S. 101 at Leggett. Without a highway, the northwest corner of Mendocino County's coast remains mysterious and hard to reach, save by foot, horseback or off the road vehicle.

The whole coast shares a common history, due to a common product — lumber. Vast redwood forests grew here almost undisturbed until the mid-nineteenth century. The Pomo Indians native to the area had developed a sophisticated culture, producing baskets that now grace museums lucky enough to own them.

Then word of the great stands of timber spread, attracting lumberjacks from around the world. The cemeteries along the coast bear witness to immigrants from Finland, Sweden, Germany, England, the Azores, Portugal, Italy and elsewhere. Sawmills dotted the coast;

Mouth of the Big River

Barbara Mullen

blacksmith shops, livery stables, hotels, saloons, breweries, general stores, schools, churches and post offices grew up around them. The towns were linked by narrow and muddy roads, served by stagecoach. Lumber was sent to market in San Francisco and beyond via small schooners, loaded at small wharves or by means of rickety chutes, stretching out from the cliffs. The crews were brave for the waves could be savage, the weather unkind and the rocky cliffs cruel to ships and sailors.

After the first great cuts swept hillsides bare, the area began to suffer an almost chronic depression. Old houses and barns stayed because new ones were too expensive.

In the forties and fifties, artists began to discover the area and tourists followed. Now, though lumber is still important along with fishing, beauty is perhaps the Mendocino Coast's most important "crop," the natural beauty of beaches and streams, hills and headlands and the made beauty of artists, depicting the area or influenced by it. There are many galleries, studios and gift shops at Mendocino and elsewhere along the coast, together with lovingly restored old houses (ranging from simple salt boxes to Victorian showplaces). There is also the famous Mendocino Art Center (in the town of Mendocino). The Art Center offers a full year's schedule of classes, concerts, poetry readings, films, wine tastings and art fairs. The town itself has old streets to explore (mid-week is quietest) plus a healthy complement of restaurants and shops.

Albion and Noyo are centers for fishing (crab and salmon are the most important catches). Fort Bragg, western terminus of the Skunk railroad, is the largest town on the coast, a shopping center with a fine new hospital, architectural treasures and galleries of its own.

While a number of side roads lead to the coast (the Greenwood Road, Comptche Road, Low Gap Road),

The lumber chute was used for loading lumber from shore to ship.

Calif. Historical Society

the main access is via either Highway 128 which turns west at Cloverdale or Highway 20, swinging west over the mountains at Willits. There is once-daily service by Greyhound Bus (Highways 128 and 1 to Fort Bragg), a scenic train ride to Fort Bragg on the Skunk and an airport at Littleriver. Main roads are narrowish and shared with lumber trucks.

Accommodations range from the elegant to the ordinary; reservations are advised.

The coast is an area of fog, especially in summer when it usually burns off in the afternoon. In a normal year, the rains are apt to be heavy from October through May; when rains are scant, local water shortages are common. The winds can be high but frosts are rare and snow is rarer.

Although there are many scheduled events (from art shows and crab suppers to rodeos and flower shows) throughout the year along the Mendocino Coast (a subscription to the Mendocino Beacon or The Mendocino Grapevine, an alternate weekly published in Ukiah, will keep you posted), some of the most memorable events are unscheduled — gulls drifting above an ocean as blue as lapis lazuli, the excitement of a sudden storm lashing the cliffs or the soft sheen as fog burns off above rail-fenced meadows.

So far, the area has been fortunate in resisting neon signs and other tokens of progress. Local naturalists invite visitors to join them in keeping flowers and trees in the woods, birds in the air and litter someplace else.

Weather-worn water
tower in Mendocino

Barbara Mullen

A wild berry blossoms
into full flower

Barbara Mullen

LEDFORD HOUSE
Built 1862

"To your health" the young man states with a big smile across his face. He is right, for it is here you can experience some of the best a Northern California restaurant has to offer. The reason is simple. Here the priority is the spiritual rejuvination of the inner being. With that as a guidepost all else falls into place. For original owner Barbara Mastin and new owners Michael and Bella Brother preparing and serving innovative dinners became a joy.

Expect a wait to be seated, but I think you'll find the framed parchments and original art displayed throughout the dining room of interest. All breads, pastries, and pasta dishes are homemade and everything is prepared to your order. The fragrance of delicious food that wafts from the kitchen is unbearable, but have patience for you will leave Ledford House with pleasant memories. The dinner menu is limited to five consistently superb entrees - the fresh catch of the day, Shrimp Cannelloni (homemade pasta), Costolettine di Agnello fritte (tender baby lamb chops sauteed in a light crust of asiago cheese), filet of beef, and the chefs special which ranges from Pork Normande to Salmon Kouliback. All dinners include homemade brioche rolls and butter, garden salad, homemade soup, your entree served with fresh vegetables and range in price from $12.00 to $13.00. For dessert a variety of mousse's are served. The wine list consists of a good selection of premium California wines. At your table a bouquet of fresh cut flowers, a bright burgundy table cloth and gently burning candle awaits you.

The time is short. From the front windows the reflection of the late afternoon sun on the distant Pacific breakers is blinding. From the side windows the tall grass waves golden in the coastal breeze and nearby pines blend into the evening sky. Late at night with the soft music and crackling fire one can't help but sense a purpose in being here - and dining at Ledford House quite often becomes a religious experience.

LEDFORD HOUSE
Country Continental
7051 No. Hwy 1, Little River
Dinners: 6pm - 9pm Mon - Sat
During winter call for information
Premium California Wines & a Ocean View
Personal Checks accepted
(707) 937-0282 Reservations advised

The Sea Gull of Mendocino

You haven't been to Mendocino unless you've sampled the fresh fruit pies in the coffee shop, dined around the restaurant's pot-bellied stove, and ordered a drink in the upstairs "cellar bar" at the Sea Gull.

The rustic inn, with its rambling complex of white, vine-covered cottages facing on the sea coast, and the newly rebuilt restaurant (after a fire in 1976 burned it down), is the center of the town's social activity, especially for the young in spirit. Always packed, it's one of the earliest establishments in town. The newly built restaurant with large fir beams, rustic wood siding, large fairy-tale paintings in the cellar bar, locally handcrafted back bar and stools of imported mahogany and outside deck, opened in June of 1977.

Rates for cottages range from $18.00 (double bed, bath) to $31.00 (three double beds, bath). All beds have electric blankets. Write Box 317, Mendocino, or phone (707) 937-5204.

SEA GULL INN & RESTAURANT
Corner of Lansing & Ukiah Sts.,
Mendocino
Continental Cuisine & Lodging

Open daily B, L, & D 8am-9pm
(707) 937-5204 Res. advised

CAFE BEAUJOLAIS
International Gourmet
961 Ukiah Street, Mendocino
Breakfast & Lunch 8am - 2pm
everyday but Tuesday
Sunday Brunch 8am - 1pm
Dinner 6pm - 9pm Fri - Mon
Beer and Wine
(707) 937-5614 Reservations advised **CAFE BEAUJOLAIS**

Cafe Beaujolais serves the finest breakfasts in Northern California, using fresh local produce and homemade bakery items. The incredible omelettes contain a variety of fillings, including Italian sausage, green chile & cheese & fresh sauteed vegetables. In addition to egg dishes, fresh fruit salad, French toast with real maple syrup, wonderful crunchy waffles and homefries made with fresh potatoes are available. Side orders include toast (from homemade bread), different kinds of muffins baked daily, buttermilk - cinnamon coffee cake and bacon or sausage. The coffee, a hearty French - Viennese roast, is the best around and the expresso machine makes delicious cappuccinos and fanciful drinks. Try the Cafe Fantasia!

Breakfast is served until 2 so even the laziest soul can get there in time. Lunch offers sandwiches, soups & salads and the beautiful outside deck overlooking the lower garden and Pacific makes for a delightful setting. The desserts are really special - owner Margaret Fox considers baked products her specialty and she is well known for them indeed. Dinners and serving times change seasonally so be sure to give a call.

Humboldt and Del Norte Counties
A Little History

by Ray Raphael

Although Spanish ships appeared off California's North Coast as early as 1543, over two centuries passed before the Spaniards made an attempt to claim the land. In 1775, the *Santiago* and the *Sonora* dropped anchor in Trinidad Bay and Captain Hecata came ashore to stake his claim:

"I set up a cross on the shore and, forming an extended front, we performed the first adoration. Then, in as orderly a fashion as the narrow trails permitted, we followed the path to the top of the hill where the chapel was made, and took possession with the most scrupulous formality... This ceremony was solemnized with several volleys of gunfire. Each of us returned to his own ship which, with banners waving, saluted with three volleys of artillery and 'Long Live The King'."

White Deerskin Dance

The Indians of Tsurai (now Trinidad) were perplexed and terrified by the strange ways of the newcomers. The Europeans, in their turn, were bewildered by the bizarre customs of the "savages".

The Spaniards never returned but soon Russian and American ships were patrolling the North Coast waters in search of sea otter furs. In 1806, sailors aboard the *O'Cain* "discovered" Humboldt Bay (the Indians had known about it all along). But the Bay was neglected by the Caucasian entrepreneurs as soon as the sea otter population had been depleted.

It was 43 years later (1849-50) when a party of gold miners rediscovered Humboldt Bay as they searched for a supply route to the inland mines. Then the back hills were quickly flooded with eager prospectors and towns were established overnight with the sole purpose of supplying the mines. Eureka, Arcata (Union), Trinidad (Warnersville) and Crescent City were all founded by and for the miner.

Mining was so dominant that Orleans Bar, a mining town along the upper Klamath River, served as the county seat for the short-lived Klamath County. In 1851, one hundred mules bearing $5,000 worth of supplies left Union every week for the mines.

The native Indians could make little sense of the strangers who passed their days looking for a yellow dust in the streambeds rather than gathering acorns and fishing for salmon. But the strangers gave them "beads, bracelets, and other trinkets captivating to the savage" in an attempt to buy Indians' goodwill. This bribery worked for a while. But, as the white

Fort Humboldt

settlements became more established, the Indians began to see what "civilization" would mean to their own way of life. Cattle and sheep grazed in fields which had formerly provided seeds for pinole. Wild pigs devoured the Indians' acorns. Deer and elk populations were quickly diminished by the rifles of miners, soldiers and settlers. Mining practices were affecting the flow of the rivers and hindering the migration of salmon. The Indians tried to adapt to the changes in their environment by hunting the introduced game—cattle! Needless to say, such a practice was not tolerated by the settlers.

Some tribes managed to come to terms with the newcomers. Most of the Yuroks, for instance, stayed friendly in return for a 20-mile reservation along the lower Klamath. But such small concessions of land were not enough, especially when bloodshed was the order of the day. On the night of February 25, 1860, every man, woman and child on Indian Island in Humboldt Bay was brutally massacred by a band of whites. After that, most of the North Coast Indians not already killed by violence or disease set aside their differences and united to oppose the white invaders.

It took five years for the soldiers based at Fort Humboldt, Fort Seward, and at Fort Bragg in Mendocino County—aided by the "Mountaineer Battalion" of private citizens—to subdue the Indians. In 1864, most of the surviving Indians were moved to reservations, along the Smith River and in Round Valley in Mendocino County. In 1868, Indians from the Smith River Reservation were transferred to Hoopa Valley.

By the time the Indians had been moved, most of the gold was gone. What could take the place of gold as the focal point of the local economy? Some thought it would be oil and, in 1865, the first oil wells in California were drilled near Petrolia. The oil fields, however, proved to be unproductive and the oil boom, like the gold rush, was over almost before it had begun.

The most significant natural resource available to the settlers was the vast redwood forest which stretched for hundreds of miles along the coast. The supply seemed virtually infinite. In the words of an early visitor to the redwood wonderland, "California will for centuries have virgin forests, perhaps to the end of Time!" The trees were quickly

Typical Mill of Northern California

utilized; by 1880, a local historian boasted that "at every available point for shipment stands a sawmill turning trees to lumber, furnishing employment for labor and investment for capital."

Although the forests predominated, there was also some fertile farmland along the lower Eel River (in the Ferndale area) as well as isolated pockets elsewhere. Much of the agricultural activity in northwest California, however, took place in marginal backcountry areas where individual homesteads dotted the landscape. "Well, when my folks came in here it was on horseback," recalls Roy Cathey from Miranda. "There was nothing. They had to raise everything to live on. About 1880, I think, when they first came in here. You take up a homestead in them days."

Throughout the hinterlands of Humboldt and Del Norte Counties, there are old-timers like Roy Cathey whose families homesteaded the land they live on today. The old-timers remember raising most of their own food, but they also remember the shopping list for imported items. According to Ettersburg rancher Fred Wolf, "Up to about 1922-23, we got our groceries twice a year. Come in by boat. You

put in your order in April for your summer supply; in September you put in for your winter. You had to stop and figure, because you couldn't go to the grocery store every day. So you had to guess how much flour and sugar that you was gonna have to have for the winter. You bought coffee green, roasted it yourself, and you bought salt in fifty-pound sacks. That was the main staples that you had to buy; meat and everything else you raised."

To make enough money to pay for the semi-annual grocery shipments, the homesteaders often worked in the woods. They trapped fur-bearing mammals, split redwood shakes and railroad ties, or peeled the bark off the tanbark oak trees for use in the tanning of leather—whatever work they could find to scrape together a few extra bucks.

Roy Cathey worked on ties and shakes: "You had to fell your own trees and then buck them too—had to buck them all by hand, then. Then split 'em and hew 'em. Used to snake 'em out by horse. Had what they called bobsleds. Put one end on the sled and let the other end drag on the ground... I used to make a lot of shakes, too. You have a mallet and a froe. Hit 'em and drive 'em out. Twenty-five in a bunch then tie 'em up."

During the heart of the tanbark boom (1900-1920), Glen Strawn worked as a teamster for the Wagner Leather Company. "I seen that whole country out by Briceland piled with bark just as high as they could pile it. They had sheds down there with driveways through it so they could drive the teams in and unload it. Then they ground it and put it in a vat and cooked it to a certain extent. Then they'd pitch it into a big distill. Christ, that distill was ten feet across. Just the same as a whiskey still. And they'd put a fire under it and chase this tannic acid out and trap it. There's more tannic acid in this tan oak than in any other kind of bark. And it's easy to peel, too, if the sap's up. Hotter the day the better the peel."

The tanbark and tannic acid, shakes and railroad ties were all carried away from the forests by sea. Around the turn of the century there were scores of landing points off the California North Coast—some with wharfs, some just with cable rigs fastened to offshore rocks.

The large redwood mills in the lowlands also relied on ocean schooners and steamers to export their lumber. Overland travel was only by mule, horse or stage on rough mountain roads. One stage line followed near the coast, coming north through Fort Bragg, Usal and Whitethorn. An inland stage passed through Round Valley, Harris and along "Mail Ridge" to Blocksburg, Bridgeville, Rohnerville and Springville (Fortuna). Even today, many of these old stage roads remain unpaved.

On October 23, 1914, the golden spike was driven into the Northwestern Pacific Railroad line to Eureka. "Joy came that morning when the link was welded that brought dear old Humboldt into rail contact with the outside," reported an enthusiastic observer.

The completion of the railroad altered settlement patterns. Small

Driving the Golden Spike October 23, 1914

Freeman Art Co./Peter Palmquist Collection

towns along the old stage routes were abandoned while Fort Seward, Alderpoint and other towns along the railroad line developed. To the south, at Willits in Mendocino County, a branch line (the still-popular "Skunk") connected the Northwestern Pacific with Fort Bragg.

By rail, fish from the North Coast found its way to San Francisco markets and, during the 1920's, an overnight passenger train carried travelers from Eureka south to San Francisco and back again.

The railroad era did not last long. The Redwood Highway was built in the 1920's along the South Fork of the Eel River. Soon the railroad towns along the Middle Fork of the Eel gave way to highway towns like Laytonville, Garberville and Weott.

The automotive engine not only altered settlement patterns—it also revolutionized the logging industry. Since powerful caterpillars could

Humboldt and Mad River Railroad

build roads anywhere and drag the trees out behind them, forests which had once enjoyed the safety of inaccessibility could now be chopped down. During and after World War II, the demand for lumber was so great that the Douglas Firs (once considered "weeds") were logged as well as the redwoods. The population of the North Coast mushroomed as workers flocked to the woods to harvest the trees that would build most of California's houses in the post-war era.

Even the logging boom did not last long. In the 1960's—when the rest of the nation was flourishing and California was becoming the most populous state—Humboldt and Del Norte counties (as well as neighboring Mendocino to the south) went into a serious depression which resulted in population declines. The reason was simple: we were running out of trees. Logging had proceeded faster than the trees could grow back. The logging bonanza had destroyed itself—and it threatened to take the rest of the local economy with it. Salmon were fast disappearing due to increased siltation in the rivers. The tourists would not come to see the trees if they were all cut down. Farms in the lowlands were devastated by the floods of 1955 and 1964, both aggravated by erosion, siltation and the absence of trees in the forests.

With our resources diminished, the fight over those that remain has intensified. Conservationists in the 1960's pushed for the creation of the Redwood National Park, which the logging industry vigorously opposed.

Now, in the 1970's, the fight continues: how best to use a handful of virgin trees and how best to manage the forests so that the trees will grow back. Populations are increasing as city-born young people come to the countryside in search of a new way of life.

Yet many of the resources that supported the Indians and the homesteaders are gone for good. Can the depleted resources support an increasing population? How can vanished resources be replenished? And who should control the land which we usurped scarcely a century ago and have since abused so badly?

These are urgent questions for the future history of the California north.

Typical Logging Crew

The Northcoast Indians perform the Red Headed Woodpecker Dance

Logs on the way to the mills

The big trees come down

Mendocino County Restaurants

THE LIDO

The guest register at The Lido gives ample testimony to why this surprising restaurant has been a dining tradition in Ukiah for more than 70 years. Accolades of "great cuisine and service" and " . . . best in 3000 miles of travel" are typical of comments by travelers from near and far. Built on the site of the original restaurant founded by Simon Casabonne in 1905, The Lido today is newly expanded and quite elegant while retaining the feeling of friendliness and warmth gained through generations of service.

The varied dinner menu ranges from succulent *prime rib, steaks* and *seafood* to hearty Italian dinners and house specialties such as *quail a la grapa* and *roast duckling l'orange.* Portions are generous and quality uniformly high, with complete dinners from $6.50. A selection of fine wines is available to complement your dinner — including a featured "Wine of the Month" from one of the great Mendocino wineries. An extensive luncheon menu is served on weekdays only, including entrees, sandwiches, salads and soups (the *french onion soup gratinee,* a house specialty, is thick and scrumptious with bubbly, melted swiss cheese and a tasty crouton!).

Dining at The Lido is always pleasant and informal in an atmosphere of warm colors, rich textures and treasured antiques. There's a cozy bar for cocktails with dining either in the intimate Cellar or elegantly-appointed Salon. On Friday and Saturday evenings there's usually live music and dancing in an area adjoining the bar. Hosts Irv and Juanita Styer and their friendly staff will make you feel welcome whenever you visit the scenic Redwood Empire.

THE LIDO
American w/Italian & Old World Specialties
228 East Perkins, Ukiah, Ca. 95482
L - Tues-Fri 11:30am-2:30pm
D - Tues-Sat 5:00pm - 10:30pm
Closed Sun & Mon. Cellar - banquets to 100.
AE, CB, MC, & Visa
(707) 462-2212 Reservations advised

PALACE HOTEL, BAR, & GRILL

In the late 1800's the Palace Hotel and Restaurant distinguished itself by serving up "a hearty table and congenial lodgings." The visions of the modern day owners and dedicated staff have been realized. To date the Palace is the most impressive hotel and restaurant along Hwy 101 between Sausalito and the Oregon Border.

The cuisine the chef and staff prepares from the exhibition kitchen is excellent. Entree's include Broiled Marinated Chicken, Rack of Lamb Provencal, Porter Valley Porterhouse (all cuts are grilled over a charcoal broiler), Veal Sweetbreads, fresh Seafood (in season), and Calamari Lombardi. Dinners are priced from $5.95 and include fresh vegetable Du Jour with soup or the special Palace salad. Appetizers ($2.25 - $6.50) include Oysters Rockefeller, escargots, iced Dugeness Crab with brandied cocktail sauce, or the Seafood Fantasy. Side orders of fresh steamed vegetables (in season), Linguini with Clams or Tortellini in cream; freshly made soups, spinach salad or Crab Louis is also served.

The Hotel staff and management have reason to be proud of the Palace Hotel's 90 rooms. Each has been individually decorated & restored to a turn of the Century of 20's - 30's motif with antiques and hand - crafted workmanship. Most have private baths, individually controlled environments, and private phones (local calls are free). Room rates vary from about $32 for a single to $38 for a double with the Bridal Suite at $80.

There is live Theater in the Palace Ballroom and convention facilities for 275. Draft beer and sandwiches are served in the Back Door, a tavern/deli which hosts live music and dancing during evenings under seven skylights. For Hotel guests a delicious continental breakfast is served each morning. Valet parking and complimentary transportation from Ukiah's airport add to the Palace's distinctiveness.

The huge vines that cling to the old brick walls no doubt once again feel the pulse beat of people from around the world. They enter and exit the stained glass and oak doors as they once did when this region of Northern California was settled and this Grand Hotel first erected.

PALACE BAR, GRILL, & HOTEL
Fresh Seafood and Steaks
272 N. State St., Ukiah, Ca. 95482
L - 11:30am - 2:30pm M - Sat
D - 5:30pm - 10:30pm daily
Sunday Brunch 10:30am - 2:30pm

90 elegant rooms - Continental Breakfast
Full Bar, Fireplaces, Air Conditioning
Valet Parking from Ukiah Airport. Dancing,
Private baths, and Private telephones.
Hotel Reservations 800-862-4698 (Toll free
in Northern California., Restaurant reservations (707) 468-9291. AE, MC, & Visa.

THE COACH HOUSE

On a grassy apron scarcely a block fro Ukiah's hectic State Street placidly sits the Coach House. On the 1st floor you enjoy a gourmet luncheon or dinner and then retreat upstairs to the Loft for som lively conversation and drink.

Owners Robert and Carolyn Savage an their children have divided the dinner m into three sections. From the broiler co New York Steaks, Filet Mignon, and Ste & Lobster. Seafood entrees include Sol Meuniere (grilled in egg batter and garnis ed with mandarin oranges; served in lemo butter sauce), Coquilles St. Jacques, and the in-season fresh catch, which is caught by the owners private boat - the Salmon Hawk. In addition thare are the Specialties of the House; which Chef Robert Simm is known for: Chicken Cordon Blue (boned breast of chicken stuffed with ham an swiss cheese), Pork Chops Supreme (baked with apricots and served with buttered noodles), and Steak Diane (flamed tableside). All dinners ($6.95 - $14.95) come with homemade soup, french bread, a choice of lettuce or Spinach salad, rice or baked potato and garden fresh vegetables. Lunch Chef Larry Aguilar prepares a variety of luncheon specials. ($2.95 - $ 5.95). Most of the desserts are made on the premises and there is a excellent wine list. Bon Apetite!

THE COACH HOUSE   *L - 11:30am-2pm M-F, D - 5:30pm-10pm M-Sat*
Continental   *Full Bar, Outdoor patio & dining, pianist 7pm-10pm*
131 East Mill St., Ukiah   *AE, MC, Visa. (707) 462-6342 Res. advised*

SCOTTY'S OLD MILL INN

It's easy to see why Scotty's Old Mill Inn has made such a hit with Ukiah's residents and Hwy 101 travelors who are lucky enough to discover this fine eating establishment. Situated eight miles north of Ukiah and down the boardwalk from Mrs. Denson's Cookie Factory; Scotty's is almost always packed weekends.

The key to their success - "Scotty" and Elives Fredrickson offer a good selection of guality entrees at a reasonable price and an excellent Sunday Brunch. Entrees include

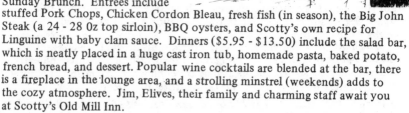

stuffed Pork Chops, Chicken Cordon Bleau, fresh fish (in season), the Big John Steak (a 24 - 28 0z top sirloin), BBQ oysters, and Scotty's own recipe for Linguine with baby clam sauce. Dinners ($5.95 - $13.50) include the salad bar, which is neatly placed in a huge cast iron tub, homemade pasta, baked potato, french bread, and dessert. Popular wine cocktails are blended at the bar, there is a fireplace in the lounge area, and a strolling minstrel (weekends) adds to the cozy atmosphere. Jim, Elives, their family and charming staff await you at Scotty's Old Mill Inn.

SCOTTY'S OLD MILL INN
Continental
9601 Hwy 101 North, Redwood Valley   *Sunday Brunch 11am - 3pm*
D - 5pm - 10pm Wed & Thur   *Beer and Wine, MC & Visa*
*   5pm - 11pm Fri & Sat*   *(707) 485-0665 Reservations on weekend*

MA'S WILDFLOWER INN

In the rapidly growing community of Willits you can dine at the homey Ma's Wildflower Inn. Binay and Mary Preston, also owners of Mad Creek Inn, recently took over the restaurant and brought as much of the rural flavor or Northern California as they could. A beautiful flower garden greets you at the entrance and during summer there is dining on the patio. Popular home-cooked meals are served.

You can choose from hearty Italian servings of homemade canne-lloni, baked lasagna, eggplant parme-san or gourmet variations of vegetables, poultry, and fresh fish from the nearby Pacific fishing fleet as well as fresh trout. Dinners ($5.75 - $10.00) include a relish dish, soup, salad & coffee. Delicious homemade pastries, espresso, non-alcholic drinks and Mendocino wines are served. Whether it be summertime dining under a starlite evening sky or intimate dining inside by candlelight - no doubt you'll leave Ma's Wildflower Inn relaxed and contented.

MA'S WILDFLOWER INN   *Brunch & Lunch 11am-3pm Wed-Sat,*
Gourmet & Italian Cooking *Sunday 9am-3pm. Dinner 6pm-10pm*
316 South Main St. , Willits *Wed - Sun. MC & Visa. Beer & Wine.*
                              (707) 459-6362 Reservations advised

MAD CREEK INN

Almost everyone wants to find a charming hideaway with atmos-phere and delicious, exciting food. The Mad Creek Inn in such a place. In 1973, Mary Cefalu reopened this quaint little restaurant reminiscent of an old-time country inn.

The menu offers gourmet home cooking with items such as the Mad Creek Combo, a hefty, tender New York Steak smothered with mushrooms and onions; and prawns stuffed with crab and rolled in sourdough. There are many other delicious dinners, which include oysters breaded in sour-dough, and other assorted seafood entrees. Complete dinners are served with fresh veggies with curry dip, French onion soup with cheese, home-made bread, crisp salad, cinnamon coffee, and your choice of ice cream. liqueur or carrot cake for dessert. There are 2 cozy cabins ($18-$20 per night). Dinner prices range from $4.50 to $10.75. The food can be summed up in one word: Superb! And it's served tastefully and with good cheer.

MAD CREEK INN   *"Look for the Windmill"*
Gourmet Home Cooking   *D 5pm-11pm (seasonal)*
14 miles north of Laytonville *Closed Mon & Tues, Full Bar.*
(Box 489, Laytonville)   *(707) 984-6206 Res. advised*
Cummings, Ca.

SHELTER COVE GROTTO

Ivy covered, sitting proudly upon knoll in north Redway, it beckons al who pass to come enjoy its colorful, nautical interior. Shelter Cove Grott for twenty-plus years has offered an extensive dinner menu featuring stea seafood and fowl, with prime rib (on Friday, Saturday, & Sunday).

Special recommendations of the chef include: Beef Medallion (Cordo Bleu) at $9.00, Sirloin Tips sauteed in wine and mushroom sauce at $9.0 and the Grotto Platter for Two (stea lobster) at $24,00. All dinners are served with clam chowder, salad, baked pot French bread, dessert and coffee or tea. The childrens menu also features a wi choice of dinners.

SHELTER COVE GROTTO
Fresh Seafood & American
410 Redwood Dr., Old Hwy 101
in Redway, just west of Garberville

Dinners: 5-10pm everyday-year roun
Cocktails, dancing, & dining
The Bar is open from 4pm - 2am
MC, Visa   (707) 923-3262
Reservations are advised

Humboldt County Restaurants

REDWOOD PALACE

In the midst of the giant coastal redwood trees lies the small village of Miranda, established 100 years ago. In Miranda, the Old West lives again, featuring "The Redwood Palace and the Jail Arcade."

The decor of the Redwood Palace is rustic, with an all-redwood interior and handhewn furniture. Your taste buds will tingle as the aroma of freshly baked breads and pies fills the room.

Specialties of the house include: homemade pizza, steaks, sandwiches, BBQ chicken and ribs. Over 40 types of domestic and imported beers awai the adventuresome, as well as wine. Young and old can test their skill on th games in the Jail Arcade.

The Redwood Palace is a unique restaurant in a breathtaking setting. Dick and Rowena Wall are the proprietors.

REDWOOD PALACE
Specialty Foods
Avenue of the Giants, Miranda
(707) 943-3174

Seasonal: Summer 0am-11pm daily
*   Winter 3pm-10pm*
Closed Tues
Beer and wine

Situated on the world famous Avenue of the Giants in the tiny community of Miranda is the Miranda Manor Restaurant. People drive from all over Northern California to have dinner here. Your hosts, John and Nora Settles, provide excellent service and atmosphere. Coastal pines and redwoods are a stones throw from the dining room windows and soft dinner music eases you through the evenings.

The Miranda Manor's stainless steel kitchen is one of the most spotless ones in Northern California. Occasionally the chef will briefly appear from the kitchen to make sure dinner guests are en-

MIRANDA MANOR

ying themselves. He carefully prepares entrees such as Veal Cordon Bleau Supreme, oast Leg of Lamb, Tournado's of Beef Bernaise, Steak and Quail, Fresh Seafood when available), Trout Almondine, and Cornish Game Hen a la Orange. Dinners e $8.00 - $14.50 and include homemade soup or salad, a loaf of fresh baked read and coffee or tea. California wines are served and there is a full bar manned y Tom Wall. A popular Champagne Breakfast and light lunch is served from 9am 2pm every Sunday. There is lodging across the street at the "Whispering Pines" For a charming dining experience in a peaceful setting I suggest you visit the iranda Manor.

IRANDA MANOR
rench - Italian Cuisine
owntown Miranda
O. Box 396, Miranda, Ca. 95553

Summertime: Dinner 5pm - 10pm, Bar from 4pm
Wintertime: Dinner Tues-Sun from 5pm - 10pm
(707) 943-3559 Reservations advised

PARLATO'S

Humboldters appreciate good food, as evidenced by the many fine restaurants in the area. There is none better than Parlato's. Family owned and operated for twenty years, they take pride in the quality as well as the quantity of their food.

The specialty of the house is their prime rib dinner for $7.50, or, from the broiler, choice steaks ranging from $9.00 to $8.00. The special homemade spaghetti and ravioli sauce, as well as salad dressings, are also packaged to take out. A full dinner includes soup, salad, garbanzos, relish plate, ravioli or spaghetti, potatoes, vegetable, bread, coffee and dessert. Even the heartiest eaters will go away satisfied.

PARLATO'S RESTAURANT
Fresh Seafood & American
320 Main St., Fortuna
D - 5pm-11pm
Bar 4pm-2am

Closed Mon & Tues
Full bar & dining
BA, MC Reservations advised
(707) 725-9961

THE WATERFRONT INC.

Through the ornate frosted etch ings on the windows you can see the daily parade of Humboldt Bay fishing boats, seagulls, and pelican

Winter or summer the Waterfro Restaurant makes the perfect spot for lunch or dinner. For lunch yo can create a delightful meal by mi ing and matching the many salad ingredients, toppings, fruits, sand wiches ($1.50 - $3.00), fresh juice coffee, teas, cakes and pies. The chef selects from 30 varieties of homemade soup ($1.50 a bowl) and serves two varieties per day during winter and three varieties per day during summer. Fresh produce is used daily. "All you should eat for all you should pay", is the philosophy of owners Jeff and Penny Bauer.

They serve Coquilles St. Jacques, Quiche Lorraine, Beef Teriyake, and Mousaka as well as other entrees. An interesting wine list and year-round picnic luncheons add to the pleasure of Waterfront Restaurant.

WATERFRONT RESTAURANT
Continental & Natural Foods
102 F. Street, Eureka
Lunch: 11am - 3pm M-Sat
Dinner: 5pm - 9pm Tues-Sat
Orders to go, catering, & wholesale
sandwich service. Checks ok.
(707) 445-2832 Reservations wk. ends

TOMASO'S TOMATO PIES
Sicilian style Pizza & Dinners
216 E St., Eureka
B - 8am-12pm Mon-Sat
L - 12pm-10pm daily
Italian dinners Sun 5pm-9pm
L & D 12pm-10pm
Pizza to go; live entertainment nigh
BA, MC, Visa   Reservations advisec
(707) 445-0100

TOMASO'S TOMATO PIES

You'll find a lively social atmosphere at Tomaso's Tomato Pies, as college students, tourists, and Old Town Eureka shop owners file in and out. They come to feast upon huge portions of nutritious, thick-crusted pizza, spinach pie, and delicious Italian dinners at unbelievable prices. The pizza crust, made fresh twice daily, is incredible.

There are hero sandwiches ($1.75-$2.65), salads ($.70-$2.25), and delicious cheese cake. Topping combinations for the thick-crusted pizzas ($2.75-$10.00) are limited only by your imagination. Single slices are also available ($.75-$1.75 The house specialty is spinach pie ($3.75-$5.75) and on Sunday a special Italian dinner is served (usually $3.95) which includes a choice of entree, soup, salad, garlic bread, and dessert. Tomaso's serves a wholesome and interesting breakfast Imported beer, wine, and expresso are available as well as something new -- blend sake drinks (milder but delicious). Tomaso's is a pleasant surpise for you and yo pocketbook. After January 1st, Tomaso's will have a new Old Town Eureka loca

LAZIO'S

The Lazio family roots are deep in Humboldt County, back to 1887, when they first came to fish and later settled in to pioneer in all phases of the industry. The restaurant was opened in 1944 and is located on Humboldt Bay on the original packing site. Broad windows offer an excellent view of the fishing boats bringing in their catch, as well as the packing operation itself.

The menu is extensive and imaginative, but the Lazio family does especially recommend fresh Filet of Petrale Sole at $6.65, or fresh King Salmon at $7.20.

Also, do not overlook the Lazio brand canned products on sale at the seafood counter.

LAZIO'S
Seafood
Foot of C St., Eureka
(707) 442-2337

Summer 11am-11pm
Winter 11am-9:30pm
Full bar
AE, BA, MC

NORTHTOWN PARK

Cozy booths named after state and national landmarks like Emerald Bay, Patricks Point, Yosemite, and Grand Teton; naturally lighted by frosted and circular windows etched with beautiful scenes as well as aquariums full of tropical fish and walls decorated with wildlife art set the stage for dining at Northtown Park. Established in 1978, Northtown Park has become a favorite dining spot for Arcata's business community, students from nearby Humboldt State University, and tourists exploring this portion of the Redwood Empire.

The menu is divided into steaks, seafood, combinations, and specials. Entrees include Filet Mignon, Roast Prime Rib au jus, Lobster Tail, New Zealand Rack of Lamb (when available) broiled with herbs and served with a piquant mint sauce, and Steak & Chicken teriyake (with special house made teriyake sauce). Dinners are served with rice pilaf and the soup & salad bar ($6.95 - $17.95). A good selection of wines are available as well as mixed drinks from the fireplace lounge.

Natures bounty, the aesthetic natural wood interior, and daily drama of the aquatic life makes dining interesting and enjoyable at Northtown Park.

NORTHTOWN PARK
American
752 18th Street, Arcata

Dinner: 5pm - 10pm M-Sat, 5pm - 9pm Sun
Full Bar & Wine List, MC & Visa
(707) 822-4619 Reservations for 5 or more

Youngberg's Restaurant, located on the third floor of the Jacoby Storehuuse in Arcata, is an elegant example of artistic hands moved through inspiration.

Here, charming hostess's seat and make you feel at home while the chef and staff expertly prepare your entree. Among the steak, chops, seafood and Italian menu items are Steak Diane $9.75 (the original recipe). Veal Scallopini $7.50, and Crab stuffed Sole $7.50. Dinner includes a relish tray. homemade soup or green salad, a baked potato, french fries or vegetable and fresh baked bread. The wine list is very adequate (rare vintages in storage are not listed) and there is an antique bar and lounge with a piano and fireplace for your further dining enjoyment.

Youngberg's restaurant is the only restaurant in Northern California of its type with truly "spirited dining"

YOUNGBERG'S RESTAURANT
Italian, Steaks & Seafood
791 Eighth St., Arcata
Lunch - 11am-2pm Tues-Fri
Dinner - 5pm-10pm Tues-Sun

Unique shops and Night Club
in 4 story rennovated building
Calif Historical Landmark 783
AE, BA, Visa
(707) 822-1712

CAFE ANTILLIES

Drawing by Michael Wilson

The comfortable cain & wicker chairs, lush tropical plants, graphic and original art, split level natural wood floors and bar with slowing turning overhead paddle fans set the stage for the cuisine that is served at Cafe Antillies.

Owners Bruce and Robin Dragge and Mark and Liz Hurt choose the name from the Islands of Antilles in the West Indies. The restaurant itself is a peaceful little island set just off the historic plaza of Arcata. For $5.00 - $11.95 the Chef will introduce you to the imaginative foods of the West Indies. You will no doubt take delight with the Chicken Carribe (served in a pinapple with mango suuce and sauteed vegetables), Fresh Jamaican Cod (with chutney and red pepper sauce), Antillies Pepper Steak (with brandy, fresh cracked pepper, chutney and demi-glace), Fresh Salmon (in season), or the Chicken Popeye (Chicken on a bed of Spinach with Hollandaise sauce). Dinners include Salad Maison and Hot Sour Dough Bread and butter. An equally delightful Sunday Brunch is served with Crepes, Omelettes and other Egg entree's. You'll also find fresh squeezed juices, delicious desserts, and an intriguing wine list. Next time you get the urge to experience a tropical island restaurant setting, dine at the Cafe Antillies.

CAFE ANTILLIES
West Indies & American
942 G Street, Arcata (on the plaza)
Brunch: 10am - 2pm Sunday

Dinner: 6pm - 10pm Tues - Thur
6pm - 11pm Fri & Sat
Beer and Wine, MC & Visa
(707) 822-0305 Reservations advised

J. BOSKOVICH 80'

MERRYMAN'S

The twisted coastal pine and redwoods march down rugged cliffs to the beach and stop. Through the large picture windows sea, sky, and sand fade into infinity. You can sit for hours at the bar and not tire of the vivid display mother nature puts on.

Sam Merryman knew this would be the ideal setting to build his restaurant; but he doesn't open the doors to just anyone off the street. If you are in a hurry then don't come here. I'm not even going to give you the address or draw you a map. You'll have to find it on your on own, just like I did, and its not easy, but it sure is worth it.

However, once you arrive you'll find 14 dinner entrees to choose from including fresh Salmon (in season), Veal Cutlets, Tournedos, Prime Rib (Saturday only), Razor Clams (when available) and Abalone King (when available) stuffed with crab and served with a delicious pimento sauce. Dinners include a seafood cocktail, clam chowder or soup of the day, tossed green salad or cottage cheese with fruit salad, baked potato and ice cream or sherbert. ($6.75 - $15.75).

Sam has beach frontage and a beach house for special parties and banquets (minimum 40 - maximum 90). He charbroils delicious prime cuts of beef over a huge sunken BBQ pit overlooking the beach. Before or after dinner you can stroll along the beach, which, by the way, is well lite at night. And if you are lucky you might witness one of those fantastic Pacific Sunsets - another reason why Merryman's is worth finding (if you can).

MERRYMAN'S
Seafood & American
On the beach south of Trinidad
Dinner 5pm - 10pm daily (Apr 1 - Oct 31)
5pm - 10pm Fri, Sat, & Sun (Nov 1 - Mar 31)
Closed major holidays
(707) 677-3111 Reservations not accepted

COLONIAL INN

Standing proud on the rugged Northern California Coast, just north of Trinidad, is the majestic Colonial Inn. The tradition of superb food and drink is carried on at Colonial Inn as it was in the late 1800's when the lovely seascape site was occupied by a Wells Fargo Stagecoach hostelry.

Good food is served here: Homemade Breads, Soups, Succulent Steaks, Prime Rib and Fresh Seafoods provide a varied menu. Complete dinners, starting at $6.25 include a choice of Soup or Seafood Cocktail, tossed Green or Salad Bar, Homemade Breads, Coffee and Dessert. A few of the outstanding selections include Combination Sole and Scallops, New York Steak, Fresh Filet of Salmon (in season) from nearby Trinidad Bay, or Prime Rib Au Jus (Saturday only). Senior Citizens plate are available for $4.00 to $6.00.

The charming cocktail lounge on the first floor provides a full array of cocktails and wines and the view of the Pacific from the second story dining room is spectacular at sunset.

COLONIAL INN
American
Patricks Point Dr., 2 mi. N. of Trinidad
Summertime open April 1 - Sept 15
Tues - Sat 5pm - 10pm, Sun 4pm - 9pm

Wintertime open Sept 15 -- April
Fri, Sat, Sun 5pm - 10pm.
Full Bar
MC, Visa
(707) 677-3363 Reservations advi

Del Norte County

JIM'S CRESCENT BEACH HOUSE

The dining room windows of the best restaurant to dine at in Del Norte County just happen to be scarcely 100 feet away from the breaking waves of the Pacific. Gourmet restaurants are rare in this part of California and grateful patrons show their appreciation by packing Jim's Crescent Beach Restaurant most summer evenings (on some evenings expect a wait to be seated).

The menu has a compliment of appetizers, side dishes, house specialties, charcoal fried steaks, and seafood. Owners Jim and Teresa Askew change the menu every so often. Creative entrees are prepared from the finest produce and meats Jim can find. One item on the menu is Pepper Steak of the House (entrecate au poivre Maisson) which is flamed with Scotch Whiskey and served with sour cream, onions, and fresh vegetables. Other entrees include Chicago Style Veal Parimgiana, Barbecued ST. Louis Pork Spareribs, and fresh seafood from the Crescent City fishing fleet. Dinners include homemade soup and tossed salad ($6.75 to $14.50). After dinner a romantic moonlite stroll along the beach is in order.

JIM'S CRESCENT BEACH RESTAURANT
International Gourmet
1455 Hwy 101 South, Crescent City
Dinner: Tues - Sat 5pm - 9:30pm
Closed the week before Xmas till Feb 10th
Beer & Wine
(707) 464-6000 Reservations advised

About Humboldt Bay

y Andy Genzoli

Dr. Josiah Gregg rediscovered
Humboldt Bay on Dec. 20, 1849

Although Humboldt Bay is large, nineteenth century explorers and adventurers played hide and seek with it for many years. It was found in 1806 when Captain Jonathan Winship sailed in, aboard the Boston ship O'Cain, under charter to the Russian-American Company. Then it was lost again until a cold and gloomy evening, December 20, 1849, when Dr. Josiah Gregg and his party of six weather-beaten and worn companions reached the sand dunes of the North Peninsula. They'd arrived following days when starvation came near being a permanent matter, weeks of struggle over mountains, across snow fields, swollen rivers and forest, coming from Rich Bar in Trinity County to their camp near the present Fairhaven.

Gregg had intended to rediscover the Bay, hoping it would provide a better and shorter route to the Trinity County gold country, for the route up the Sacramento Valley was long and expensive. Cheered by their arrival, Dr. Gregg and his party moved on, stopping for a Christmas Day encampment on or near the plaza in today's Arcata. There, L.K. Wood wrote years later, Christmas dinner "in no way resembled the repast enjoyed back home in Kentucky." They feasted on elk meat.

The next day, the expedition crossed to the eastern side of Humboldt Bay, choosing a campsite near the future Fort Humboldt, close to an Indian village. The Native Americans were friendly, providing the white men with clams for their supper.

On December 27, 1849, the party came to another river, now known as the Eel. At the junction of the Eel with the Van Duzen, there was a bitter clash and the party broke into two factions, one headed by Dr. Gregg and the other by L.K. Wood.

While trying to reach civilization by one route, Dr. Gregg fell from his horse near Clearlake and died from exposure and exhaustion. Wood and his companions reached Mark West Ranch in Sonoma County and passed along word of their discovery. Within a few days, 14 vessels were equipped by San Francisco merchants, speculators and adventurer and the great race to find the long lost harbor began. But Humboldt Bay was lost again — most of the vessels reached Trinidad Bay instead and it became a flourishing settlement.

Finally, in a cat and mouse game with competing parties, members of the Laura Virginia Association, aboard the sailing vessel Laura Virginia, dispatched a land party from Trinidad to locate the bay's entrance. When they found it, they returned to the Laura Virginia and guided the ship south to the seaward opening of the bay, sounded the entrance from a

small boat and found it safe for the Laura Virginia to cross.

That night, the ship veered away from the entrance to avoid being detected by other vessels. On the South Spit beach, several of the party were left behind to camp. Around the fire, discussion centered on a name for the newly rediscovered harbor. Stephen Lewis Shaw, first American artist to reach California in the Gold Rush, proposed they honor Baron Alexander Von Humboldt, noted German naturalist and author, and all agreed.

The next morning, with the help of the tide, the ship was guided into Humboldt Bay to an inlet near Humboldt Point, now known as Buhne Point and there founded Humboldt City, today the site of King Salmon and the PG&E atomic power plant.

When news of th Laura Virginia's success reached San Francisco, a flood of immigrants came by land and sea. They came with one purpose — to get rich and go home to the states and live like gentlemen. However, it

Fort Humboldt, near Eureka.
Where General Grant, then Captain, was stationed in 1853-4. Indicates Grant's quarters

Eureka Chamber of Commerce

Fort Humboldt, now a museum.

was not that easy. The country that would become Humboldt County was rugged and many of the would-be miners went broke. Many returned to former professions — merchants, carpenters, blacksmiths, packers, druggists, doctors, preachers and others — in the new land.

After Humboldt City was founded, Union (now Arcata), Bucksport and Eureka followed, all around the edge of Humboldt Bay. Trinidad with its head start already had a population of several hundred.

When dreams of gold proved unrealistic, the newcomers began to eye the tall trees. The first sawmill, The Pioneer, was built in the summer of 1850 by Eddy and White. Although the new arrivals eyed the giant redwoods growing close to Humboldt Bay, their size daunted them; even experienced woodsmen from Novia Scotia and Maine lacked the courage to tackle them without proper equipment so Douglas fir and spruce were cut first. William Carson (who later built the famous Carson Mansion) is credited with cutting the first redwood, though this may be only another Humboldt myth. Soon other men who had come to find gold turned to trees instead and prosperous lumber barons began to emerge.

Most of the lumber companies owned their own sailing ships, and out over Humboldt Bay for generations to come, sailed white-winged vessels, loaded with redwood lumber, doors, window frames, prefabricated houses and other products headed for such close and eager ports as San Francisco, Los Angeles and San Diego and such far away places as Tahiti, Fiji, Melbourne, Shanghai, Siberia, and Central and South American cities.

Humboldt Bay ships were famous for their sturdiness and speed; one of the great shipbuilders was Hans Ditler Bendixsen of Fairhaven.

Even the trip to San Francisco was considered perilous but the skippers were skilled and soon efficient, sturdy and commodious steamers such as the famous Humboldt, City of Topeka, City of Chester, Pomona, Corona, Santa Cruz, F.A. Kilburn and others were carrying the U.S. mail, passengers and commerce.

When the Northwestern Pacific Railroad completed its missing link between Willits and Scotia, passenger carrying ships gradually became a thing of the past. The railroad altered the sea-going complexion of Humboldt Bay, even competing to carry lumber.

It was after the railroad came that the true beauty of the redwoods was spread far and wide and the drive to save some of the great groves for posterity began and bore fruit. Now more than 100,000 people populate the roomy acres of Humboldt County with many thousands more visiting each year. There is much to see — the redwoods, salmon fishing out of Trinidad and Humboldt Bays, fishing on the Trinity and Klamath Rivers, the lowlands and antiques of Ferndale, the new College of the Redwoods, south of Eureka and the older Humboldt State University at Arcata, historic spots, small towns that still maintain a frontier atmosphere, quiet creeks and beaches, Old Town and the Redwood Acres Fair in June in Eureka . . .

For those with time to explore side roads, lane and trails, present day Humboldt County offers no end of surprises and delights, together with clues to a roistering past.

"The Mystery of the Forest" by Tibbitts in the late 1890's

Avenue of the Giants *By Barbara Dorr Mullen*

Although the beauties of the Redwood Highway start a long way south on U.S. 101, they reach their forest peak among the big trees along the Avenue of the Giants. This is a magnificent 33-mile bypass of 101, roughly paralleling the course of the Eel River as it twists through towering groves of redwoods.

The Avenue, a well-maintained section of the old Highway, starts some 200 miles north of San Francisco, just south of the tiny town of Phillipsville (population, 250). It winds through thousands of acres of virgin redwoods (over a hundred separate groves), interspersed with lush groves of young trees, springing up around the stumps of trees lost to fire, flood or ax. Many of the trees, tall even at the time of Christ, are now more than 300 feet high, stretching so far skyward it's hard to see their tops.

Although the redwoods (*Sequoia sempervirens* or coast redwoods) are the star attractions along the Avenue of the Giants, there are many seasonal shows. In the spring, you'll catch the lace of dogwoods, rhododendrons, wild azaleas and the soft blues of California's wild lilacs against evergreen hills as well as wild flags and trilliums hiding in the woods. In the summer, you'll find sticky monkey on shady hillsides and redwood sorrel or oxalis and other shy flowers in the shadows of the groves. Fall is spectacular with great flaming splashes of color, including the turning leaves of maples and wild grapes, the bright berries of madrones and that Dr. Jekyll and Mr. Hyde of the western plant community, poison oak, marvelous to look at, often poison to the touch.

Since there are a number of access roads from the freeway to the more leisurely Avenue of the Giants, you can see as much or as little as you wish. Though you can cover the entire thirty-three miles in less than an hour, there's enough here to keep an outdoor lover busy exploring all summer long.

The Avenue of the Giants is a vacation area, with a wide choice of motels, old family-style resorts, private and public campgrounds and trailer parks. Centered around the small towns, you'll find restaurants, roadside stands, gift shops, lauderettes, service stations and redwood burl factories. You'll also find tennis courts, horses for riding and trails through the redwood groves, inviting exploration. The Eel is a favorite for swimming and rafting in the summer, and for steelhead and salmon fishing in the fall.

Starting in the south and following (more or less) the South Fork of the Eel, the first town is Phillipsville. From there, it's a short hop between towns, including Miranda (population 350), Myers Flatt, Weott (including the new area on the hill, built after the flood of 1964), Redcrest and Pepperwood. In between, there are groves and parks, including the almost 43,000 acres of Humboldt State Park, Burlington Unit Campground, Hidden Springs State Campground and Rockefeller Forest. Strange or outstanding trees — Founder's Tree, Eternal Tree, Chimney Tree, Shrine Drive-in Tree and others — are special stops along the way.

Redwoods thrive on wetness and welcome the morning fogs (which usually burn off early), the sixty inches of rain per year, even the occasional winter flooding of the Eel.

At the north end of the Avenue, Pacific Lumber Company maintains a Demonstration Forest. From there, it's less than 40 miles north to Eureka, unless you choose to stop and explore Ferndale, Humboldt County's restored Victorian town. Or turn around and head right back to see a redwood tree you missed on the way north . . .

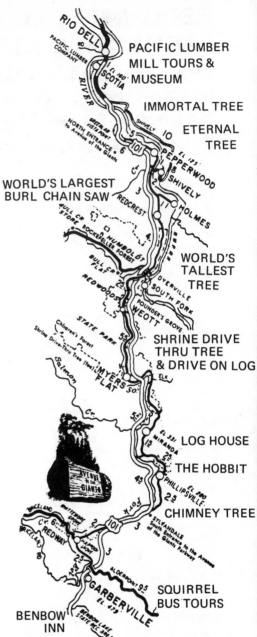

MAP of the Avenue of the Giants with mileage numbers in place. Summertime the redwood corridors are conjested with eager visitors. The peace and tranquility the Avenue has to offer can best be experienced in late fall & early winter or late winter & early spring. During late summer and early fall the South Fork of the Eel River runs crystal clear and baby trout wait on the sandy bottoms of emerald blue swimming holes to nibble on your toes.

RECOMMENDED LODGING FACILITIES & RESTAURANTS

from the Golden Gate Bridge to the Oregon Border (covering Mari Sonoma, Napa, Mendocino, Humbold & Del Norte Counties)

For those of you who havn't experienced the shelter of a country inn or cozy lodging facility in Northern California, I would encourage you to do so. I know for some of you a vacation is limited to a few weeks each year, and that usually means a hectic pace, but isn't that what you are trying to escape from in the first place?

The lodging facilities I write about are best enjoyed over a period of days-even weeks. Most offer special rates to encourage just that. From Sausalito to the Oregon Border is an endless adventure in relaxation, discovery, intimacy, contemplation, and above all a place for the vacationer to renew their relationship with loved ones and life itself. I have selected a group of inns and lodges North of San Francisco that are above average; some you'll find even extraordinary. The stage has been carefully set for you. Be considerate and you'll have a considerable vacation. What do you say? The proprietors and innkeepers are thoughtfully waiting for you to knock on their doors. I hope you find what you're looking for.

When the wheels of your car hit the last few bumps of the north side of the Golden Gate Bridge you will have entered Marin County. A few miles up the Redwood Highway ("Freeway 101") you will enter the only tunnel between San Francisco and the Oregon Border. Its south wall has a rainbow painted on it - I doubt if you'll find a pot of gold on the other side, but you will have entered one of the most controversial and spectacular regions of the United States, Northern California. And hope-

fully, you'll leave with a treasure ches of pleasant memories. Here you'll see the redwoods - coastal sentinels that reach 350 feet into the sky, you'll hea the Pacific waves thunder against coast outcroppings during winter storms, sea lions bark and migrating whales break s the sea's surface - and just maybe on s foggy night you might glimpse the sillouette of Bigfoot. Winetasting, golden sunshine, sandy beaches, swimming in crystal clear streams and rivers - there's plenty to do, but you're going to need an appropriate shelter. A place the fingers of civilization have reached, but not destroyed. A warm crackling fire, crystal decanter of wine, a firm bed and soft pillows to lay your head on at days end. A place where one journey ends and another begins.

MUIR BEACH TO LEGGETT ROUTE 1:

Up the hill, through the tunnel and down the north slope (Waldo Grade) and to the right is the Sausalito Exit. You'll find excellent restaurants, unusual gift shops and botiques and three very elegant hotels - the Alta Mira, Sausalito, and Casa Madrona. One of the more elegant Victorian hotels on the West Coast is the Casa Madrona. It is perched on a steep hillside overlooking Sausalito Harbor. Thirteen elegant rooms like the Barbary Room with its bright reds and lace, the Fireside Room with its original mahogany mantel & brass bed, and the Mariner Room decorated in a nautical theme and overlooking the harbor, range in price from $32 to

0 for two. There are also several
stored cottages.

Route 1 goes by many names
it winds its way up the coast be-
een Muir Beach and Leggett. To
e south it is the Shoreline Highway,
rther north it is referred to as High-
y 1, Coast Highway 1, or Route 1.
uth of San Francisco it is referred
as the Cabrillo Highway.

Less than 2 miles north of the
usalito Exit on Hwy 101 you'll
tice a green & white exit sign mark-
g the way to Stinson Beach & the
oreline Highway (Hwy 1) into Mill
alley. The Buckeye restaurant lies
rectly to the left of the freeway
it. Once through Mill Valley you
ill encounter sharp hairpin turns
nked by thick trunked Eucalyptice
ees. Stay on the road and head for
eautiful Muir Beach & John Muir
oods National Monument. Here you
n eat drink, & be merry at the
lican Inn.

Bed & breakfast innkeeping dates
ck to 13th century England. The
lican Inn is as authentic as you can
t. The ancient legends and super-
itions of 16th century England are
pt alive by Publicans Charles & Brenda
elix. To keep the "Witches" at bay,
lly has been placed in the window
lls and a thimble of red ribbons placed
the fireplace chimney. A bowl of
lt at the doorway passifies the "Little
eople". In the Pub loyal patrons feast
n sheppard's & cottage pie, toast with
oblets full of mead wine and then re-
re to one of the 6 spotless rooms
rnished with half & full testors,
nglish antiques, and private baths.
andlelight dining on tables over 300
ears old in front of the Inglenook
earth with the minstrels music in the
ackground brings a twinkle to your
ye and a song to your heart.

From here Coast Hwy 1 climbs
everal hundred feet up as it snakes
nd hugs the cliffs above the Pacific.
inally the road levels at Stinson
Beach, but still twists and turns as it
ugs the contours of the shoreline.
fter several miles of this it heads
nland to Inverness & Point Reyes
where you can stay at the Holly Tree
Inn or the Inverness Lodge (Mankas).

The Holly Tree Inn is a delightful
setting for parents with small children.
When its foggy elsewhere in Point Reyes
the sun often shines here in this protected valley setting. Three rooms,
a delicious continental breakfast,
courtyard, gardens, babbling brook and
floral scented air awaits you.

Hwy 1 goes through the town of
Point Reyes and then turns left at the
Y junction to Petaluma (drive east)
or Marshall & Tomales (drive north).
Go north to Marshall. On the way
you'll pass Tony's Seafood Restaurant.
Here the proprietors affectionately
bark out orders to waitress's and
customers alike. Tony's is a popular
place to anchor and enjoy fresh crab
(en season) or BBQ Oysters; while
outside the dining room windows the
boats of the fishing fleet bob up and down.
At Marshall is the Marshall Tavern, a
colorful dining establishment with a
full bar and dance floor. The Marshall
Tavern sits over the waters of Tomales
Bay and you can hear the waves lap
against the wooden pilings beneath
the dining room. Tomales is famous
for the annual shark festival. The bay
is a prime breeding ground for the great
white shark. One of the previous
owners used to boast of an 11 foot
shark that was caught near the
tavern. Just to the north is Nicks
Cove Restaurant. Owners Al & Ruth
Gibson serve delicious platters of
seafood and BBQ Oysters in the packed
dining room on weekends and during
the week. Al was the first to turn
BBQ'd Oysters into a ritual for guests
who drive out from San Francisco
and Sacramento, to feast on the
tasty morsels covered with his special
sauce and served on a half shell. In
Tomales you'll find one of the most
trusting innkeepers in Northern California. His name is Byron Randall and
his inn is called Byron Randall's Famous Tomales Guest House and Art
Gallery. When you arrive you'll see
what I mean. It was he and Emy Lou
Packard who started the very first
country inn in Mendocino, (now the
country inn capitol of the West Coast),
in the late 1950's. Byron's paintings
of consumate integrity grace the walls
of the guest house. Even the most

insensitive guest can't help but wonder about and appreciate the graphic feelings and effort put forth to create his lush victorian environment where we are encouraged to put trust & sharing before superficial formality. The three story victorian with it's 8 cozy antique furnished rooms, kitchen priviledges and large living room/library with brick fireplace and candled chandeler await you.

North of Tomales, Hwy 1 rambles over the rolling hills of dairyland and past flocks of sheep and herds of cattle. Just south of Valley Ford you'll enter Sonoma County. In Valley Ford be sure to stop at Dinucci's. The restaurant and owners, Betty and Gene, have lots of personality. At the junction of Hwy 1 and Bodega Hwy you can either head north into Bodega Bay or take a side trip into the famous town of Bodega. Alfred Hitchcock filmed "The Birds" at the Potter School House which has since been rennovated into a restaurant & art gallery.

South of Bodega Bay (not Bodega town) on a hillside is the modern two story Best Western - Bodega Bay Lodge. The manager, Randy Rollin, and his staff will insure that your stay is as comfortable as possible. They are quick to point out gas availability, where to dine, weather and road conditions, as well as any other questions you may have. Past Bodega Bay is Chanselor Ranch with it's 7 course dinners, riding stables and thoroughbred horses. In Jenner is River's End Restaurant and it's handfull of rustic cabins overlooking the mouth of the Russian River where it flows into the Pacific Ocean. It's not uncommon to spot pelicans, terns, sea lions and whales from the cabin windows. The setting is very peaceful and the German cuisine Chef/owner Wolfgang Gramatzki serves is exquisite.

From here north to Fort Ross the going can get rough, but I want to point out that what lies ahead at Timber Cove, Stillwater Cove Ranch, Salt Point Lodge, Saint Orres, the Old Milano Hotel, and Whale Watch are well worth the trek. During winters & foggy evenings this is one of the most hazardous

stretches of Coastal Highway 1 in Northern California. The hair-pin turns, sheer cliffs, grazing sheep, cattl deer, rock & mud slides, fog, high wir macho truckers, hot rodders, and Sun drivers all take their toll yearly. Alo this stretch is also the most spectacule Pacific scenery, but drive carefully - t is no room for error.

At Fort Ross the Russians built the Fort Ross Outpost to secure their holdings in this region of the West Coast. They established the first chur North of San Francisco Bay. The orig inal church was leveled by the 1906 quake and rebuilt, only to be destroye by fire; but once again rebuilt. A Russian Princess once lived there. The reconstructed buildings are perfect reproductions of the original fort and make for a very interesting journey through time.

You can gas up at the Fort Ross Store or at Ocean Cove Store (both are north of Fort Ross). A few miles to the north is the spectacular Timber Co Inn. Timber Cove Inn is a architectur brilliant work in wood and stone. Glas follows the countour of the huge boulo that cradle the lodge. It almost seems as if someone dropped a seed in the g and up popped Timber Cove. The rugg isolation and harmonic relationship wit the natural environment sought by its designer, Dick Clements, works wonders on guests who stay there. Sadly it was neglected in recent years, but now is being completely remodeled by new owners Richard and Carroll Hojohr The cuisine is excellent. The most unique gift shop on the coast is here also - the Timber Cove Craft Gallery.

North of Timber Cove is Salt Point Lodge. At the entrance is a huge stone and wood sculpture that depicts sky, water, and earth. The owner, Bill Lafeber, has the only hot tub open to the public on Hwy 1 between Sausalito and Mendocino. Evenings in the hot tub, with the sea calling in the distance and the starlite sky overhead, are memorable. The 16 rooms were recently remodeled and there is a gourmet restaurant with a fireplace lounge. At Salt Point State Park north of the lodge you can climb over the moon rocks. The cliffs were sculpted into bizarre formations when lava & sea boiled together eon's ago. Just south of Salt Point Lodge at a sharp right angle turn is the charming Ocean Cove Store. Across the highway from the store is a private campground (inquire at the store for rates). You may have seen a picture of the 118 year old building a few years ago when Time, Playboy, and Reader's Digent ran a Honda advertisement with the store as a backdrop.

A large white ram horn logo clearly marks the Sea Ranch Restaurant & Offices. Sea Ranch was designed to be a coastal vacation home community, as a "portrayal of man's wish to live with the beauty of his environment and beyond it." However environmentalists and the coastal commission curtailed the lofty plans of the developers. Today their are about 500 homes instead of the planned 5,500. Sea Ranch is a tight-nit community of intelligent and environmentally aware retired couples. The natural environment has cast it's spell on them. The beautiful lodge provides accomodations and the bar and restaurant have a spectacular view of the Pacific sunsets.

You can gas up at Stewart's Point Store (3miles south of Sea Ranch) or in Gualala to the north. The folksy Gualala Hotel is an important landmark on the coast that has provided accomodations, lumberjack breakfasts, and Italian dinners. Dependably unchanged for years, the food is good, but the rooms are run-down. Just north of Gualala is the Old Milano Hotel and Saint Orres. Once a roadhouse, the Old Milano Hotel has been carefully rennovated into a elegant country inn. Saint Orres is a architectural showplace. It resembles a Russian Castle. It reminds me of the "New Fort Ross." In Anchor Bay there is a grocery store, laundry, gas station, and a couple of good restaurants. Just past Anchor Bay, high on a cliff, sits Whale Watch, a rustic, tree-shrouded, luxurious condominium complex with fireplaces, kitchen facilities, and private decks with ocean views for whale watching.

Gas and lodging wise there is not much between Anchor Bay and Point Arena. However at Manchester there are several privately owned homes at Irish Beach. Fully furnished $68,000 to $200,000, 2 to 4 bedroom homes with spectacular ocean views, fireplaces; some with hot tubs, & saunas can be rented by the day or week to small groups or families. Irish Beach is the ideal place for seminars or important conferences. The natural environment acts to inspire logical and creative thought.

The tiny coastal town of Elk marks the southern border of a region I call the Country Inn Capitol of the West Coast. This region extends from Elk through Albion, Little River, Mendocino, Casper, and into Fort Bragg. Here you'll find 25 of the best the West has to offer. In Elk there are three fabulous country inns and restaurants - the Elk Cove Inn, Greenwood Pier Cafe, and Harbor House. Delicious quiches, fresh seafood and a variety of gourmet entrees are served at the Greenwood Pier Cafe. Next door is their lodging facility. The rooms are very comfortable and the beds are so relaxing you can almost sleep forever. Harbor House is special. It has all the ingredients for a perfect country inn. A homey living room & fire, dining room view of the sheltered cove with emerald blue water and sea caves, a continental breakfast and home-cooked full course dinner (all included in your room rates. Owner Trisha Corcoran and her charming staff hosbitably tend to your needs in the warm environment of country elegance they have created.

South of Little River you have a choice between the Heritage House, S.S. Seafoam Lodge, Andrion Lodge, Fools Rush Inn, or the Victorian Farm House. Heritage House has been such a coastal mainstay that it is now famous. The quaint setting has been used as a motion picture set for at least two major motion pictures in recent years. The four antique furnished rooms of the two story Victorian Farmhouse are complimented by a sauna & hot tub. The com-

continued on page 220

CASA MADRONA

One of the more elegant Victorian Hotels on the West Coast is perched on a a steep hillside overlooking Sausalito Harbor. Built in 1885 by lumber baron William G. Barrett, the 13 room Casa Madrona Hotel has been completely restored by owner John Mays.

Individually furnished, each room reflects the unhurried ambiance of yesterday. Take for example the "Fireside Room". The fireplace has the original mahogany mantel: a brass bed, private bath and a spectacular view of the Bay through shuttered windows. The "Mariner Room", with its breathtaking harbor view is fitted with nautical lighting, Armoire and queen sized brass bed, a private bath and natural redwood floor and trim. Room rates are $32 to $60 for two and include a continental breakfast (served from 8am - 9am) and complimentary wine and hors d' oeuvres from 6pm - 7:30pm. In addition John has restored several cottages which can accomodate families up to 4 ($65 - $70).

During evenings contented guests sip wine and chat in the fireside lounge or on the balcony overlooking the shimmering lights of Sausalito Harbor and nearby San Francisco. At Casa Madrona you can truly experience the best of two worlds.

CASA MADRONA HOTEL
156 Bulkley, Sausalito 94965
Reservations 8am - 10pm
Spectacular Harbor View and
Continental Breakfast
(415) 332-0502 Reservations advised

HOLLY TREE INN

On a secluded 19 acre estate, close-in to Point Reyes Park Headquarters sits the two story Holly Tree Inn. When its foggy elsewhere in Point Reyes the sun often shines here in this protected valley setting. Three - second floor rooms; the Laurel Room, Ivy Room and Holly Room provide both elegant and practical accomodations for couples or small families. Gracious hosts and owners Diane and Tom Balogh serve a delicious continental breakfast of home baked coffee cakes and scones filled with melted butter and English jams; fresh fruit and juice with cheese from a local dairy, either by the dining room fire or in the cozy confines of your bedroom. Breakfast is served from 9am - 10am and room rates are $30 & $35 (shared bath) and $40 for the Laurel Room (private bath). The rooms of the Holly Tree Inn open into a light and airey living room furnished with overstuffed sofas and a huge brick fireplace.

The four Holly Trees in the courtyard, plush landscaped grounds and gardens, babbling brook and floral scented air provides a peaceful setting. There is much to see and do around Point Reyes, but I doubt if you'll want to leave the Holly Tree Inn once you've laid eyes on it.

HOLLY TREE INN   *Box 642, Point Reyes 94956*
3 Silver Hills Road, Point Reyes   *(415) 663-1554 (3 wks in advance)*

BYRON RANDALL'S FAMOUS TOMALES GUEST HOUSE

Between the small towns of Bodega and Point Reyes on Coast Hwy 1 is the sleepy community of Tomales. On a knoll overlooking Tomales is a beautiful Victorian that has been carefully secluded by trees and landscaped grounds. The owner, Byron Randall, was the first to open a guest house in Mendocino 20 years earlier and notes that Tomales today, is much the same as Mendocino was then. Byron calls his inn Byron Randall's Famous Tomales Guest House and Art Gallery.

In an Old World sense he has created one of the more honest country inn environments in California. Eight cozy rooms are furnished with antiques, comfortable double beds and Byron's original paintings - works of consumate integrity which grace each and every wall. There are three bathrooms, one on the first floor for rooms 6 & 7 ($30 - $35) and one on the second floor for rooms 1 thru 5 ($25 - $30); room 8 has the master bedroom and a private bath ($40). All rooms share the large fully equipped kitchen and living room with its brick fireplace. You can relax by the lilly ponds and green bowers of the handsomely landscaped grounds. Here in this unique guest house, you feel free to enjoy . . . . .

BYRON RANDALLS FAMOUS
TOMALES GUEST HOUSE
25 Valley Street, Tomales 94971

8 cozy rooms - kitchen priviledges
fireplace in the living room and
beautiful landscaped grounds
(707) 878 - 9992 Reservations advised

Fear knocked at the door,
Faith answered - no one was there

PELICAN INN

Bed & breakfast innkeeping dates back to 13th century England. In recent years bed & breakfast inns have become a West Coast phenomenon, but not one is as authentic as the Pelican Inn. Thanks to British Publicans, Charles & Brenda Felix, the real spirit of 16th Century England lives in Northern California.

The 6 spotless rooms are furnished with half & full testors (elevated and canopied beds), private baths, massive beams, leaded windows, and English antiques dating back to the 16th century. A full English breakfast of bacon or sausages, eggs any style, imported Scottish & English marmalade with toast, orange juice and coffee or tea is served the following morning by the fire or in your bed from 8am - 10am. Room rates are $65 weekends and $55 during the week. In the Pub, loyal patrons feast on hearty servings of shepherd's pie, cottage pie, paté & cheese plates, homemade desserts and quench their thirst with cider, ports, mead wine, and a selection of domestic and imported English beers on draft or bottled. Candlelight dining on tables over 300 years old in front of the Inglenook hearth with the minstrels music in the background brings a twinkle to your eye and a song to your heart. There is one more thing . . . . Innkeeping has been a tradition for the Felix family for 4 generations. Ancient legends & superstitions are kept alive here, but necessary precautions have been taken to prevent the uninvited entry of witches & the little people. Indeed, pleasant dreams and sleep tight.

PELICAN INN
No. 10 Pacific Way, Muir Beach 94970
20 minutes Northwest of the Golden
Gate Bridge. Take Hwy 101 N. to the
Stinson Beach Exit, drive west on Shore-
line Hwy 1 to Muir Beach. (415) 383-6000

NAPA VALLEY LODGE

   The Napa Valley Lodge - Best Western is in the heart of the Napa Valley
eight miles north of the city of Napa and eight miles south of Saint Helena -
off Highway 29 at Madison Street in historic Yountville.

   The Lodge is new and its rooms are charming, spacious, air conditioned
and sound proofed. The AAA has awarded it the Four Stars ****, the
highest rating possible in its category. Plush carpets, painted Mexican tile
bathrooms, vaulted ceilings, fireplaces, refrigerators (in each room) and
very comfortable beds (kings and queens only) are just a few of the
nice things. Room rates range in price from $28.00 to $48.00 - a real bargain
for such convience and comfort.

   Every room has its own private balcony overlooking vineyards and a
quaint park with swings and slides for children. The large swimming pool
and hot, whirlpool spa actually border the grape vines. In the charming
Yountville area (a walking community) you can visit more than 50 shops
and enjoy some very fine and special restaurants. After exploring the
Valley's great wineries, this is the place to stay - and relax!!

NAPA VALLEY LODGE-BEST WESTERN

Hwy 29 at Madison Street, Yountville   *(707) 944-2468; for toll free reservations*
54 rooms (conference facilities for 50) *at the Lodge or any other Best Western, call*
Spa and Swimming Pool   *(800) 528-1234.*
Kitchenettes, fireplaces, free in-room coffee
AE, CB, DC, Exon, MC, Sohio, Visa

SILVERADO COUNTRY CLUB

Get away to Silverado! All the romance and history of a century-old estate set in the breathtaking Napa Valley. The 1200 acres of the present resort were originally part of the holdings of Mariano Guadelupe Vallejo. After the Civil War, General John Miller, a former U.S. Senator, acquired the land and in 1870, built a great mansion on the property. In 1966, the AMFAC Corporation bought the property in order to create this harmonious resort.

It is a vacationer's delight with two championship Robert Trent Jones Golf Courses. Tennis, swimming, clear air, and blue skies. Along with every civilized pleasure, from a champagne brunch to a crackling fire in a very private suite. All less than an hour from San Francisco. Come to our country. It is the perfect escape.

SILVERADO COUNTRY CLUB
1600 Atlas Peak Rd., Napa
Restaurant, Golf Course, Tennis Courts, Swimming
AE, BA, DC, MC
(707) 255-2970 Reservations advised

BURGUNDY HOUSE

What is luxury? Fresh fruit and flowers by the bed, a glass of wine on an antique table, silk sheets from Saks? Pamper yourself with a night's stay — or longer — at the charming Burgundy House, a five-bedroom country inn within walking distance of the Vintage 1870 shops, Yountville.

Built from native fieldstone in the 1870's by Charles Ronvegneau, the inn has been carefully restored by its present owners, Mary and Bob Keenan. Original stone walls have been exposed in the rooms, which are cool in summer and cozy around the hearth in winter. Like the French country inns, Burgundy House has planter boxes at the windows and an old-fashioned clawed tub where you can relax and look out at Napa Valley's famous vineyards.

Wine, breakfast on the house, and antique table games are included in the room rates ($24 — $38) — also a selection of wines. Some of the old treasures are sold out of the entry room shop.

BURGUNDY HOUSE COUNTRY INN
6711 Washington, Yountville
Bread, Breakfast, Wine
Open Year Round

(707) 944-2711 Reservations — First night deposit in advance

HARVEST INN

How many of us ever truly pursue our dreams? In 1972 Richard Geyer decided to move to Northern California to do just that. He had been raised near Valley Forge, and in a way the spirit he reflects reminds one of the same spirit which gave Washington's Army the perseverance to stick it out in the name of freedom of individual expression. Under the warm California sun Richard began to design a country inn for the total enjoyment of humanity. He would use the finest materials available with Old World craftsmanship. It would be located in the Napa Valley - he would call it the Harvest Inn.

On January 20, 1979 Richard's dream became reality and the gate to the Harvest Inn opened. On the 23½ acre estate sit three houses – White Haus, Rose Haus, and Red Haus. Inside are 18 suites appropriately named after varietals of wine. Each room has a ladies valet, built-in bar with refrigerator, stone fireplace, queen or king size beds and early American antiques. There are also two telephones and hidden in antique cabinets are remnants of technology– an AM-FM radio and color television.

The Harvest Inn is flanked on two sides by a 15 acre working vineyard where during December & January an expert vineyardist will teach you to prune vines. There are also 2½ miles of walking and jogging trails, a swimming pool, jacuzzi, barbecue pits, large patio and arbor. A continental breakfast is served and there are fresh flowers the ladies may take with them. Overnight rates for two are $50.00 to $97.00.

Richard states "the Great Spirit gave me the materials and inspiration and with them I built the Harvest Inn." In any event this earthy individualist pursued his dreams and has created one of the finest country inns in California.

HARVEST INN
One Main Street, Saint Helena, 94574
18 luxury antique furnished suites,
telephones, continental breakfast,
color TV, AM-FM radio, vineyards
for walking or jogging, swimming pool
jacuzzi, BBQ pits and patio, fireplaces.
MC, Visa (707) 963-WINE Reservations advised

CHALET BERNENSIS

In the heart of the Napa Valley, center of the world famous wine country, is the small town of St. Helena. Located just south of the city limits on Hwy 29 is Chalet Bernensis, a lovely Victorian home built in 1884 by prominent wine maker John Thoman.

Jack and Essie Doty opened this home as an Antique Shop and followed a year later by restoring and opening the upstairs for the enjoyment of over night guests. In June of 1979 a replica of the original tank tower was completed and four guest rooms added, each with private bath, air conditioning and fireplaces. The rooms are a step into the past. Lace curtains, doilies, handmade quilts on ornate brass or iron beds and Early American and Victorian furnishings complete the comfortable decor. The bathrooms have restored claw foot tubs, pedestal sinks, as well as conventional showers. Breakfast may be homemade bran muffins or scones, fresh fruit, coffee, tea, juice with homemade jams & jellies. Sorry, no children or pets and smoking is discouraged.

CHALET BERNENSIS
Bed & Breakfast
225 St. Helena Hwy, Saint Helena
Open 8am-10pm for callers

5 rooms, $49 for 2 (private bath)
4 rooms, $42 for 2 (shared bath)
(707) 963-4423 Reservations advised
MC, Visa (24 hrs. notice to cancel)

THE WINE BIBBER'S INN

Gracious hospitality, tradition and warmth describe well the environment of the Winebiber's Inn. Jayne and Don Headley opened the 6 cozy rooms of their bed & breakfast inn in October of 1979. Jayne, an interior decorator, has received many compliments from guests who marvel at the decor of the rooms she and Don christened after the names of local wineries - Hop Kiln, Windsor, Johnson, Simi, Geyser Peak, and Souverain.

The Winebiber's Inn is situated on a knoll overlooking Healdsburg, which means numerous conveniences are nearby. Summertime guests can sun and read on the balcony or enjoy the full moon as it climbs above Fitch Mountain and traverses to the west across the broad wine valley. In the truest tradition of innkeeping, Don & Jayne keep a warm fire and room ready; the following morning serve a delicious continental breakfast, and if you need it - a spare gallon of gas.

WINEBIBER'S INN
603 Monte Vista Ave, Healdsburg
6 rooms, $40 - $55, Continental
Breakfast, vegetable garden, BBQ&
patio, bicycles, canoeing, fishing, &
swimming nearby. MC, Visa
(707) 433- 3019 Reservations advised

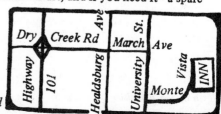

SONOMA HOTEL

A late 1890 writer refers to this structure (Sonoma Hotel); "as one of the most important buildings on a corner facing the plaza". The present structure was built as a two-story adobe across a dirt road from the Sonoma Stage Depot, sometime in the 1870's.

The building has had a checkered and colorful career over its ten decades of existence. It has housed a bar, mercantile store, a meeting hall, boarding house, and, so legend has it, even today, an occasional ghost from the days of the wild West. Sonoma Hotel has been recently restored and refurnished by the present owners, John & Dorene Musilli. The rooms are furnished with authentic items from the days of the Barbary Coast and the Gay Nineties. To spend a night at this most comfortable wine country inn is to step back into the past; a romantic period of California's history. Each room in the Hotel is furnished in antiques in the flavor and decor of the nineteenth century. Seventeen elegant rooms are available from $28.00 to $45.00.

One of the most outstanding rooms in the hotel is the Vallejo room which is furnished with pieces which once belonged to the Vallejo family. All chandeliers are authentic to the period. Five rooms have their own private bath, complete with clawfoot tubs and water closets. Twelve rooms are European Style. Continental breakfast is served in the lobby of the Hotel between 7:00am and 10:00am. "Old Fashioned Hospitality at it's best", sets the mood. There isn't a more elegant place to stay in the Sonoma Valley Wine Country than this old Hotel.

SONOMA HOTEL
110 West Spain Street, Sonoma
seventeen rooms available
elegant antique furnishings
AE, BA, MC, Visa
(707) 996-2996 reservations advised

RIDENHOUR RANCH HOUSE INN

The only Country style bed and breakfast inn in the Russian River area lies five miles east of Guerneville on River Road. The inn was originally a large family home built by Louis E. Ridenhour in 1906. The Ridenhour family farmed the 900 acre ranch consisting of land on both sides of the Russian River and adjacent to historic Korbel Winery. Today the ancient gravenstein apple trees, hollowed by time, still yield an abundant crop as well as persimmon, plum. pear, and fig trees. Travelers will note that here rambling orchards become redwoods.

The 11 room country house has 5 bedrooms (2 with private bath), a large country kitchen and formal dining room. Secluded river beaches are a short walk away and a hot tub is available to guests. A complimentary breakfast of freshly ground coffee, hot rolls and nut breads, fruit and cheese is served to overnight guests. Each room is decorated intimately and individually with antiques, quilts, flowers, plants and crystal decanters of wine. Guests are invited to sip wines from nearby wineries in front of the comfortable living room fireplace. Informally landscaped grounds with meandering paths under redwoods and oak trees invite guests to stroll. Overnight rates, including breakfast, are $40 - $65 per room. Your hosts are Martha and Bob Satterthwaite and daughter, Deirdre.

RIDENHOUR RANCH HOUSE INN
12850 River Road, Guerneville
(entrance 500 yds east of Korbel Winery)
Open Mar - Nov, special group arrangements Dec - Feb. Numerous restaurants
& recreational facilities nearby, Hot Tub.
(707) 887-1033 Reservations advised

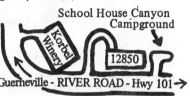

School House Canyon Campground

Guerneville - RIVER ROAD - Hwy 101 →

RIVERWOOD RESORT

Riverwood Resort in Guerneville has been carefully restored by Bob & Rosalie Hope. Six elegantly furnished hotel rooms and eight housekeeping cottages are available from mid May thru September (Hotel rooms year round).

A very diverse recreational environment has been created with the addition of a campground amid the redwoods (shower facilities available) and RV & trailor hook-ups, (22 full service spots including cable TV which are $10 per night with monthly rates from $135-$150 depending on length of stay. The Hotel rooms retain a intimate country inn charm. The rustic housekeeping cottages are $30-$40 for 4, while the antique furnished Hotel rooms are $30-$40 for 2, which includes a delicious homemade continental breakfast prepared by Rosalie, who also with her daughter Kerri operate a gourmet catering service called Oui Cater at Windsor Vineyards (433-9727).

In addition there is a small vineyard of Pinot Chardonnay and Pinto Noir grapes, and a olympic size swimming pool. Riverwood Resort is a carefully planned recreational community where families or couples can truly partake in the beauty this region has to offer.

RIVERWOOD RESORT
16180 Neeley Road, Guerneville

(707) 869-9978 Reservations
accepted from 8am-8pm. MC & Visa

BODEGA BAY LODGE Best Western

Overlooking beaches, the harbor, and misty, bird-filled marshes, the Bodega Bay Lodge is a convenient headquarters for exploring the waters and wonders of Bodega and Tomales Bays. From every room one can watch whales in migration, sea lions, fishing boats, thrashing waves and glorious sunsets, and view a world not very different from the one that welcomed Sir Francis Drake over 400 years ago.

Bodega Bay has the largest harbor between San Francisco and Eureka. Bodega Head is the University of California's Marine Biological Research Center, and is open to the public. Nearby is a string of Sonoma County parks, marinas, and the Russian River resort area. Fort Ross' historic Russian settlement is a leisurely drive north, and the Point Reyes National Seashore is a scenic drive south.

The rural villages of Occidental, Freestone, Bodega, Marshall, Tomales and Valley Ford provide galleries, craft shops and unusual places to explore. Artist Christo chose this area for his famous running fence.

Adjacent to the Lodge is the Bodega Harbor Country Club, which offers golf to the public in a spectacular setting.

The Lodge's immaculate rooms have their own balconies, color television, queen-sized beds, free in-room coffee and kitchenettes. Open all year, the Lodge is a ready retreat with an ever-warm and friendly welcome from the host. Under Best Western standards, Bodega Bay Lodge provides "lodging at its best."

BODEGA BAY LODGE-BEST WESTERN
Highway 1, Bodega Bay
Open 24 hours daily, year round
Ocean view rooms, color TV, kitchenettes
AE, BA, CB, DC, MC
(707) 875-3525
Reservations advised

FERNGROVE

Neatly tucked in a pocket of 100 foot high redwoods are the charming cottages of Ferngrove Resort. The 18 rustic knotty pine cottages, grounds, and large heated pool are beautifully maintained by owners Jay Milo and Bob Leech; much to the contentment of their guests. Ferngrove is located scarcely two blocks from downtown Guerneville, but you wouldn't know it, for a corridor of redwoods blocks out the busy view. Consequently the cottages lie in quiet seclusion. Ferngrove is ideal for honey mooners and couples who are looking for unique lodging facilities from which to take walks in the redwoods, winetaste, or go swimming in the Russian River and explore the nearby Pacific Coastline.

There are 4 duplex units and 14 individual housekeeping cottages. The cottages are equipped with one or two bedrooms, cable TV's, kitchens, one or two bathrooms, and eight have fireplaces. Rates vary from $27 a night for two to $60 a night for 4 (2 bedrooms, 2 baths, large kitchen, family room with fireplace; $5/ additional guest - up to 6). Le Chalet, an excellent French Restaurant is located next door and the chef takes pride in arranging special wedding receptions or parties for the guests of Ferngrove Resort. At Ferngrove Resort you'll soon discover that the owners priority is your pleasure.

FERNGROVE RESORT
16650 River Road, Guerneville, 95446
Reservations accepted from 8am-10pm
year-round. MC, Visa. 18 cottages -
some with fireplaces. Numerous rest-
aurants and outdoor activities nearby.
(707) 869-9992 Reservations advised

SALT POINT LODGE

A lodge for all seasons awaits you less than 90 miles from the Golden Gate Bridge. A huge sculpture depicting sky, water and earth marks the entrance. At Salt Point Lodge you can get back to basics, but with the civilized comforts of fine lodging, good food at the Cove House, hearty libations in front of a roaring fire, and the only hot tub and sauna on Route 1 between San Francisco and Mendocino.

Owner Bill Lafeber has tastefully remolded the 16 rooms of the lodge

($28 - $55 a couple per night). Four of the rooms are equipped with fireplaces, a queen sized bed and couch, FM Stereo, and picture window views of the Pacific. In the Cove House you can choose from a selection of American and Seafood entrees. Dinners ($6.25 - $15.95) include chowder or salad, baked potato or french fries, dessert and coffee or tea. California wines are served.

Best of all - on special nights, from the surging waters of the hot tub, you can see a ring around a mist shrouded full moon; and with the sea calling in the distance you can feel the spiritual f⋯⋯s of mother nature take hold of your soul, making this one of the gr⋯

SALT POINT LODGE   ⋯iles N. of Jenner
America & Seafood (orders to go)   ⋯-3234 Res.

BLACKBERRY INN

In the sleepy little town of Occidental, nestled against a steep hillside is the Blackberry Inn. The two story Victorian, built in the 1860's, has been carefully restored by its energetic owner, Charles Tomka Jr. After doubling the size of the home Charlie added his private antique collection, Persian rugs, stained glass windows and a jungle of lush plants. Finally, after 4 years, he opened the French style doors to the public in the summer of 1980.

Seven of the elegant guest rooms share three bathrooms with claw-foot tubs, brass fixtures and oak tiolets. The luxurious second floor suite, with its sunken tub & fireplace, has been affectionately christened the Blue Angel. The living room with its overstuffed sofa & chairs and crackling fire makes it easy to shake the chill of those cold & foggy Occidental winters or discuss exploration of the nearby countryside on a warm summer day. From a crystal decanter you can sample complimentary wine from one of the local boutique wineries. Needless to say, lively conversation soon spreads among adventureous travelors who come from all over the country to stay at the Blackberry Inn.

The next morning a continental breakfast of French pastries, fresh fruits, homemade jams, herb teas and coffee is served early morning in the dining room. Rates are $38 - $50 per night for two; the Blue Angel is more. *Charlie points out that special extended stay and off-season rates are available for area residents and visitors.*

A stroll through Occidental, once a booming lumber town in the 1800's, is still today a step back in time; especially the unhurried Victorian elegance young Charles Tomka Jr. has revived at his Blackberry Inn.

BLACKBERRY INN
3657 Church St., Occidental
P.O. Box 266, Occidental, Ca. 95465
Reservations received year-round
7 rooms (shared bath) $38 - $50 per
couple per day, Blue Angel suite $55

Restored Victorian, numerous restaurants & wineries nearby, redwoods & Russian River Resort Area, Pacific Ocean all within 15 miles. AE, MC, Visa (707) 874-3023 Reservations necessary

The new and very elegant Chalet Bernensis.

Saint Orres Inn and Restaurant sits just north of Gualala.

Bruce and Theadora McBroom who restored the Old Milano Hotel.

New and convienent is Hill House of Mendocino.

Glendeven is as warm as toast on those chilly winter days on the Pacific Coast.

Joshua-Grindle has been furnished with early American antiques.

WHALE WATCH

High above the Pacific from outside the large picture windows of your room something catches your eye. You scan the horizon, and suddenly you see it. A large gray body breaks the surface followed by the graceful flip of a huge fin. As suddenly as it happened it ends, but the memory of first sighting nature's largest mammal, the Gray Whale, lasts forever. . . .

One of the best locations to observe this natural phenomenon is from one of the four luxurious rooms of Whale Watch, a cozy condominium lodge perched on a cliff 90 miles north of San Francisco. Besides the view there are spectacular winter storms, strolls along the beach, evenings in front of your fireplace, and the private environment of redwood, glass, skylights, and cozy furnishings of your room. Rates vary from $60 (studio), $75 (one bedroom unit), to $90 for 4 (with hide-a-bed). There is a 2 night minimum on wk ends. You can isolate yourself in your room and prepare special dinners in the fully equipped kitchen or enjoy excellent food at nearby restaurants. The peace and quiet coupled with the natural events surrounding Whale Watch act as stimulis to rekindle relationships or fire new ones.

WHALE WATCH
35100 Hwy 1, ¼ mile north of
Anchor Bay, Box 127 - Gualala 95445
Luxurious Condominium with 4 units

each with fireplace & equipped kitchen.
cash or checks accepted, reservations
received from 9am - 7pm
(707) 884-3667

OLD MILANO HOTEL

On a cliff overlooking Castle Rock stands the Old Milano Hotel. When Bruce and Theadora McBroom left Hollywood to restore the Old Milano Hotel, located 1.84 miles north of Gualala, they definitely knew what they were doing. Thanks to a lot of elbow grease and painstaking reconstruction, the hotel is now listed in the the National Register of Historical Landmarks.

Inside you will find seven elegantly furnished Victorian bedrooms and outside an old renovated railroad caboose. Each room has its own name and the furnishings and colors within depict different moods.

Room rates are $35, $45, and $55 (double occupancy) per day. Ocean views and luxurious European style baths add to your pleasure. There is nothing like Thea's fresh baked continental breakfast, followed by an early morning stroll along the private Pacific beach beneath the Old Milano Hotel.

OLD MILANO HOTEL
1.84 Mi. north of Gualala
Spectacular setting; 7 cozy

Victorian bedrooms and a
caboose; European baths
(707) 884-3256
Reservations advised

Looking for a secluded mount-aintop cabin? Where the only night-time sounds are cool breezes whispering through the trees. Where you can bask on a sundeck followed by a dip in a heated pool. Where you can cook your own meals in the completely equipped kitchen of your cabin or savor charbroiled Filet Mignon, Top Sirloin, or Gourmet Chicken Breast accompanied by fresh garlic bread, a crisp green salad and premium Mendocino Wine - all in the intimate dining room of the lodge.

Where can you find such a cozy oasis? Bear Wallow! Located scarcely two and a half hours from San Francisco and 23 miles from the Mendocino Coast. You can taste premium wines at nearby wineries, or hike amid streams and red-woods. You can drive or fly in (the 2900' Boonville airstrip is four miles away). Such a vacation spot would seem priceless, but its not. Dinners are $5.95 - $10.95 and seven cozy one and two bedroom cabins with fireplaces are $35 - $45 a night for two to six people. Bear Wallow is ideal for seminar groups or vagabond couples.

BEAR WALLOW RESORT   *Dinners: 6pm - 9pm Thur - Sun*
American & Continental   *Seven rustic cabins available*
4 miles West of Boonville   *Checks accepted*
on Mountainview Road   *(707) 895-3295 Reservations advised*

VICTORIAN FARM HOUSE
BUILT 1877

In the guest book at the Victorian Farm House a couple from New York wrote "very nice, more like New England than California." One of a party from New Zealand inscribed, "a home away from home".

From the parlor of this Century Old Victorian Inn the warm glow of the eve-ning fire soothes your soul. It's four cozy antique furnished rooms with private baths and a delicious homemade contin-ental breakfast further restores you. There is the Library Room (up to 4) with it's cache of books, plush blue carpet, redwood, and imported French wood-burning stove. Upstairs is the Regal Room (up to 4) and Gold Room with their shared sitting room and ocean views. The Garden Room has a large bathroom with victorian motif and plans for a sauna in the future. Room rates are $30 - $45, there is a hot tub, and occassionally complimentary wine is served. Innkeepers Curt and Carlene Acker state "the blend of past and present is so natural that you'll wonder why such a place is rare on this earth."

VICTORIAN FARM HOUSE - Built 1877   *(707) 937-0697*
3 miles south of Mendocino on Hiway 1   *BA, MC*
P.O. Box 357, Little River, CA. 95456   *4 rooms, 2 fireplaces, private baths &*
Reservations received from 8am - 10pm   *continental breakfast, Hot Tub - Spring 1980*

HARBOR HOUSE

For the discriminating traveler, looking for peace, relaxation, and an unparalleled view of ocean topography and surf, Harbor House is the place to stay.

Built 60 years ago, the inn itself is an architectural curiosity. Formerly a lumber company's executive guest house. It's an enlarged replica of the Redwood Model House at the 1915 Pan American Exposition in San Francisco. All rooms have private baths and most have fireplaces or Franklin stoves.

The ocean has carved a large natural arch that opens toward the sea. At the turn of the century, lumber schooners were loaded by chute from this point. Close to the beach a grotto from which seawater surges through three tunnels adds to the breathtaking view at Harbor House.

Homecooked, full-course dinners, as well as hearty breakfasts are provided for the enjoyment of the guests. Also available is a fine wine list featuring Mendocino County's finest wines. This fine inn is owned by Trisha Corcoran.

HARBOR HOUSE
5600 S. Hwy 1, Elk (PO Box 167)
Lodging & Meals for guests

Rooms with fireplaces &
Franklin Stoves
Private Beach

(707) 877-3203 Reservations

MENDOCINO VILLAGE INN

Weathered by time and north coast sea winds, the Mendocino Village Inn blends comfortably into the unique postcard setting of Mendocino's main street. Known as the House of Doctors because of a succession of owners in the medical profession, it was built by Dr. William McCornack in 1882. Sold to Dr. James Milliken in 1903 for $1,800, it housed the last doctor, Frank Peirsol, in the 1930's. In the 1960's it served as the home and gallery of famous artists Byron Randall and Emy Lou Packard.

Hosts Robert and Beverly Sallinen restored the inn in 1972. The 1800 Cape Cod styling with Mansard roof and windows open to the sea characterize the two-story white frame house. It has 13 guest rooms, 7 fireplaces, 2 hall baths, 8 private baths, 2 attic rooms - one with a breath-taking view, and even a parlor alcove in some of the rooms. Reasonable rates for rooms and coffee are $18 - $24 per night for two.

MENDOCINO VILLAGE INN
Main Street (P.O. Box 626), Mendocino
Open 24 hours a day
(707) 937-0246 Reservations advised

1021 MAIN STREET GUEST HOUSE

"Take the foundry - some people stay out there for a week and we never see them - others leave in tears." Those are the words of Marilyn Solomon speaking of the guests to her country inn, 1021 Main Street Guest House.

1021 Main Street Guest House is what I call an authentic California Country Inn. The architecture, decor, furnishings are a melting pot of many cultures and eras. Above all, it portrays the Mendocino Mystic well. It hugs the coastline. From the table where a delicious breakfast is served (9am - 10am) you can see the Big River where it flows into the Pacific. Just down from the house there is a sandy drift-wood scattered beach to stroll on. Evenings in the hot tub, with the stars and moon overhead, and the sirens of the sea calling in the distance, are unforgetable. Original art & sculpture, such as hot lips, an unusual fireplace, reflect the ingenuity of the Mendocino artist. One of Marilyn's sons, Carl, will even wax your car professionally to protect it from the salty Pacific air. Another son, Eric, manages the inn in Marilyn's abscence.

Of all the beautiful inns in Mendocino County, it was here that I wished I did not have to leave - not because of the breathtaking view, or the elegant bedrooms, or the grand piano, the kitchen facilities, nor the abundance of creative stimulus throughout the house, but because Marilyn is a guide who truly knows what a country inn should be and do for people. You can "leave your cloak of formality" at the doorstep. If necessary, it is here that your mind, body, and soul can begin the restoration process that our society and ourselves so often prevent. However, you must call and make a reservation in advance. 1021 Main Street Guest House is my favorite retreat. I hope you'll go there. I know if I left right now for Mendocino, it would be there, at 1021 Main Street Guest House that I would begin my journey.

1021 MAIN STREET GUEST HOUSE
Main at Evergreen, Mendocino
Write: Box 803, Mendocino, Ca. 95460
Res. accepted from 9am - 9pm, check
in time is 2pm. No children under 16
& no pets. 3 rooms & 2 cottages with
ocean front, wood burning sauna, and
hot tub with jacuzzi. $48 - $58 for 2
per day. (707) 937-5150 (unlisted)

MacCALLUM HOUSE

For the Mendocino experience, watch whales, browse in the galleries, and then dine at the elegant MacCallum House. The three-storied American Victorian, restored as an inn, was built by William H. Kelley for his newlywed daughter, Daisy MacCallum.

Set back on Albion Street behind a white picket fence, its verandas command a sweeping view across spacious lawns and twisting cypress to the crashing waves of Mendocino's headlands. It's a favorite subject for artists and photographers.

Now the rooms have been cheerfully restored in flower prints, the original furniture rearranged to accommodate guests, quaint wooden beds laid with handmade coverlets, and rich Persian rugs and paneled walls. The easy-going hospitality is reflected in the Grey Whale Bar, where you can sip a cocktail, look out at the view, and imagine yourself in another time.

Dinners are served in a library study that is complete with huge fireplace, wall to wall books, oil lamps, and fresh flowers on the tables. Specialties include fresh salmon (in season), stuffed cornish game hen, seafood crepes. and other gourmet entrees. For an additional treat, start with the French onion soup ($2.25), or Oysters Casino ($2.95) and top off the dinner with a Swedish cream (a rich pudding topped with berries). Complete dinners start at $8.95. Continental breakfast is included in the room rates ($34.50 - $75.00). Special family & weekly rates are available on request.

Guests are invited to stay over in the main house, where some of the baths are "down the hall" or in the Carriage House, two separate units with fireplace and adjoining baths; in the Greenhouse, now a rustic cottage or in the Water Tower, a split level lodging with ocean view. The Gazebo, once a child's playhouse, is now a guest lodge, nestled in a bed of geraniums. The Old Barn offers luxurious suites with ocean views & stone fireplaces.

MacCALLUM HOUSE
Continental Cuisine
740 Albion St., Mendocino
D - 7pm-10pm except Mondays

Lodging, Bar, & Restaurant
MC, Visa Reservations advised
Inn - (707) 937-0289
Restaurant - (707) 937-5763

North of San Francisco 150

MENDOCINO HOTEL

The Mendocino Hotel was built in 1878. It is the central structure in the historically preserved coastal village of Mendocino. Located just off state highway 1 on Main Street (which is four blocks long), the century old building faces Mendocino Bay and Big River. The Mendocino Hotel was completely rennovated in 1975 by Don Bruce & Company.

The spacious waiting room is furnished with a large fireplace and overstuffed antique sofas and chairs. In the lobby bar you can set at semi-private tables for two to six people or drink at the stand up bar with its huge overhead stained glass valance (try the Mendocino Fog Fizz). On many evenings lively conversation soon envelopes the room.

You can dine in the formal dining room or more casual sunlite garden room with its long bar. Lunch and dinner is served daily, year-round. For lunch you can choose between a selection of fresh homemade soups & salads, sandwiches, specialties like Flautas (rolled tortillas, with a spicey beef filling, deep fried, and topped with guacomole and sour cream - $2.75) or the fresh catch as well as desserts like the deep dish fruit pie. Regular dinner entrees include Abalone Steak, Lobster, Hotel Chicken Glace or Prime Rib (on Sat & Sun). The selection of House Specialties change monthly and include Cod Terriyake, Shrimp Creole, Veal Picatta and Fresh Seafood. Dinners are ($7.00 - $18.00) and include a choice of soup or salad. There is also an interesting selection of appetizers & homemade deserts. deserts.

The three story hotel, with its 26 spotless rooms await you. Rooms with shared bath start at $30.00 and rooms with private bath are from $50.00 (2 room suites are $80.00). Some have ocean views. A continental breakfast of fresh fruit and freshly squeezed orange juice together with homebaked fruit and nut breads is included in the room rate. Since accomodations are limited, careful planning and advance reservations are recommended.

MENDOCINO HOTEL
Modified American
45080 Main St., Mendocino
P.O. Box 587, Mendocino, Ca. 95460

L- 11:30am-2:30pm, Sat 5:30pm to
10pm, Sunday Brunch 10:30am-2:30pm
Hotel, Restaurant, & Full Bar. MC & Visa
(707) 937-0511 Reservations advised

HILL HOUSE INN

Many of the 21 rooms of Hill House Inn have sweeping views of the Pacific, Mendocino Headlands and meadows. Modernized victorian elegance is a good way to describe the decor. A continental breakfast of coffee cake, fruit juices and coffee is served each morning from 8am - 10pm. If you so wish then you can enjoy breakfast in bed. Fifteen of the rooms have king sized beds, six rooms have 2 double beds each, and the luxurious suite has a sitting room with view and a fireplace. Room rates are $46 - $65 for two nightly. Rates include a private phone, television, and private bath. The historic community of Mendocino is within walking distance as is the near-by Pacific Ocean. Because its off the beaten path, its not unusual to find movie crews or stars lodged at the Hill House Inn while they are filming the Mendocino landscape. The Hill House Inn is located on a knoll just north-west of downtown Mendocino.

HILL HOUSE INN
Bed & Breakfast Inn
10701 Palette Dr., Mendocino
Box 625, Mendocino, Calif. 95460

21 rooms, continental breakfast
private phones & TV ($46-$65)
(707) 937-0554 Reservations advised

THE GREY WHALE INN

The Grey Whale Inn of Fort Bragg like its namesake, has spacious accom dations for one to six guests (four roc have kitchens and one has a fireplace) Room rates range from $22 (for 1) $24-$38 (for 2), $45 (for 4), and $55 (for 6), and include a continental brea of pastries, fruit juice and coffee. Be the inn was built as the Redwood Coa Hospital by lumberman C. R. Johnso 1915, guests in wheel chairs have ramp access to the main floor and one roor being re-modeled with special shower facilities.

One of famed Mendocino artist, Byrd Baker's Grey Whales, carved from a nine f redwood log, is proudly displayed in front of the inn. From the ocean view rooms can see migrating whales spouting in the nearby Pacific (December-March), so brin your binoculars and enjoy the comfortable accomodations that have been created John and Colette Bailey at the Grey Whale Inn.

THE GREY WHALE INN
615 N. Main St., Fort Bragg, Ca. 95437
(2 blks from Skunk Train Depot)
Open daily from 8am-11pm year round

13 rooms, no pets
Restaurants and facilities nearby
MC, Visa
(707) 964-0640 Res. Advised

Best Western VISTA MANOR

Major motion picture companies have made Vista Manor their headquarters while photographing the Fort Bragg - Mendocino area. Prepared for year - round tourists, the motel maintains a tradition of comfort and hospitality on magnificent cliffs alongside Highway 1, north of Fort Bragg.

There's never an off - season at Vista Manor. During the long Indian summer, visitors can enjoy the miles of natural beaches, hunt driftwood or swim in protected surf or lagoon. In fall, the weather stays steady, crisp and clear. In winter, guests can watch the wild ocean waves, the whale migration or swim in the large indoor heated swimming pool with its huge mural depicting the local environment that was painted by the Fort Bragg Senior High art class. In spring-time, rhododendrons and wildflowers highlight the fields, dunes and forests and carefully placed flower gardens around the Vista Manor bloom spectacularly.

Recently the spacious 54 rooms were remodeled with natural wood, bright colored carpets, drapes, and bedspreads and the bathrooms were modernized. Also a continental breakfast (served 7:30am - 11am) of Danish rolls,. juice, and coffee or tea has been added. Telephones equip each room and a comfortable two bedroom cottage complete with a kitchen and fireplace provides a rustic setting for small conferences or social gatherings. Room rates for two are $35 - $65 and the cottage (for 8) is $90 per day.

There are many attractions within a few miles driving distance such as the Pygmy Forest, California Western "Skunk" Railroad, and the fishing fleet at Noyo Harbor. Luxury planning and thoughtful attention make Vista Manor a wonderful place to stay. A phone call or card will assure you of the accommodations of your choice. Write 1100 No. Main ST., Fort Bragg, Ca. 95437, or call toll free 800 - 528 - 1234.

VISTA MANOR
1100 No. Main St., Fort Bragg
Open 24 hours
(707) 964-4776

Indoor heated pool, color TV,
numerous recreational areas nearby
AE, BA, CB, DC, MC, EX, Visa

A beautiful garden of delicate flowers with every color of the rainbow embrace this old Victorian. Carefully restored and painted shades of blue, the Blue Rose Guest House, once a run-down home clearly does not belong in the middle of Fort Bragg. The proprietor, Ann Samas and her daughter Christine, have lovingly brought this old home back to life and spared nothing in the process.

After registration, guests are served red or white wine and a tray of Hors d' deuvres of cheeses, salami, pickles, olives, etc. An overnight stay in this enriching and placid environment will work its magic on your soul. The following morning you'll find a variety of delicious breakfast items such as waffles with melted butter and syrup, fresh orange juice; or eggs, quiches, special hams and sausages, with coffee or tea. You will delight in preparing these breakfast items the way you like at the hour most convenient for you in the morning. The five rooms are tastefully appointed (two rooms upstairs have a shared bath and the rooms downstairs have private baths). Room rates are $35 to $50. A stay here will leave you refreshed. Your host, Ann Samas, is as pleasant as her name-sake, the Blue Rose.

BLUE ROSE GUEST HOUSE   *5 elegant rooms and a complete breakfast*
520 N. Main St., Fort Bragg   *(707) 964-3477 Reservations advised*

COBWEB PALACE INN

Back in the 1880's, when it was the largest seaport between San Francisco and Eureka, there were 14 hotels and 17 saloons in Westport. Today there is only one of the originals still standing; it houses the Cobweb Inn, picturesque as the seacoast it overlooks.

The Inn specializes in homecooked food, seafoods fresh from nearby Noyo Harbor, as well as succulent steaks and chops from the grill. Dinner prices range from $6.95 - $10.50. The dining room is open to the public on Saturdays and Sundays from 6pm - 9pm and Sunday Brunch 9am - 1pm. Lodging, breakfast, and dinner is available to those who stay over six days a week (everyday but Friday).

By fall of 1979 two more 2nd story rooms will be opened bringing a total of six cozy accomodations ($25- $30) to guests, two with balconies situated 100 yards from the rugged Pacific Coastline. There's a full bar and an antique shop as well. Presiding over all are gracious hosts Dave Cantley and Peter Husk.

COBWEB INN
Home Cooking, Sun Champagne Brunch Full Bar and adjoining antique shop
Westport, California   BA, MC
Hotel - Amer Plan B&D - 6 rooms   (707) 964-5588 Reservations require

IRISH BEACH

How would you like to have the comforts of a luxury home overlooking the Pacific Ocean. At Irish Beach you can have just that. Completely furnished homes that sleep 6 to 12 people with a variety of conveniences can be rented from 2 days to a week or longer. Rates range from $80 - $170 for 2 nights to $210 - $455 per week. Each home has a fireplace (firewood is furnished); many have panoramic views of the beach, and some have private phones, sunken tubs, saunas, hot tubs, wet bars, dish-washer, washer/dryers, sound systems, private sun decks, and equipped kitchens. Each $68,000 to $200,000 home is privately owned and managed by the Irish Beach Rental Agency.

The setting is spectacular. A forest of redwoods & coastal pines are laced with meadows and a variety of flora & fauna. The ocean beach ranges from an expanse of smooth sand to rocky outcroppings and cliffs. There are hiking trails and pathways, two parks, a trout lake, and surf fishing. Irish Beach occupies a dream like setting on the Pacific 8 miles north of Point Arena and just a ½ hours drive from Sea Ranch and a ½ hours drive from Mendocino. There are numerous gourmet restaurants along this stretch of Hwy 1. In nearby Point Arena are several stores, markets, and gas stations. The staff at Irish Beach Rental Agency are more than happy to answer any questions you may have.

IRISH BEACH
Star Route, Manchester, Calif. 95459
located 8 miles north of Point Arena
on Coast Highway 1. 24 luxury homes
for 6 - 12 people by the day or week.
(707) 882-2467 Reservations necessary.

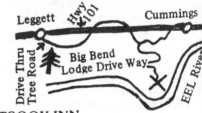

BIG BEND LODGE

In a secluded pocket canyon a mile off the highway where the South Fork of the Eel River cuts sharply into a solid rock cliff, gives up, and bends to the right, you'll find the 10 cozy cottages of Big Bend Lodge. The one and two bedroom cottages are furnished with double beds and housekeeping kitchens with room for five per cottage (special group & extended stay rates are available).

"If you are looking for a place where there are a lot of people and activity, souvenir stands and artificial things to do, then don't bother with us," state owners Jack & Ken; "Big Bend is not for you." During summer there is a communal campfire and several emerald blue swimming holes; and in the winter a wood fire and coffee pot awaits the steelhead and salmon fishermen who stay at the Big Bend Lodge. Some families have been visiting the lodge for over 20 years. Jack & Ken have a soft spot in their hearts for animals so don't be afraid to bring your pet. The Big Bend Lodge is located five miles south of Leggett & three miles north of Cummings off the Drive-Thru-Tree-Road. Look for the Big Bend Lodge mailbox - your stay will be pleasant.

BIG BEND LODGE
located 3 miles north of Cummings
Box 111, Leggett, Ca. 95455
10 cozy cottages - 2 with fireplaces
hike, swim, fish or relax
community campfire & BBQ facilities
(707) 984-6321 Reservations advised

HARTSOOK INN

At night in the heart of the redwood forests, the lights of the big Hartsook Inn will welcome you.

The resort is 8 miles south of Garberville, on scenic Redwood Highway 101.

The original inn, built in 1920 by photographer Fred Hartsook, was destroyed by fire. Successive owners have rebuilt, added to the properties, and now the lodge, cottages, and network of trails and recreational facilities occupy 30 acres of park land.

All cottages are designed with baths, veranda, and view in an individual setting. Property borders on the Eel River.

In the main lodge, you can shop for an outstanding array of gifts, relax on the terrace or in front of the stone fireplace. A tempting array of old family recipes is offered in the sunny dining room.

HARTSOOK INN
8 Mi. So. of Garberville, Piercy
All year - some cottages
River swimming, croquet, hiking
Dining room 5/1 to 11/1
BA, MC
(707) 247-3305 Reservations, deposit.

SINGING TREES RESORT AND RESTAURANT

Bordering one of the most spectacular redwood groves in Northern California is the Singing Trees Resort and Restaurant. Family owned and operated, the atmosphere at Singing Trees is friendly and casual.

Rustic accomodations consist of 29 modest to delux units; some with sundecks overlooking the Eel River. Nine have kitchenettes with prices ranging from $20 (couple) to $60 (for 8) and all are discounted 10% for extended stays of a week at a time or more. Sorry, no fireplaces due to summertime fire hazards, but there is a communal campfire accompanied with movies or singing 3 nites a week.

You can occupy your time with walks through Richardson's Grove, swim, boat, or fish on the famous Eel River, and 4 miles to the north is Benbow Golf Course. Redwood Gift shops and markets are nearby. After you have worked up a appetite you can enjoy a good selection of American and Mexican food at the Singing Trees Restaurant. Beer and Wine is also served. Several gas stations are located nearby (1-7miles) so you can easily make Singing Trees your vacation headquarters for a pleasant and memorable stay in this portion of the Redwood Empire.

SINGING TREES RESORT
AND RESTAURANT
American and Mexican Food
Located 7 miles South of
Garberville on Hwy 101
Open May 15 - Oct 1st
B - 7am-11am, L - 11am-1pm

D--5pm-9pm, dining room
open everyday but Monday,
Sundays 7am-1pm
29 Units, kitchens, sundecks
in the Redwoods on the Eel
River. Beer & Wine, MC & Visa
(707) 247-3434 Reservations

SHERWOOD FOREST MOTEL

Beautiful Sherwood Forest Motel, in downtown Garberville, offers urban comfort in the midst of redwood country. Set back on gentle slopes behind pools and fountains, the feeling is one of utmost privacy though tourist facilities are within a short walk.

In the 33 luxury rooms, sound-proofed and air-conditioned, are cable color TV, taped music, tile showers (some tubs and kitchens available), long beds, thick carpets, phones; all have covered walkways. Baby-sitting arrangements, patio barbecues, and attractive lobby are all signs that people care.

The inn is a popular one with steelhead fishermen (December, January, February). Open all year, with Earl Mitchell, the owner-manager who takes great pride in his motel and serving you. Rates are $19 - $44 per night for two.

SHERWOOD FOREST MOTEL
814 Redwood Dr. Garberville
Open all year, pool & hot spa, air
conditioning, golf nearby as well
as restaurants. MC & Visa.
(707) 923-2721 Reservations advised.

BENBOW INN

The stately Benbow Inn, a 70 room hotel in the heart of redwood country, combines the rhapsody of the 1920's art nouveau period with the grace and style of architecture in Tudor, England. It has been recognized as one of the finest country inns in the West for more than 50 years and has provided lodging for many greats in business, theater, politics and the arts.

Famous San Francisco architect Albert Farr designed Benbow in 1924 utilizing massive stairways and spacious halls. New owners, Chuck and Patsy Watts commissioned skilled Northern California craftsmen to rennovate the inn. The stairways and hall wings have been refinished with cherrywood and Wool carpeting from England. Rooms have been individually furnished with a variety of antiques and twin, queen, or king size beds with spreads that match the drapes and wallpaper. Guests can stay in the main building or neatly tucked away in the garden rooms overlooking lush grounds and a massive stone bridge. The adjoining garden rooms have shared baths making them ideal family units ($60.00); the 2nd and 3rd floor rooms (private baths or showers are $42.00 to $48.00 for two).

For your dining pleasure Benbow's chef prepares delicious entrees like Veal Ala Marsala (Wisconsin milk fed veal), Prime Ribs of Beef, New York Pepper Steak, Rack of Lamb, Scallops St. Michael, Fresh Fish (in season), or the Benbow Classic Lobster Mornay. Dinners ($7.95 - $13.95) include bread baked daily, homemade soup, Salad L Maison or chilled spinach salad & fresh vegetables. The desserts, Crepe Patissiere and Benbow's Fabulous Chocolate Mousse Pie ($1.95 - $2.25) are homemade. The wine list is excellent.

The Benbow has its own nine-hole golf course, 2 tennis courts, swimming, rivers on all sides and a lake at the front door. Guests can relax on the wicker chairs of the veranda, rent a boat and float under a stone bridge reminiscent of the Thames. Under vaulted ceilings, game tables are set for bridge or chess.

The four-story inn spans a hill at the fork of the Eel River two miles south of Garberville on Hwy 101.

BENBOW INN
Lodging and Gourmet Dining
2675 Benbow Drive (2 miles south of Garberville)
Open March 28 - November 30
Sunday Brunch: 10am - 1pm
Dinner: 6pm - 9:30pm Mon-Fri
7pm - 10pm Sat & Sun
70 rooms, private lake, swimming, tennis,
hiking, boating and a full bar
MC, Visa (707) 923-2124 Reservations advised

MIRANDA GARDENS

On the Avenue of Giants, Miranda Gardens Resort offers motel and housekeeping cottages in the woods at reasonable prices. Guests relax in the quiet of dense redwood forests, amid an exotic array of flowers and shrubs, or take short walks to the Eel River, swim in the heated pool, or dine around the patio barbecue.

Other conveniences are the beamed lounge, outdoor terrace, comfortable rooms with TV, children's playground, and grocery store. Fully equipped kitchens, cribs, and rollaways are optional.

The resort is located at Miranda, four hours drive north of San Francisco, between Garberville and Scotia. Open all year. Rates from $25 to $36 single motel room, to $30 to $50 per cottage per night. Deposit required. Major credit cards accepted.

Write Box 186, Miranda, Calif. 95553, or call (707) 943-3011.

MIRANDA GARDENS RESORT
Located on the Avenue of the Giants
(P.O. Box 186) Miranda
Preferably 8am-11pm daily
BA, MC
(707) 943-3011 for summer reservations
Special winter rates available; call for information

BISHOP PINE LODGE

Located two miles north of Trinidad and just west of Hwy 101 on Patricks Point Drive placidly sits Bishop Pine Lodge.

Secluded paths, meticulous gardens a and a small bird sanctuary provides the setting. A romantic trail winds 1,200 feet through redwoods to the edge of a cliff high above the Pacific. This spectacular view works its magic to rejuvinate your soul.

Owner Steve Kopf has carefully restored 13 rustic cabins with natural redwood and added comfortable full sized beds with Canadian Hudson Bay blankets to keep you warm and cozy. There are modern bathrooms and fully equipped kitchens ($3 extra/day - 2 day minimum). The cabins are family orientated and the daily rates vary with the seasons, but plan on spending $18.50 to $20 for small cottages, $23 - $29 (1-4) for medium cottages, and $29 - $33 (1 - 4) for large cottages (per day). Baby cribs are $3 extra and weekly rates are available. Surrounded by cozy stone benches is a large outdoor fireplace for BBQ's of steaks and fresh salmon; and for intimate gatherings under the starlite summer sky. As a added treat Steve occassionally shows an outdoor movie.

BISHOP PINE LODGE
2 miles north of Trinidad
at 900 Patrick Point Drive
Guests accepted from 9am - 10pm

daily all year.   MC, Visa
13 rustic cabins & ocean front trail
(707) 677-3314 Reservations advised

EUREKA INN

While polite society would never question the age of a gracious lady, the fact is the 150-room Eureka Inn just refuses to grow old. Like a fine wine, she improves with age; mellowed perhaps, but still charged with the effervescence of her youth.

The Eureka Inn was born into society as a showplace of elegance and sophistication for a young, growing city. Her charm and ambience carry over from that era. She remains queen of this city, with her Tudor-type architecture, high-beamed half-timber construction with rambling garrets, and the look of another era...a little of England, a lot of Europe. Summer visitors find the Inn impressive, bridging the gap of generations and weathering the storms of time. A continuous refurbishing program gives her the look of having just been built last week.

There's a motor entrance with convenient parking facilities for guests.

Today, the Eureka Inn is undergoing remodeling with the addition of luxurious 4th floor suites for 4 to 8 people. The conveniences of today have been blended with Old World charm. There is a coffee shop, fireplace lite cocktail lounge, and in the adjacent Rib Room you can dine elegantly on choice cuts of beef, veal, poultry, and Humbolt Bay crab and fresh fish (in season). Banquet facilities can accomodate from 10 to 600 and there is room service. The Eureka Inn and staff are proud to be part of this colorful and dynamic area and invite you to join them soon. Welcome!

EUREKA INN
7th & F Sts., Eureka
Inn hours: 24 hrs. a day
Coffee shop hours: 6:30am-2pm daily
Rib Room: L - 11am-2pm Mon-Fri
D - 5-11pm daily
(707) 442-6441

Banquet facilities
Heated swimming pool
Beauty parlor
Lounge and pub
Laundry & valet service
AE, BA, DC, MC
Dinner reservations advised

PATRICK CREEK LODGE

There is a place near the Oregon Border where you can cup your hands and drink from the swiftly flowing waters of the second cleanest river in the USA – the Smith River. The air is pure and scented with Douglas Fir and Virgin Redwood. A rugged range of mountains shoot up on all sides to salute the sky. In this beautiful setting you'll find Patrick Creek Lodge.

The owners, Neal and Liz Haley searched long to find such a rare dining and lodging facility. Luther Burbank himself would approve of the fresh produce Neal brings in from Oregon farmers and vendors. Everything is made fresh from scratch in the kitchen from pure, natural ingredients. Mouthwatering Barbecued Spareribs, Pan-Fried Rainbow Trout, Fresh Salmon (in season) or Fresh Red Snapper Almondine, Roast Turkey with dressing/cranberry sauce, and Chateaubriand for two is served. Dinners are $5.95 - $23.00 (for two) and include a relish tray, homemade soup & bread, baked potato and garden fresh vegetables. For breakfast you might try the Huevos Rancheros (the specialty), three egg omelettes, or Birchermusli (a delicious natural Swiss cereal topped with fresh fruit). A large variety of sandwiches and a la carte luncheons such as the Oregon Mountain are available. There is also a full bar.

Overnight accomodations $18.50 (for two) - $50 (for 7 - 2bdrm suite) are provided in the rustic lodge or motel, but be patient when making telephone reservations: because of the primitiveness of the area, party lines are still in service. Patrick Creek Lodge is quite the retreat for city slickers who want to experience comfortable lodging and excellent home cooking in the middle of wilderness.

PATRICK CREEK LODGE
American & International
U.S. Hwy 199, 27 miles East
of Crescent City, within the
boundaries of Six Rivers
National Forest.
May - Sept open everyday
B - 8am-noon, L - noon to 5pm
D - 5pm - 9pm (Sun 2pm - 9pm)
Mar - April & Sept - Nov open
Fri, Sat, Sun & Holidays

Lodging: 10 rooms in Lodge,
6 Motel Units, Full Bar, Live
music occasionally, game room,
living room/library with fireplace
swimming pool, clear creek & river,
fishing, golf course, and airport.
Telephone: Go through Crescent
City operator and ask for Patrick
Creek Toll No. 5 - be patient for
there are still party lines here.
MC, Visa,Reservations advised.

NOTE: At present the Pioneer Inn does not exist, but hopefully the right people will build it. It is needed. There are millions of Americans who hunger for such a harmonious and simplistic Inn to escape too. The Pioneer Inn can put them back in touch with their biological heritage and give those that have been city locked and swallowed by insensitive technology new hope. If you are interested then write the Pioneer Inn, %Robert W. Matson, Box G, Santa Rosa, Calif. 95402. I might be able to steer you in the right direction.

THE
PIONEER INN

"They are the Pilgrims that will enable the renewal of a tired society. A society where the individual has lost the grip on his own destiny."

They escaped from a culture that had been swallowed by high capitol, high energy and high technology systems. They reintroduced common sense and peacefully lived in simple elegance with the land and natural environment. With appropriate technology they designed and built five attractive 2 story energy efficient cabins at a fraction of the cost of traditional housing. A 12volt DC power pack and inverter replaced the unattractive and costly overhead power lines. Lights and household appliances run on 110 volts AC or 12 volts DC. The batteries are recharge-able through any number of ways - wind, solar, hydro, compost, auto-mobile; even peddle power (a good way to get 30 minutes of exercise each day). Fresh water comes from a spring and there is a creek nearby. Solar heated 55 gallon drums and wood fired agua-heaters in the bath house provide plenty of hot water. Two of the cabins have private baths.

Best of all - a large well managed solar heated greenhouse provides fresh organic produce year-round. Besides pollinating the plants, a small hive of bees make delicious honey. There is also a trout farm, crayfish pond and pens of fresh escargot. Fresh milk comes from Bessie and Nanny Bell. Herbs from the garden spice up the homemade jack cheese. Fresh eggs come from the chickens and from the small orchard comes fresh fruit (in season).

Each cabin is furnished with a fireplace and cozy bedroom loft with skylight. There is a communal kitchen. Guests are also encouraged to learn rural skills during their stay at the Pioneer Inn. "We all need to rekindle basic survival skills so we can become more self reliant and better able to cope with a world full of uncertainties in the 1980's." A library of books on history and alternatives will further enlighten you.

PIONEER INN
Farm Lodging
Box G, Santa Rosa, California 95402
1776 Independence Road, Freedom, California
Rates for two $50 shared bath, $65 private bath.
Farm fresh continental breakfast & delicious
fresh produce right from the farm. Five cabins
elegantly set in a self sufficient community in
harmony with the land and natural environment.
Children and pets ok. Reservations are required.

The fog adds a magical touch.

Some Napa Valley Wineries

By Deborah Erb

Most Napa Valley days begin in a thick cool fog. The rare but fortunate early morning visitor who enters the valley from the north descending from Mt. St. Helena may transcend time in the spectacular, primeval view below.

Layer upon layer of receding mountain ridges form the valley boundries on the east and on the west. Throughout the sea of fog which covers the valley floor float islands of higher hilltops. The disembodied camelback of San Francisco's Mt. Diablo, some 80 miles in the distance, looms on the southern horizon. The clarity of first light above the dense blue fog is startlingly bright; the eerie contrast, quiet, timeless. This is one recurring image of the Napa Valley which has remained unchanged for centuries.

But beneath the fog the changes have been many, as the land has answered to the demands of successive populations: native Indians, Mexican explorers, farming settlers, gold digging prospectors, and many others.

As the sun warms, dissipating the timeless fog, the present Napa Valley is revealed. The carpet of vineyard meeting vineyard is interrupted only by the wineries and the small communities which they support. The agriculturally-based wine industry has kept the Upper Napa Valley a greenly growing place. Where grape vines flourish, sub-divisions do not.

Looking down on the valley with its great expanse of vineyards, anyone would find it difficult to believe that this place attracts more tourists than any other place in California — with the incongruous exception of Disneyland. But come they do, in an ever increasing stream, and the explanation for this — the wine industry.

Spring Mountain - total elegance

Buller

Sterling Vineyards - high above
the Napa Valley.

Thanks to increased profits, production, and prestige, some of the biggest wineries have been acquired by large corporations but new small wineries start or old small ones are reborn, dedicated to preserving individuality and a personal touch in wine making.

Throughout the Napa wine country, the new name of the game is "Premium Varietal Wines." In the European tradition, a wine's name was derived from the area where it was produced. A *true* Burgundy, for instance, came only from the Burgundy district of France.

When California winemakers first borrowed the old names from their European heritage, they used them to describe similar wines of their own making. Such generic names do not identify the variety of grapes used to make the wines.

The names of varietal wines are more precise for they refer to the specific grapes used rather than a region thousands of miles away. By law, a varietal wine must contain at

least 51 percent of the named variety of grape, although most varietals contain a much higher percentage.

The prestige of and demand for varietal wines continues to grow. Twenty-five years ago, there were three or four Cabernet Sauvignons available. Now there are perhaps forty.

Bob Trinchero, winemaker at the family owned and operated Sutter Home Winery, grew up in the wine business. He comments on some of the changes he has seen: "The industry educated itself to the tastes of the consumers. Back in the old days, the wine business was strongly ethnic and fairly local. We made wine to suit ourselves and we drank it.

"But let's face it, American kids grow up on Kool-Aid and Coca-Cola, and it's a big step from Kool-Aid to Cabernet." In 1959-60, U.C. Davis conducted a study to find out what Americans liked in wine. What they came up with was something pink and slightly sweet. Believe it or not, in 1959 there was only one California rose — Almaden's Grenache rose'. But the industry picked up on it. Gallo suggested that you put a rose in your glass and others followed.

More and more people are drinking more and better California wines. Their interest brings them to the wine country and its queen, The Napa Valley. They come to see the vineyards, to learn how grapes become wine, to drink wine where it is made and to enjoy the countryside.

Since the big, don't-miss wineries like Charles Krug, Beringer Brothers, Beaulieu, The Christian Brothers, Inglenook, Louis M. Martini and Souverain are well known to most visitors, we've concentrated our tour on smaller wineries, with a few exceptions. The big wineries all have full schedules of tours, tasting rooms and retail sales. The smaller wineries, often more personal in their welcome to visitors, are also busy places. If you want a chance to talk to the people that make wine, small wineries are ideal, but advance appointments must often be made.

Most visitors come to the Napa Valley from the San Francisco Bay Area so this guide follows Highway 29 north along the western edge of the valley and returns south along the Silverado Trail at the eastern edge.

The Napa Valley's most southern winery is Carneros Creek Winery (1285 Dealy Lane, Napa). "Carneros climate is ideal for a true Burgundy," says winemaker Frank Mahoney. He and his partners, Balfour and Anita Gibson, are particularly committed to a "true Burgundy" because in California there are many good Cabernets and Zinfandels, but rarely a good Pinot Noir.

Frank Mahoney is a young winemaker: experimental, enthusiastic and hard working. Virtually a one-man winery, he has since 1973 worked nearly unassisted in the cellar and in the vineyards. Even so, he tries to find time to talk to knowledgeable visitors who have called for an appointment.

Completed in early 1977, Domain Chandon (California Drive, Yountville) marks the arrival in the

Daryl Sattui of V. Sattui Winery.

Napa Valley of the prestigious French firm of Moet-Hennessey. In their new 3-½ million dollar winery, they are making "sparkling wine in the French tradition." Loyalty and French law (not American) reserve the champagne label exclusively for the sparkling wine made in the French district of the same name. French money, French expertise and the traditional French methode Champenoise set the style at the enormous new winery, which is open to the public everyday but Tuesday and Wednesday.

Mayacamas Vineyards (1155 Lokoya Road, Napa) is secluded in the Mayacamas Mountain range from which it takes its name. The winery is surrounded by 45 acres of mountain vineyards; it is the only cultivated mark on the otherwise untamed hills. Mayacamas is an Indian name, said to mean "howl of the mountain lion."

Bob Travers puts great stock in the European emphasis on mountain vineyards but admits that "the best place to grow grapes is always in your own vineyard, no matter what the terrain." This man, who seems so much a part of his surroundings, has been at Mayacamas only since 1968, following a first career as a financial analyst. His wife, Elinor, takes an active part in winery work, handling bookkeeping, advertising and co-wine tasting. "She's a miscellaneous worker — like me." Visitors to this mountain haven should call one day in advance and are encouraged to ask for directions.

Robert Mondavi Winery (7801 Highway 29, Oakville) is a newish winery, bearing a well-established name. Robert Mondavi opened the winery in 1966, following a family disagreement which caused him to leave the Mondavi-owned Charles Krug Winery. Robert's branch of the family continues the tradition of a family-run operation. His son Tim is in charge of production while Michael shares the winemaker's title with his father.

Unlike many father and son teams, the Mondavis have a high regard for the talents of women in this traditionally male dominated industry. The important positions of head enologist and director of public relations are held by Zelma Long and Margrit Biever. In addition, in the cellars, women are proving that they can "drag hoses" as well as the next general winery worker.

"Making good wine is a skill, fine wine an art" is the Mondavi motto, explains Michael. "My father, Robert, believes it natural to blend the arts and wine in community service." The beautifully skylighted Vineyard Room offers rotating art exhibits, open to the public. Every year, a summer program of jazz concerts and a winter program of chamber music are hosted by the Mondavis.

Tours are frequent and wines are available for tasting.

Sutter Home Winery (227 St. Helena Highway South, St. Helena) is what many other small Napa Valley wineries can only pretend to be — family owned and operated. Bob, Vera and Roger Trinchero and even Steve Bertolucci, their only permanent employee, grew up in Mario and Mary Trinchero's home on the winery grounds. "We have none of the corporate problems," says eldest son and winemaker Bob, "but we have all the problems of a family business."

In the old days, the winery drew its customers from the local Italian community and sold good red wine for $2 a gallon to customers who provided their own bottles. "Back then, we were just making a living," says Bob, "but we've become a little serious about it now." In 1960, Bob's first vintage as a winemaker, they were producing 52 wines and eight vinegars. Eighty-five percent of their

FREEMARK ABBEY WINERY , St. Helena

production is now reserved for their specialty, Amador County Zinfandel, one of the finest Zinfandels the county offers.

There are no tours at Sutter Home, but their wines are offered for tasting and there's nearly always a member of the Trinchero family on hand to talk about wine.

The name of the V. Sattui Winery (White Lane, St. Helena) goes back to the 19th century when it was founded by Victorio Sattui. Now his great great grandson, Daryl Sattui, has revived the old name at a new winery built in an old walnut grove in the Napa Valley. His first crush was in 1975.

At this very early stage in its new history, V. Sattui Winery has perhaps more cheese than wine on hand in an excellent cheese shop. Visitors, always welcome, are invited to make use of the picnic area.

Freemark Abbey Winery (3022 St. Helena Highway, St. Helena), reopened in 1967 under the new ownership of a limited partnership of seven men, operates in the building of hand-cut stone, first opened as Lombardo Cellars in 1895.

The philosophy of winemaking at Freemark is "to provide an environment which allows the natural winemaking process to proceed to the greatest potential of each vintage."

To ensure the best quality grapes, Freemark Abbey relies heavily on the partnership's own vineyards where they may harvest with confidence. Only four wines are made here: Cabernet Sauvignon, Pinot Noir, Pinot Chardonnay and Johannisberg Riesling. All wines are barrel-aged in small French cooperage. In addition to retail sales and tours, Freemark Abbey houses a restaurant, gourmet shop and candle factory.

Hanns Kornell Champagne Cellars (1091 Larkmead Lane, Calistoga), while very much a working winery, hosts a full schedule of tours and tastings. Owner and winemaker Hanns, a fourth generation champagne maker, arrived in this country nearly

Winemaker Philip Togni of Cuvaison.

penniless from Germany in 1939. He was, however, determined to continue his family reputation by establishing an internationally recognized wine cellar in California. Hanns, proud of his traditional "in this bottle" method of champagne making, is teaching his children everything he knows so they may continue in his name.

For further information on that most misunderstood of wines, champagne, visit also Schramsberg Vineyard (Schramsberg Road, Calistoga). "Champagne is nothing more than wine with bubbles in it," explains owner Jack Davies. "Any grape, any fruit can be made into wine. The art is in the essential blending of wines to produce a cuvee which will benefit from secondary fermentation and the interesting tactile dimension added by its by-product — bubbles."

Schramsberg Champagne is made by the traditional *methode Champenoise* — fermented, aged, hand-riddled, disgorged, topped with a cognac dosage, recorked and delivered to the consumer in the same bottle.

Visitors, welcome only by appointment, should call in advance.

Stonegate Winery (Dunaweal Lane, Calistoga), a small winery with a present production of 5,000 cases,

Hanns Kornell, a fourth generation champagne maker.

aims to make "the smallest amount of modestly priced quality wine possible and still survive," says David Spaulding, winemaker, general manager and son of the owners, James and Barbara Spaulding.

Open since the spring of 1974, the winery now offers seven different varietals because "good wine is made only from good grapes so we find the best grapes available and make our wines from them." David is glad to see visitors when he has the time.

Al Brounstein of Diamond Creek Vineyards (1500 Diamond Mountain Road, Calistoga) is determined to "have something really, really good" and is willing to pay "the price of patience." A very small winery, it produces one varietal, Cabernet Sauvignon bottled under three different Diamond Creek labels which derive their names from the three distinct soil conditions found in the twenty acre hillside vineyard — Volcanic Rock, Red Rock Terrace and Gravelly Meadow. This jewel of a winery located beneath Diamond Mountain has a small mountain lake for boating and swimming.

At present, Al and Boots Brounstein can only accommodate

organized groups of wine lovers. For an appointment, write well in advance.

Phillip Togni, winemaker at Cuvaison (4560 Silverado Trail North, Calistoga) has impressive credentials. A cosmopolitan winemaker with a Swiss passport, Togni was educated in England and France and came to this country via Chile. The first wine made completely under his direction, a Chardonnay, has a release date of March 1977. The small white winery has an arched veranda which frames the view of the western slopes of the valley, "our daily recompense for being located on the hot side of the valley."

Visitors to the white hilltop winery of Sterling Vineyards (1111 Dunaweal Lane, Calistoga) arrive via a tramway (fee, $2.50) and begin a self-guided tour of the winery. Placards which dot the walkways of the four passages emphasize the historical beginnings of wine and winemaking, relating them to the modern methods used in the winery. The tour is highly informative and efficient. Tours end in the tasting room, where the dry table wines of winemaker R.W. Forman are offered.

Burgess Cellars (1108 Deer Park Road, St. Helena) is located in a stone and redwood winery that dates back to the 1870's. Thomas E. Burgess, a former corporation airplane pilot, bought the winery in 1972. It overlooks 22 acres of hillside vineyards and a panoramic view of the northern end of Napa Valley. Bill Sorenson, a '72 graduate from Fresno, is the winemaker. He believes that a winemaker belongs in the cellar with the cellar workers as much as in the lab.

"We learned the practical part as we went along," Burgess says. A big problem in winemaking is that you must wait three years for the results of your experiments. It's in individual attention to wines that the promise of Burgess lies. "People are welcome to walk through our cellars anytime we're not too busy working." Limited tastings of Burgess wines are offered on weekends, and there is a picnic area.

In 1972 Arlene and James Devitt bought and refurbished the old Sam Haus Winery, founded in 1909. It's now called Pope Valley Winery (6613 Pope Valley Road, St. Helena) and is managed by the two sons, Bob and Steve Devitt. The "wine guys," as they refer to themselves, are as refreshingly unpretentious about their wine as they are about their jobs. "We make table wine — red, white and rose'." Visitors are invited to taste wine anytime and people can "poke around" the winery which is built from redwood timbers salvaged from the Oat Hill quicksilver mine.

James Nichelini, a third generation winemaker, remembers when Nichelini Winery (Highway 128, St. Helena) in Chile's Valley had dirt floors and hand pumps. He adds that "Twenty years ago, if you went into a bar and asked for a glass of wine, people thought you were crazy. In 1960 I went out of the gallon business and in 1968 I went out of the half

Pope Valley Winery

Buller

Chateau Montelena

Buller

Burgess Cellars dates back to the 1870's.

gallon business. Now I'm making 18—20,000 gallons per year, all distributed in fifths."

Jimmy is a winemaker who works at every part of the operation — crushing, cellar work, hand bottling and delivery. Of his wines, all produced from the 170 acres managed by his partner in the vineyards, Cousin Joe Nichelini, Jimmy says they're all good. "Everybody has their own taste and has gotta pick their own favorite."

Joseph Phelps' first career gave him a good start on his second. His new winery building at Joseph Phelps Vineyards (200 Taplin Road, St. Helena) was constructed by his own national contracting company., The four story building is made of redwood cut from the timbers of a 100 year old bridge. The surrounding acreage is planted with "major noble varities" — Cabernet Sauvignon, Zinfandel, Johannisberg Riesling, and Gewurtztraminer. "The natural air drainage of our enclosed terrain assures us of a climatic distinction in our vineyard," Phelps says. The first Saturday of every month, there's open house from 11 to 2:30; otherwise visitors should come by appointment only.

At Clos du Val (5330 Silverado Trail, Napa) Bernard Portet is the young and energetic winemaker,

manager and one of the limited partners. He has an impressive family background in winemaking in France. Bernard came to California determined to make the highest quality wine outside of Beaulieu. Of his homeland, he says "The French structure does not bend much. In France, a winemaker does not work; he does the thinking and someone below him does the work. Here in California, I get to do both. It has been a great and enjoyable challenge to build a winery from scratch." The winery, set up for red wines only, crushed its first grapes in '74. Visitors come by appointment only.

In Europe, winemaking has long been accorded a respect which is only lately being bestowed upon American wines and winemaking. An offshoot of this recently sprouted respect is a full blown romanticism. A great wine, even a good wine, is a remarkable achievement and the valley does foster a rewarding life style.

Visitors now flock to the valley. They come to learn about and to taste wine and they come to explore the romantic image that now surrounds the art of Napa Valley winemaking and the people who make it. In a culture where creative individuality and excellence have grown elusive and country life enviable, this image is sure to flourish.

Buller

Mike Mondavi, son of
Robert Mondavi.

Buller

Nichelini Vineyards, founded 1890.

NapaCounty Wineries

Vineyard after vineyard meet on
the floor of the Napa Valley
and the eye and heart
appreciate it's green expanse.

R Thompson JR
NSF

CHRISTIAN BROTHERS

The Christian Brothers Winery is operated by a lay teaching order of the Roman Catholic Church, who take vows of poverty, chastity, and obedience and dedicate their lives to educating others in the community. The Brothers support thirteen schools on the West Coast with their wine operations.

Winemakers since 1882, in Martinez, the Brothers initiated their wine production in the Napa Valley moving to Mont La Salle in 1930. With the building of the modern crushing and fermenting facility in South St. Helena in 1973, the Brothers have grown to become a leading producer of premium wines, Brandy, Champagne, and Vermouth, not only in the Napa Valley, but throughout California and the world. Visitors are always enthusiastically received by the Brothers, who have produced their wine with personal dedication to quality.

THE CHRISTIAN BROTHERS
2555 Main Hwy. 29, St. Helena
(707) 963-2719, 10:30-4:30 daily
tastings and tours
generic and varietal wines, Champagnes,
vermouth, brandy

1978

NAPA

CHARDONNAY

100% Chardonnay grapes
from Carneros, Napa

Produced and Bottled by

SONOMA, CALIFORNIA

ALCOHOL 12.5% BY VOLUME

ZD WINERY

During 1979, the very small ZD Winery was moved from Sonoma to the heart of the Napa Valley Wine Country. All equipment and cooperage was moved into the new facility just in time for the 1979 crush. Though the facilities have more than quadrupled in size, it is refreshing to know that owners Gino Zepponi and Norman C. de Leuze maintain the same style and philosophy of winemaking - that of a family run operation. The winery is now managed on a full time basis by Norman, with his son Robert acting as cellarmaster. Gino participates whenever time allows from his very hectic schedule as Director of Operations at Domain Chandon, and other family members work enthusiastically on a part time basis.

The wines produced are primarily 100% varietals, and the label carries a vintage date and an appelation of origin of the grapes. In their quest for grapes with full varietal character, ZD has produced wines using grapes from a number of areas in the state. Each wine is kept separate, fermented in small batches, aged in 50 and 60 gallon barrels, and bottled seperately. The primary wines produced have been Chardonnay and Pinot Noir, although a Gewurtztraminer, a Merlot and a Cabernet Sauvignon were sold in 1979, and a Zinfandel will be bottled in late 1980. Each of these wines is treated as an individual, and the resulting wines reflect the particular flavors and aromas associated with the grape variety, the area it was grown in, and the vintage year, as well as the wine-making technique.

ZD WINERY
8383 Silverado Trail, Napa 94558
(707) 963-5188

tours & tastings by appointment only
Hours vary seasonally so be sure to call
varietal wines

CLOS du VAL

"Like Father, Like Son . . . is more than just an idle aphorism in the case of Clos du Val winery. This small, select winery, located in Napa Valley, is run by Bernard Portet, son of Andre Portet, "regisseur" (manager) of France's most esteemed vineyard, Chateau Lafite Rothschild. The skilled winemaker is determined to produce wines as fine and rich in quality as those of his father's vineyards.

Monsieur Portet's credentials are impressive: graduate of his father's alma mater, the Ecole National Superieure d'Agronomie de Montpellier in France, Bernard received degrees in viticulture, enology, and agronomy. In 1972, the talented young Frenchman came to California and crushed the first grapes for Clos du Val. The resulting Zinfandel and Cabernet Sauvignon, released to the public in 1974, were well received.

Clos du Val is a handsome winery, with the construction reflecting clean, straight lines highlighted by arched windows. Surrounded by quiet rolling hills and vineyards, the winery creates a striking picture as its strong form proudly juts out against this quiet, rustic background.

Napa Valley was selected as the site for Clos du Val for a precise reason; the rich, sunny land is like no other for growing wine, save that of the vineyards of France. The Valley is famous for its Cabernet Sauvignon grape, which Portet uses to its fullest advantage. The Clos du Val Winery has determined to specialize in the Cabernet Sauvignon and the Zinfandel wines. This specialization results in a finer quality wine for your table.

Clos du Val is still a relatively new winery, especially when compared to the years of tradition embodied in the older wineries of France. Yet, this Napa winery carries the proud legacy of the Portet tradition of quality winemaking. The rich Napa Valley grapes, combined with the unique skills of Bernard Portet, prove that, in the case of fine winemaking, the whole can be greater than the sum of the parts.

CLOS DU VAL WINE CO., LTD.
5330 Silverado Tr., Napa
(707) 252-6711, 8am-5pm M-F
tours by apt., no tasting
varietal wines

NICHELINI VINEYARDS

We're sure there is only one individual like Jim Nichelini in the wine world. "Jimmy Nick", as his friends call him, is a hard working, gritty, and colorful man who possesses a hearty laugh and outlook on life you won't soon forget. He takes pride in making fine vintages of Chenin Blanc, and Sauvignon Vert (his specialities) and Zinfandel.

The winery was founded in 1890 by Antone Nichelini, Jim's grandfather. It was William Antone Nichelini who took over the winery in 1933, kept it going through the hard times and passed on what he knew to his son Jimmy. Nichelini Vineyards still has the only Roman Press in the Western Hemisphere. Visitors are always welcome at Nichelini's.

NICHELINI VINEYARDS
2349 Lower Chiles Rd., Rutherford
(707) 963-3357, 10am-6pm Sat & Sun
Tasting & Tours
Varietal Wines

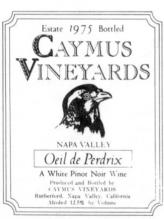

CAYMUS

Caymus Vineyards was established in 1972 by the Charles Wagner family. The name Caymus was taken from the Mexican land grant to George C. Yount, who named his grant Rancho Caymus after a sub-tribe of Indians who resided in the area now called Yountville.

The Wagner family has many years of experience in both viticulture and wine making, dating back to the mid 1880's. The buildings at Caymus are plain and functional with none of the austerity found in many wineries because good equipment and cooperage are more important to them. At Caymus the wines speak for themselves, each is 100 percent of the variety so named. Authenticity and quality are never compromised at this family operated winery.

CAYMUS VINEYARDS
8700 Conn Creek Road, Rutherford
(707) 963-4204
Tasting
By appointment, case sales only
Varietal wines

ROBERT MONDAVI WINERY

California wines did not always have the alluring reputation they carry today. Thirty years ago a young, energetic winemaker named Robert Mondavi found, in his repeated travels to the East Coast, that California wines held a poor image with the sophisticated Easterners. Intrigued with the concept of making quality table wines which would earn California quality reputation, Robert Mondavi spent the next seventeen years collecting data, facts, and, more importantly, experience in winemaking, in order to develop the kind of table wine which would earn applause from the winemaking world. His efforts as an Ambassador for California wines proved successful. By the early 1960's, thanks to his dedication and energy, the California winemaking industry was receiving recognition for high quality table wines, and a definite nod of approval and esteem from the East.

Today, the Robert Mondavi Winery, established in 1966, stands as a formidable leader in Napa Valley winemaking. Approximately eight hundred acres span the rich Robert Mondavi Vineyards in the Oakville-Yountville area. Robert Mondavi runs the winery with his sons Michael and Timothy and his daughter Marcia. The team works hard and well together to preserve the prestigious reputation of the famous Robert Mondavi label. The Mondavi's firmly believe in aging their wines in wood in order to bring out the special flavor of the wine, thus all Robert Mondavi wines have the "kiss of the wood." This subtle touch of oak which appears in all of their wines is one of their signatures of quality. Their distinctive list of table wines is impressive: Chardonnay, Pinot Noir, Gamay, Chenin Blanc, Johannisberg Riesling, Cabernet Sauvignon, Gamay Rose, plus the dessert wine, Moscato d'Oro.

The impressive Mission-style winery, with its rich paneled walls and smooth Spanish-tiled floors paving long, cool corridors has become a center for community events. Concert series are held summer and winter during which time patrons may savor the famous **Robert** Mondavi wines.

ROBERT MONDAVI WINERY
7801 St. Helena Highway
Oakville
(707) 963-7156, 10am-4:30pm daily

Tasting, Tours, Catered Dinners
Varietal Wines
BA, MC

FRANCISCAN

"Aging smooths the sharp qualities of youth." Aye, now there's hearty admonishment for quality wine. Within the spacious, modern, Franciscan Winery located on Highway 29 on the fringe of St. Helena, you will find the rewards of such an admonishment taken to heed. The Franciscan Winery offers a whole learning as well as wine tasting experience. A leisurely, self-guided tour is offered for all visitors to fully explore for themselves all the phases of wine-making which makes Franciscan wines, quality wines. Informational signs are posted at each of the crushing, fermentation, aging, finishing, and bottling sites, which briefly explain an overview of each process. As you complete your tour and pass by the impressive racks of wine-filled oak barrels in the finishing room, and the winery's bottling line, you will find a sunny, enclosed flower filled courtyard beyond which lies the tasting room. Here, beneath high redwood beam cathedral ceiling, you have the opportunity to taste the products of the Winery.

The variety of Franciscan Wines range from Napa Valley White Riesling (1974), Napa Valley Chenin Blanc (1974), limited bottling of 1975 Carnelian Nouveau, and 1973 Napa Valley Burgundy and 1972 North Coast Cabernet Sauvignon. Special selection wines include 1975 California White Riesling, 1975 California Chenin Blanc (medium sweet), Napa Valley Rose, 1973 California Zinfandel, and 1973 Napa Valley Pinot Noir. Dollar wines and Friar's Table Half-Gallons are also offered for the budget minded. All wines are available for purchase.

Visit the Franciscan Winery and explore for yourself the rich rewards of the process of patient aging. It's an opportunity well worth experiencing.

FRANCISCAN VINEYARDS
1178 Galleron Rd., Rutherford
(707) 963-7111, 10am-6pm daily
tasting, tours
generic and varietal wines
AE, BA, MC

LOUIS MARTINI WINERY

Just as the qualities of fine wines deepen and become enriched with age, so does the character and accomplishments of fine men increase and multiply with the passing of years. Spanning the 87 years of his life, Louis Martini made striking achievements in the field of winemaking. Born in 1887 in Genoa, Louis Martini immigrated to San Francisco at the age of 13. Following a disillusioning failure at a backyard winery, Louis returned to Italy in 1906 to learn firsthand the fine art of quality winemaking. He completed his studies at the Alba School of Enology in a year, and eagerly returned to America to use his new found knowledge. Producing a rewarding vintage, he sold the wine door to door in the Italian community of San Francisco's North Beach. As the years passed, Louis's interest and participation in winemaking steadily grew, deepened, became enriched. His first winery was built in Kingsburg during Prohibition, when he produced grape concentrates, sacramental, and medicinal wines. By 1934 he had built a second plant at St. Helena for the production of dry wines, and subsequently moved all operations to the Napa Valley plant in 1940. The wines he then proceeded to produce stunned the winemaking world; they were of the finest quality and the Martini reputation for fine wines skyrocketed to the top of the list of quality California winemakers.

Today, the winery and vineyards are still family owned and operated. Louis P. Martini, a son, has been in charge of production for the past 20 years and continues today as the President and General Manager. A grandaughter has just joined the firm in an administrative capacity and a grandson is studying Enology at UC Davis, and plans to join the family enterprise when he completes his studies. Another grandaughter plans to eventually come into the business also. Their vineyards now include over 800 acres of fine grapes grown in the best locations near the towns of St. Helena, Napa, Sonoma, and Healdsburg. Louis M. Martini produces a wide array of very fine and moderately priced red and white varietal wines and some inexpensive generics.

LOUIS MARTINI WINERY
254 S. St. Helena Hwy., St. Helena
(707) 963-2736, 10am-4pm Daily
Tasting & Tours
Generic & Varietal Wines   North of San Francisco 179
BA

Est. N°. 69 *of a total of 5,300 Bottles* *1885*

UNFINED
UNFILTERED

1975
NAPA VALLEY

Cabernet Sauvignon

Produced and Bottled By

V. Sattui Winery

ST. HELENA, CALIFORNIA

Alcohol 13%   By Volume

V. SATTUI WINERY and the ST. HELENA CHEESE FACTORY

No where else in the Napa Valley can one visit a charming family winery, inexpensively purchase the makings of a gourmet picnic lunch from an extensive cheese shop on the premises and enjoy, in the European manner, food and wine on the winery picnic grounds.

The St. Helena Cheese Factory purveys more than 150 quality cheeses from throughout the world. It features sour dough French bread, quality Italian dry salami, homemade French pate' and liver sausage. Fresh fruits and nuts are also available along with a host of other delicacies.

Outside on the picnic grounds one can sit under the shade trees at tables made from old wine casks or relax in the grass adjacent to the winery and an old Zinfandel vineyard.

V. Sattui Winery was founded in 1885 by Victorio Sattui and was well known in the area until the advent of Prohibition when it was compelled to close its doors. With the approval and encouragement of the family, Daryl Sattui, the great grandson of the founder, recently realized his life-long dream by giving the old winery a rebirth.

Daryl wishes to follow in the footsteps of his great grandfather by making small lots of fine varietal wines which shall be sold only at the winery. He intends to concentrate on producing: Zinfandel, Cabernet Sauvignon, and Napa Valley Riesling.

For those who enjoy visiting a small, family operated winery come to V. Sattui Winery where from its handsomely rugged tasting room with its massive timbers and beautiful redwood doors guests may view the entire winemaking operation.

V. SATTUI WINERY
S. St., Helena Hwy. at White Lane, St. Helena
(707) 963-7774, 10am-5:30pm daily June—Oct.

North of San Francisco 180

Tasting, tours, retail sales, picnic area
gift & cheese shop
Varietal
BA, MC

Spring Mountain was founded in 1968, using the basement of a stately old home that was built in 1876, just north of Christian Brothers at St. Helena.

The vineyards and buildings had fallen into disrepair, but caught the eye and imagination of Michael Robbins, an engineer from Iowa, during his trips to the valley in 1963. He spent the next few years restoring and assembling a winemaker's dream of a winery from its below-level basement. His first Spring Mountain wine was introduced in 1970.

The first wines, a Chardonnay and a Sauvignon Blanc, were proclaimed excellent by connoisseurs. Spring Mountain also released a Cabernet Sauvignon with great promise.

The proprietors, Mike and Shirley Robbins, feel the Napa Valley is a great place to make fine wine because of climate and soil, and "a great tradition which motivates winemakers to achieve the highest form of the winemaker's art."

The proliferation of small wineries is an ecological as well as an economic asset. It is, in the highest sense, the result of man's sincere desire to produce something pleasurable to man and the environment.

SPRING MOUNTAIN VINEYARDS
  2805 Spring Mountain Rd., St. Helena
  (707) 963-4341
  Visitors by appointment
  Varietal wines

FREEMARK ABBEY WINERY

Located in the beautiful Napa Valley, just two miles north of St. Helena, is the Freemark Abbey winery. The building was constructed out of stone block hewn from the adjacent countryside. In 1967 the winery was sold to its present owners--a partnership of seven men.

The policy of Freemark Abbey is to produce fine wine through the most natural means possible. They have minimized the use of filtration, heavy fining, and complex stabilization.

At Freemark Abbey, 75% of the grapes used in wine production are grown in their own vineyards. They believe that quality is best achieved through specialization; consequently, emphasis is placed on the production of four varietals: Johannisberg Riesling, Pinot Chardonnay, Cabernet Sauvignon, and Pinot Noir. This winery is a small one: production level is not expected to exceed 20,000 cases per year.

A visit to the well-noted Freemark Abbey winery is strongly recommended because it offers not only a fine winery tour, but the adjacent Abbey restaurant, a gourmet shop, the Hurd candle factory and the newly constructed Wine Country Inn.

FREEMARK ABBEY
3022 St. Helena Hwy., St. Helena
(707) 963-7105

Scheduled tours daily
BA, MC

CHARLES KRUG

"Old timers believe the quality of a man's wine depends on his own quality and character, a little bit of himself going into every bottle. To gain lasting fame, he has to be a poet, a philosopher, and an honorable man as well as a master craftsman." These are the words of Peter Mondavi, general manager of the family owned and operated Charles Krug Winery.

In 1943 when the Charles Krug estate was originally acquired by the late Cesare Mondavi, he faced the challenge of rehabilitating and expanding the winery and vineyards. Older wines were replaced with finer wine grape varieties and additional vines were planted. By 1959, when Cesare Mondavi died, he had left to his family one of the best equipped and most efficient wineries in the country.

It is the fact that Charles Krug is family owned and operated that adds to the wine's special essence. Peter Mondavi feels that "It is impossible to overstress the value of family ownership and operation in any line of endeavor which calls for fine workmanship and consistently high quality."

In the last few years the Mondavi family has increased the vine acreage of Charles Krug by adding another 900 acres. Most of these have been planted in Cabernet, Sauvignon, Pinot Noir, Gamay Beaujolais, Pinot Chardonnay, Johannisberg Riesling, and Gewurtztraminer.

For the Mondavi family, quality is the watchword. Their goal has always been to make the finest wines in California, and to offer them proudly for comparison with wines made anywhere else. The winery slogan aptly describes the sound values of the Mondavi family in the production of Charles Krug wines: wines of character, dependability, reputation.

CHARLES KRUG WINERY
St. Helena Hwy, St. Helena
(707) 963-2761, 9am—4:30pm daily
tours and tastings
generic and varietal wines
BA

NSF

HANNS KORNELL CHAMPAGNE CELLARS

Hanns Kornell first arrived in the United States from Germany in 1940. He is the third generation of a family of fine wine and champagne makers from Mainz. Hanns Kornell bought his present winery on Larkmead Lane in 1958, where through his great knowledge, hard work, and dedication to producing only the finest champagne, he has achieved success and international recognition. Today, his champagne cellars contain over one and a half million bottles of these international award winning champagnes.

Champagne making is still a family enterprise at Hanns Kornell. Hanns is instructing his children in champagne production, knowing that the fourth generation will continue with the family heritage with pride. Hanns Kornell Champagne is produced in the traditional methode Champenoise. Here the wine remains in the same bottle. Only in this traditional method of production can the label state that the Champagne has been "Naturally Fermented in this Bottle".

Since 1959 champagne sales have shot up approximately 600%. Sparkling wines are now popular for all occasions. What is more pleasing than a perfectly chilled bottle of Champagne — the crowning touch, for example, to a picnic!

Legend has it that champagne was discovered some 300 years ago by Dom Perignon, a Benedictine cellarmaster. Perignon is supposed to have shouted out to his fellow monks "Come quickly, I'm drinking stars". Thanks to men like Hanns Kornell this great discovery can be as exciting for you as it was for Perignon and his fellow monks three centuries ago.

HANNS KORNELL CHAMPAGNE CELLARS
1091 Larkmead Lane, St. Helena
(707) 963-2334, 10am-4pm daily
Champagne tasting and tours
AE, BA, MC

STERLING VINEYARDS

Sterling Vineyards is one of the newer wineries in the Napa Valley but word about the wines has spread quickly. Each year since 1973, more than one hundred thousand visitors have experienced a unique aerial tramway ride to the hilltop winery, taken a self-guided tour, then enjoyed a comfortable tasting in rooms high above the valley.

The winery building itself was designed in the spirit of monastic architecture of the Mediterranean, and it fits naturally into the foothills of Mt. St. Helena. From the winery one can take in spectacular views of the north end of the Napa Valley as attendants pour and discuss the wines in as much detail as each visitor desires.

Under the Sterling Vineyards estate bottled label there are eight dry wines, four white and four red, several of which are produced in limited quantities. Four other varietal wines as well as a generic red and a white are sold under the Sterling Cellars label.

The winemaker is Ric Forman. Forman has made all of the Sterling Vineyards wines, beginning in 1969. Sterling is privately owned by four families, two of whom manage the daily operations.

STERLING VINEYARDS
1111 Dunaweal Lane, Calistoga
(707) 942-5151, 10:30am-4:30pm daily
$2.50 fee for tours, tasting, retail sales
Varietal and generic wines
AE, BA, MC, DC

POPE VALLEY VINEYARDS

Estate Bottled

ℙope Valley Ⓦinery

1973
Napa Valley

Dry Semillon

The Pope Valley Winery was founded in 1910 by Sam Haus. In 1972, James and Arlene Devitt purchased the winery. They have renovated the building and added the latest equipment for quality wine production. The delightful old world essence of the few Napa Valley wineries owned and operated by a family, can be found here. Pope Valley Winery is one of the last wineries in California to operate with a gravitational flow system. The wines produced are both generic and varietal types. The Devitt's wine is sold at the winery, at outlets in Northern and Southern California, and of course, at the Pope Valley General Store. Visitors are welcome to enjoy the wine tasting facilities, and picnic amidst the gracious natural splendor of the Pope Valley Winery.

POPE VALLEY WINERY
6613 Pope Valley Rd., Pope Valley
(707) 965-2192, 10am-5pm Daily
Tasting
Generic & Varietal Wines

CHATEAU MONTELENA

Rising impressively from the base of Mount St. Helena stands the striking Chateau Montelena, built in 1882. The surrounding 140 acres of land feed the winery its distinctive supply of wine grapes. The famous Chateau was built by Alfred A. Tubbs, who came to California in 1850 and subsequently became a State Senator. Demanding excellence in all aspects of his winemaking, Senator Tubbs brought to Chateau Montelena a French winemaker, Jerome Bardot, who became famous for producing several superb vintages.

The winery is now owned and operated by Chateau Montelena Associates, a California partnership-the standard of excellence still reigns today. Their goal is to produce four varietal wines which will be recognized for their merit: a Cabernet Sauvignon, a Chardonnay, a Johannisberg Riesling, and a Zinfindel. Tours and visits are by appointment only.

CHATEAU MONTELENA
ESTABLISHED 1882

Late Harvest NAPA & ALEXANDER VALLEYS
Johannisberg Riesling
1974

PRODUCED AND BOTTLED BY CHATEAU MONTELENA WINERY
CALISTOGA, NAPA VALLEY, CALIFORNIA • ALCOHOL 12.5% BY VOL.

CHATEAU MONTELENA WINERY
1429 Tubbs Lane, Calistoga
(707) 942-5105
Tours by appointment only, sales 10-4 daily
Varietal wines
BA, MC

A rare snow fall covers the vineyards of Napa Valley.

Frederick Beringer, co-founder of Bering Brothers Winery, was a close friend of President Cleveland. This picture shows Cleveland (second from left) and Beringe (third from left).

Wine Institute

V. Sattui Wine Cellar in 1911. (left to right) Mario Sattui and three cellar workers.

Sattui Collection

Colonel Haraszthy - Father of California Viticulture

by Mike Topolos

Colonel Agoston Haraszthy came to America in 1840, eventually arriving in Wisconsin on a horse, wearing a velour hat, silken shirt, lustrous beard, and possessing a commanding bearing that captivated the citizenry of what is now Sauk City.

His every endeavor met with success except for the propogation of the grapevine that had allowed his family to prosper for centuries in his homeland. This one defeat led him to San Diego in search of a more hospitable home for the vine. Here, he met with more personal success, but his attempt to grow grape vines was once again stymied by an unsuitable climate, which finally prompted him to transplant his 13,000 vine cuttings to Buena Vista in 1856.

In Sonoma, the Colonel found a climate even more suitable to the vine than his native land. 85,556 vines were planted in the next two years, three large cellars were dug into the mountain rock, and the grapes grown by Haraszthy were pressed in 1857.

A friendly rivalry, which endured for several years, existed between General Vallejo and Haraszthy. The results of the State Fair of 1860 found Vallejo with five firsts and Haraszthy with six. Two of Haraszthy's sons married the daughters of Vallejo on June 1, 1863, and the next year Colonel Haraszthy became the head of the Buena Vista Vinicultural Society, in possession of 5,100 acres of land, 362,000 grapevines, and 6 mountain side cellars, each 125 feet long.

Wine Institute

Colonel Haraszthy

The Colonel left Sonoma in 1869, to establish a sugar plantation in Nicaragua, the society having charged him with extravagance, and the newspaper Alta disclosing that the "Buena Vista Vinicultural Society has the largest winegrowing estate in the world, and alas, the most unprofitable; at least the most costly." His life ended that same summer — attempting to cross a stream near his plantation, a tree limb broke, and the alligators below left not a trace.

Colonel Agoston Haraszthy was officially recognized on June 15, 1946, when a plaque commemorating "The Father of California Viticulture" was dedicated during the Bear Flag Centennial at Sonoma. Idwal Jones, speaking of Haraszthy, says it well in one glib sentence; "This Hungarian, who somewhere on the rough journey dropped the title of count for the more democratic title of colonel, could breathe only the air of hazard and strife; he was a chevalier with a dash of Mephisto, yet behind him he has left much that solidly endures."

Hank and Linda Wetzel stand amidst the grape vines that will determine their future, at Alexander Valley Vineyards.

Joan Diane Goode watches the crush with John and Jim Pedroncelli of Pedroncelli Vineyards.

Matson

Gino R. Zepponi of ZD Winery in Sonoma.

Leo Trentadue takes a short break and samples his fine product.

Silverek

Gundlach - Bundschu of Sonoma, established over 118 years ago.

Frank and Antonia Bartholomew standing in the same field where the California wine industry began.

A Wine Tour of Historic Sonoma County

By Joan Diane Goode

Sonoma County is rich in beauty and history, and the wine industry has contributed greatly to both dimensions. A resident or visitor of the County who does not visit at least a few wineries is missing a truly precious experience.

There are a good number of wineries in Sonoma County — both large and small. Names like: Sebastiani, Italian Swiss Colony, Geyser Peak, and Souverain are familiar to most wine enthusiasts. These large wineries offer: a wide variety of tour schedules, ample tasting facilities, and a comfortable atmosphere. Smaller wineries on the other hand provide a more individualistic view of the wine industry. The visitor to a small winery may usually converse freely with the winemakers themselves, and enjoy

an unhurried and sometimes self-guided tour. Some family owned wineries are so small, however, that visitors must make appointments for tasting and tours in advance.

This article focuses on twenty-one wineries in Sonoma County, chosen either for the richness of their heritage or the enthusiasm of their youth. All but two are small wineries, and most are family owned ventures.

The tour begins in Southern Sonoma County where the California wine industry first began, then moves West, and concludes with the rapidly expanding Northern portion of the County.

The oldest winery in Sonoma County is Buena Vista (18000 Old Winery Road, Sonoma). It has been declared an official Historical Landmark by the State of California. The land was originally planted to the mission grape by General Vallejo in 1832. In 1840, Count Agoston Haraszthy came to America from Hungary and in the mid-fifties, he settled in the Valley of the Moon. Convinced that he could produce premium wines from European grapes grown on this land, he bottled his first wine in 1857 and the results surpassed his own hopes. Haraszthy became known as the father of the California wine industry.

Buena Vista remained in the Haraszthy family for many years. In 1943, it was sold to Frank Bartholomew, past president of United Press International and now Chairman Emeritus of the Board. In 1968, the winery was sold to its present owners, Youngs Market Company, a Los Angeles-based firm. The Count's grandson, Jan Haraszthy, still works at the winery.

Tours and tastings are offered daily in the beautiful ivy-covered stone winery. Guests are also welcome to picnic on the terrace and survey the land where wine production first began in northern California.

Hacienda Cellars (1000 Vineyard Lane, Sonoma) was established in 1972 by Frank Bartholomew, former owner of Buena Vista. This small winery, located next to Buena Vista, shares that winery's colorful background. Bartholomew retained the original vineyard where grapes were first planted by Haraszthy.

Frank Bartholomew is a man who takes pride in a job well done. That is why he decided to produce only a limited amount of wine so that its quality could be controlled through each phase of production. He finds winemaking the perfect compliment to the harried schedule he must sometimes keep, working on projects for UPI.

Although Hacienda was established recently, Bartholomew has had thirty-four years experience in winemaking in Sonoma County. The winemaker and general manager of Hacienda is Steve MacRostie who holds his Master's in food science, specializing in enology, from the University of California, Davis. Both Bartholomew and MacRostie are enjoying success with the winery — last year, Hacienda won two of the three gold medals awarded at the Sonoma County Harvest Fair.

The winery itself is a two-story Spanish style brick building with a tile roof and a balcony. There is a tasting area and tours are available by appointment. A popular feature at Hacienda is the picnic ground, overlooking a small lake and vineyards which stretch as far as the eye can see.

ZD Winery (Burn Dale Road, Sonoma) is owned and operated by Gino R. Zepponi and Norman C. de Leuze. Though winemaking began as a hobby for them, it's grown into a successful business. ZD was started in 1969 when both families worked to install winemaking equipment in an old farm house. Almost every member of both families is involved in maintaining the winery.

This winery concentrates on the production of four wines: Pinot Noir, Chardonnay, Zinfandel, and Gewurztraminer. The wines are 100 percent varietals. Almost all of the grapes used in their Pinot Noir are purchased from the Carneros region of Napa. Tours and tastings are available on Saturdays and Sundays by appointment only.

Gundlach-Bundschu (3775 Thornsberry Road, Sonoma) is an old winery, newly reopened. At its peak, this 118 year old winery produced 175,000 gallons a year. And, exactly 100 years ago, Gundlach-Bundschu was awarded a gold medal at a Centennial celebration in Philadelphia. In the quake of 1906, the winery was hit by disaster when its San Francisco warehouse was destroyed, along with all the wine it contained. It took the winery years to recover and then along came Prohibition so the operation was discontinued.

Jim Bundschu, great grandson of the winery's founder, and his brother-in-law, John Merrit, along with Barney Fernandez, decided to reopen the old winery and worked fervently for the July 1976 opening. They produce four wines: Zinfandel, Cabernet Sauvignon, Sonoma Riesling and Klienberger, a German wine so rare that Gundlach-Bundschu is the only winery in the United States producing it. All grapes are grown in their own vineyards. The winery is open to the public only on week ends.

Valley of the Moon Winery (777 Madrone Road, Glen Ellen) was founded in the 1880's by Eli Sheppard. Since then it has had several illustrious owners: Generals William Sherman, Fighting Joe Hooker, and Charles P. Stone, and Senator Randolph Hearst. Valley of the Moon's current owners are Enrico Parducci and his son Harry.

All of the grapes used in production of their wines are picked either from their own 200 acre vineyard or from surrounding vineyards. The wines produced include: Burgundy, Claret, Rose', Chablis, and estate bottled Semillon, French Colombard, and Zinfandel. You may meet one of the Parduccis in the tasting room, open every day of the week except Thursday.

Grand Cru Vineyards (1 Vintage Lane, Glen Ellen), was established in 1970. This young winery is a corporation under the direction of Al Ferrera, President and Bob Magnani, head winemaker. They keep their wine list small in order to better control production. Grand Cru Wines include Zinfandel, Cabernet Sauvignon, White Pinot Noir, Gewurztraminer, and a Pinot Noir Champagne, not to be released until the 1980's. Many of the grapes used here are bought in Alexander Valley. Their late harvest 1974 Zinfandel received a gold medal at the Los Angeles County Fair this year.

Tours and tasting are offered at the winery only on Saturdays and Sundays.

Kenwood Winery (9592 Sonoma Highway, Kenwood) has been in operation since 1970. It is owned by Martin Lee and his two sons, Mike and Marty, along with John Sheela and Neil Knott. It was formerly the old Pagani Winery, established in 1906.

Like many other small wineries, Kenwood chooses to concentrate on a small number of wines, conscious that the quality of the wine can go down if a winery attempts to produce too many. Kenwood produces Cabernet Sauvignon, Zinfandel, Pinot Noir, Petite Sirah, Burgundy, Johannisberg Riesling and Chenin Blanc. Their wines are growing in popularity as they gain recognition among the best wineries of Sonoma County. The year, Kenwood took two gold medals at the Sonoma County Harvest Festival.

Kenwood Winery, great people — great wine.

The tasting room inside the tiny wood frame winery is open from 9 to 5 daily. There are no formal tours but guests are free to examine the winemaking facilities.

Chateau St. Jean

Another new winery in Kenwood is Chateau St. Jean (8555 Sonoma Highway, Kenwood). It is owned by Robert and Edward Merizoian and Kenneth Sheffield with Dick Arrowood as winemaker. Their first release was a 1974 vintage Johannisberg Riesling. They plan to concentrate on fine white wines, some reds and a traditional French method champagne. Chateau St. Jean is also enjoying early success — they won seven awards for the seven wines they entered in the Sonoma County Harvest Festival this year, along with a gold medal at the Sonoma County Fair.

The tasting facilities and offices are located in a beautiful French-Mediterranean style mansion; the winery itself will be constructed in keeping with the French motif of the mansion and will conform to the natural beauty of the countryside. There is tasting, but no tours as yet pending completion of the winemaking facilities. Elegant catered dinners are available in the mansion for groups of no more than twenty-five.

Korbel Winery (River Road, Guerneville) was established in the 1880's by the three Korbel brothers: Francis, Joseph and Anton. The brothers moved to Sonoma County in 1862 to log the huge Redwoods along the Russian River. They discovered the location was perfectly suited to the growing of grapes demanding the coolest wine growing conditions. Korbel is a name well known in Sonoma County and beyond for both fine wines and French method champagne.

The winery itself is a beautiful old ivy-covered red brick building, overlooking the river. Tours and tastings are available from 10am to 4:30pm daily.

Russian River Vineyards (5700 Gravenstein Highway North, Forestville) was established in 1964. This winery is located in the beautiful countryside near the Russian River. Among the interesting features at the winery is the restaurant where guests may enjoy a fine meal while looking out over vineyards. The winery is currently undergoing a change in management — so appointments are a must.

Davis Bynum Winery (8075 Westside Road, Healdsburg) has one of the most talked about labels on the California wine market — a bare foot. However, it is a rare occasion when any wine is bottled under that label today. The Davis Bynum and River Bend labels are featured both at the winery and in selected retail shops throughout the country. Davis, a journalist turned winemaker, founded the winery in 1965 and is the winemaker. His son, Hampton, formerly co-winemaker has recently gone out on his own leaving Gary Farrell as asst. winemaker and cellarmaster.

The winery operates a retail room on the premises and will arrange guided tours by appointment. A Napa Valley vineyard has recently been sold so that total production now comes from local Sonoma County vineyards, primarily near the winery on Westside Road.

The Hop Kiln Winery is a charming and tiny new winery owned by Dr. L. Martin Griffin, Jr. (6050 Westside Road, Healdsburg). It is housed in a lovingly restored hop kiln, built in 1905 when the hop industry still flourished in Sonoma County. Most of the old kilns have been destroyed or left to deteriorate but this one is still a beauty, standing amidst acres of vineyards with Mount St. Helena in the background.

The Hop Kiln Winery offers both varietal and generic wines. Tours and tastings are available from 10am to 5pm, Saturday and Sundays and by appointment during the week. For large groups touring, there is a service charge of $2 per person. There are picnic facilities as well as two nature walks — one which leads down to the Russian River and one through the orchard. Catering services are also available by appointment.

Bynum Winery (left to right) Julie Johnson Hampton Bynum, Ron Pace and Gary Farrell.

Silverek

Hop Kiln Winery on Westside Road, Healdsburg

Silverek

RUSSIAN RIVER VINEYARDS

SONOMA COUNTY
GRAVENSTEIN
BLANC
DRY APPLE WINE

Selected and bottled by TOPOLOS at Russian River Vineyards
Forestville, California BW 4855 Alcohol 12% by volume

The dream of a fine winemaker is to have his own winery. In the natural environment the creativity of the winemaker is enhanced. Michael Topolos, author, lecturer, and teacher of winemaking, now has his own lable—"Topolos at" Russian River Vineyards. At the restaurant you can enjoy fine cuisine and taste the premium wines of Topolos

Mill Creek Vineyards and Winery (1401 Westside Road, Healdsburg) is a small family owned and operated winery, long the dream of Charles Kreck. For fifteen years, the family sold its grapes to surrounding wineries. Finally, they decided to crush their own grapes and make their own wines. Most of the operation is conducted by Bob and Bill Kreck, Charles' two sons and their families.

The winery will produce only 100 percent varietal wines. Their first crush was in 1974. Mill Creek will produce only four wines: Pinot Chardonnay, Pinot Noir, Cabernet Sauvignon and Merlot.

· Dry Creek Vineyards (3770 Lambert Bridge Road, Healdsburg) is another young winery which began in 1972 with three varietals — Chenin Blanc, Fume' Blanc and Chardonnay. David Stare is the owner of this winery and David was the President of Sonoma County Wine Growers Assn.

Dry Creek was among the wineries to win gold medals at the 1976, '77 and '78 Sonoma County Harvest Fair.

At Dry Creek, tasting facilities are located inside the winery. Visitors may get a first hand glimpse of the winemaking process and speak to the winemakers. There is also a picnic area next to the winery.

Foppiano Vineyards (12781 Old Redwood Highway, Healdsburg) is one of the oldest remaining wineries in Sonoma County. It began in 1864 when great-grandfather John Foppiano came to the Russian River Valley from Italy. The winery is presently run by Louis Joseph's two sons, Lou and Rod. Louis Joseph was born at the winery in the room which now serves as his office. The Foppianos take great pride in their wine. Their motto is: "At the Foppiano Winery we make wine the way we Used to."

Louis Joseph says that much of their success is due to the location of their winery. "Our white grapes are as good as any, and our red grapes are better. You notice it in the flavor when you taste the wine." They use grapes grown on their own land in the production of varietal wines. The only Dry Sauvignon Blanc to receive a medal at the Sonoma County Harvest Fair this year was the Foppianos! Lou Foppiano is 1976 vice-president of the Sonoma County Wine

Growers' Association. Lou says there are no plans for expansion at their winery because "When you get bigger, you lose control of quality."

There is tasting at the winery and tours are given by appointment. Something you won't want to miss is Lou's office, a restored Northwestern Pacific Railraod caboose.

Simi Winery (16275 Healdsburg Avenue, Healdsburg) is another old timer, established in 1876 by Guiseppe and Pietro Simi. They named the winery "Montepulciano" after their native village in Italy, but it became known as Simi. Simi was owned by the family until 1970 when it was bought by Russell Greene. Greene installed new equipment so that the winery could take advantage of new winemaking techniques but retain its old features. Simi was then sold to Scottish and New Castle, a British firm. Last year, the winery again changed hands. Currently it is owned by Schieffelin and Co., a New York based firm.

Although Simi is no longer a family operation, their winemaker, Mary Ann Graf, believes that the winery will continue to produce quality wines. "If the wine isn't up to par, the firm will not sell it," says Mary Ann.

Isabelle Simi Haigh, the only remaining Simi, still greets customers in the tasting room even though she is in her eighties. The tasting room, located in the old winery, is open to the public daily.

Johnson's Alexander Valley Wines (8333 Highway 128, Healdsburg) is owned by three brothers: Tom, Jay and Will Johnson. The family originally sold their grapes to surrounding wineries. In 1966, they began to replant their land to the varieties they wanted to make. In 1975, they released their first wine, a Pinot Noir. Johnson's will continue to concentrate on the production of four white wines and three reds. All of the grapes used in the wines will be their own.

The winery is open for tours and tastings from 10am to 5pm daily. You will have a chance to speak with the winemakers if you wish. This is the only winery with a 1924 pipe organ in the tasting room. Once each month, there is a special tasting, with a session of organ music as a treat for guests.

Alexander Valley Vineyards (8644 Highway 128, Healdsburg) is a young and enthusiastic winery, only in operation for a year. The winery is owned by Harry Wetzel and his family. His son Hank, a graduate of U.C., Davis, is the winemaker.

Alexander Valley Vineyards plans on producing only three wines: Chardonnay, Cabernet and Riesling. All are 100 percent varietals, except for the Cabernet which is 12 percent Merlow.

The land itself was formerly owned by Cyrus Alexander who once owned the entire Alexander Valley. Hank's parents live in Cyrus' old mansion.

The winery itself is an attractive modern structure, set amidst acres of vineyards. Because the winery is so small, tours and tastings are by appointment only.

Trentadue Winery (19170 Redwood Highway, Healdsburg) has been in operation since 1969 and is owned by the Trentadue family. Leo and his wife, along with their two daughters and son, all work long hours.

The vineyards at Trentadue Winery are organic. No sprays are used on their vines and the only chemical additive to their wine is sulphur. Other than their Burgundy, their wines are 100 percent varietals and all are estate bottled.

In the brick and wood winery, tastings are available from 10 am to 5 pm daily. There is also a gift shop. Personalized labels may also be ordered at the winery — they're perfect for special occasions.

Pedroncelli Vineyards (1220 Canyon Road, Geyserville) was

Lou Foppiano's office, a remodeled caboos

Silverek

Sonoma Vineyards—a daring piece of design.

Silverek

established by John Pedroncelli, Sr., in 1927. It is currently operated by Jim and John Pedroncelli, Jr. Jim was born at the winery. For the Pedroncellis, wine production is more than a business — it is their life. The two sons work hard to maintain the fine wine production which their father began.

Pedroncelli is noted for producing quality wines at a price much lower than competitors. Jim says the reason they are able to keep their prices down is that they put very little money into advertising and sales. Everything goes into wine production.

They produce fourteen wines in all, eight varietals and six generics. The tasting room is open daily but there are no tours.

Pastori Vineyards (23189 Geyserville Avenue, Geyserville) is another Sonoma County winery which is family owned and operated. It was established in 1914 by Constante Pastori. Constante's son, Frank, now continues in the footsteps of his father. He believes the quality of his wines to be superior to others produced in California because his vineyards lie in the "Chianti" region of Sonoma — named after a prime grape growing region in Italy. The "Chianti" area was one of the first to be successfully planted to grapes in California.

The Pastori's now offer tastings in their retail room. Visitors will be able to meet Mrs. Pastori and perhaps Frank — provided he's not too busy — they will at least be able to catch a glimpse of him riding about the vineyards on his tractor.

This Author sincerely hopes that this article has encouraged you to visit the wineries of Sonoma County. By visiting the wineries where wine is produced, you will be able to talk with the winemakers themselves and view the winemaking process first hand.

Traveling to a place where one can see only gently rolling hills of vineyards, hear only the sounds of wildlife, smell the warm earth during a summer's day, and taste wine that is a product of this environment, is an experience no one should miss during his or her lifetime.

The Old World skill of building hand crafted wooden tanks is vital to the aging of premium wines. Pieter Kloos of Spring Mountain Cooperage is an expert. The wooden tanks he builds are not only for wine cooperage, but also can be used as hot tubs and rural water storage tanks. He and his wife Linda own Spring Mountain Cooperage and have a show room in Saint Helena. In the show room is displayed a hot tub and wood fired hot water heater called an Aqua Heater., (see page 162). Such alternative heating devices cut down on the high cost of using gas & electricity to heat water, are very efficient on a demand basis and can be used anywhere there is a source of kindling wood. If you would like to tour their show room and pick up some good ideas for saving money and adding healthy alternatives to your lifestyle then stop by 1216 "C" Church Street in Saint Helena which is located in the heart of the Napa Valley Wine Country, or call (707) 963-7451. There are several excellent restaurants within walking distance.

BUENA VISTA WINERY

Buena Vista, once the largest vineyard in the world, has been declared an official Historical Landmark by the State of California. The land was first planted to the mission grape in 1832, by General Mariano Guadalupe Vallejo. In 1840 Count Agoston Haraszthy came to America to escape the Hapsburg Revolution in Hungary. He brought with him cuttings from his family's vineyards - convinced that in America there was a place to grow fine wine. After searching 12 years for wine land, he found the Valley of the Moon. He became good friends with General Vallejo and bought from him hundreds of acres of land on which to establish his vineyards and winery. In honor of Vallejo, Haraszthy named his vineyards *Buena Vista* - beautiful view. Two massive stone buildings were constructed with underground tunnels in which to store the wines at a constant cool temperature. In 1857 Count Haraszthy bottled his first wine and its quality surpassed his highest expectations. In 1861 he proposed to the California government that he travel to Europe and bring back cuttings from the finest vines. Although the trip was at his own expense, he offered cuttings to all the wine growers. Haraszthy was truly the father of California's wine industry.

Shortly after his death in 1869, several disastrous events struck the winery. The grapes of Sonoma County were contaminated with phylloxera, a disease which withers the vines and hardens the grapes. For twenty years, Haraszthy's two sons struggled to maintain the winery to no avail. Buena Vista was also hit hard by the 1906 earthquake. The underground tunnels containing hundreds of bottles of premium wine being aged collapsed, destroying the wine. The winery was finally shut down for 40 years.

In 1943 the winery and vineyards were bought by Mr. Frank Bartholomew, past president of United Press International, and in 1968 the winery was sold to Young's Market Co. of Los Angeles. Through slow, hard work the vineyards of Buena Vista were brought back to productivity, and Californians may once again enjoy fine wine from Buena Vista. Visitors are always welcome to come see the place where premium California wine production first began. Today the winery upholds the tradition of fine wine production set forth over one hundred years ago by Count Haraszthy.

BUENA VISTA WINERY
18000 Old Winery Rd., Sonoma
(707) 938-1266

Tastings and tours
Generic and varietal wines
BA, MC
10am-5pm daily

BUENA VISTA WINERY

Buena Vista, once the largest vineyard in the world, has been declared an official Historical Landmark by the State of California. The land was first planted to the mission grape in 1832, by General Mariano Guadalupe Vallejo. In 1840 Count Agoston Haraszthy came to America to escape the Hapsburg Revolution in Hungary. He brought with him cuttings from his family's vineyards - convinced that in America there was a place to grow fine wine. After searching 12 years for wine land, he found the Valley of the Moon. He became good friends with General Vallejo and bought from him hundreds of acres of land on which to establish his vineyards and winery. In honor of Vallejo, Haraszthy named his vineyards *Buena Vista* - beautiful view. Two massive stone buildings were constructed with underground tunnels in which to store the wines at a constant cool temperature. In 1857 Count Haraszthy bottled his first wine and its quality surpassed his highest expectations. In 1861 he proposed to the California government that he travel to Europe and bring back cuttings from the finest vines. Although the trip was at his own expense, he offered cuttings to all the wine growers. Haraszthy was truly the father of California's wine industry.

Shortly after his death in 1869, several disastrous events struck the winery. The grapes of Sonoma County were contaminated with phylloxera, a disease which withers the vines and hardens the grapes. For twenty years, Haraszthy's two sons struggled to maintain the winery to no avail. Buena Vista was also hit hard by the 1906 earthquake. The underground tunnels containing hundreds of bottles of premium wine being aged collapsed, destroying the wine. The winery was finally shut down for 40 years.

In 1943 the winery and vineyards were bought by Mr. Frank Bartholomew, past president of United Press International, and in 1968 the winery was sold to Young's Market Co. of Los Angeles. Through slow, hard work the vineyards of Buena Vista were brought back to productivity, and Californians may once again enjoy fine wine from Buena Vista. Visitors are always welcome to come see the place where premium California wine production first began. Today the winery upholds the tradition of fine wine production set forth over one hundred years ago by Count Haraszthy.

BUENA VISTA WINERY
18000 Old Winery Rd., Sonoma
(707) 938-1266

Tastings and tours
Generic and varietal wines
BA, MC
10am-5pm daily

SEBASTIANI

Winemaking is a family tradition at Sebastiani Vineyards. They have been involved in producing fine wines for over three-quarters of a century. Samuele, the founder, who learned the art of winemaking from his father, immigrated to the United States from Italy when he was only eighteen. With ambition and knowledge he pursued a dream which was realized in the founding of the Sebastiani Vineyards. In 1903, Samuele bought land originally owned by General Mariano Vallejo. It included the land first planted to grapes in 1825 by the Mission fathers. Samuele trained his son, August, in wine production. Today August is the winemaker of Sebastiani. August's sons, Sam and Don, plan to continue the family heritage. Even Sam, Jr. (August's grandson) is being taught the rudiments of the wine industry.

The Redwood Rancher chose August Sebastiani as vintner of the year in 1973. The award represents a winery which has proven itself to be a producer of superior wines, economically sound, and one which holds a respected position among peers in the community. August Sebastiani easily fulfills these qualifications.

Only 30% of the grapes used in Sebastiani wines are grown on their own vineyards, 70% are bought from other vintners. The grapes are tested for proper sugar/acid content and only the finest are used. Sebastiani Vineyards has a large aging cellar, and the family is able to hold their red wines until they have achieved proper maturation. Sebastiani Vineyards, with the most fully aged wines in America today, is now in world competiton.

Guided tours are offered from 10:00am to 5:00pm at the Sebastiani Cellars. After the tour guests are taken to tasting rooms where they may sample a variety of fine wines. When you see the extra care that goes into producing their wine and taste the finished result, you'll know why the name Sebastiani Vineyards on the label is the sign of quality wine.

SEBASTIANI VINEYARDS
389 - 4th St. East, Sonoma
(707) 938-5532 10am-5pm daily
tours and tasting
generic, varietal, and sparkling wines
BA, MC

HACIENDA WINE CELLARS

The Hacienda Wine Cellars, est. 1972, is a small, new winery, yet it carries a colorful and romantic past. The development of this winery emerged after owner Frank Bartholomew, past president of UPI, sold his impressive Buena Vista Winery, the Haraszthy property which he and his wife owned since 1943. He still retained, however, the rich Buena Vista vineyard.

The history of Buena Vista vineyard began in 1861 when its original owner the Hungarian Colonel Haraszthy brought back from Europe 300,000 cuttings and distributed them not only to his own Buena Vista vineyard, but to vineyards throughout California. This marked the first time European cuttings were used in California.

Additional viticultural experience was acquired when A Crawford Cooley joined Hacienda Wine Cellars in 1977 as an investor and its President. His family has owned vineyards in Sonoma County since 1860. Vintner Bartholomew once described Hacienda Wine Cellars as "an experiment in quality and nothing else ... a wine can be technically perfect and still not give pleasure, so we add the pleasure quotient."

To produce wines with that quotient is the responsibility of Winemaker Steven MacRostie, whose imaginative philosophy has earned the winery 15 silver and gold medals over the past few years. Eight varietals are grown in the 50 acres of grapes with seven wines currently marketed under the Hacienda Wine Cellars label.

Wine by the case at a 10% discount may be ordered at the Tasting Room, and delivery can be arranged anywhere in California. The Hacienda Wine Garden can accomodate about 60 persons under its spreading oaks. This popular hillside retreat is a very scenic spot for enjoying a bottle of fine Hacienda wine. Ducks and geese come up from the pond adjacent the 100 year old vineyards for a tidbit from visitors. Wine glasses may be borrowed from the Tasting Room and picnic tables may be reserved for large groups.

HACIENDA WINE CELLARS
1000 Vineyard Lane, Sonoma
(707) 938-3220, 10am-5pm daily

tasting, tours by appt., retail sales, wine garden
varietal wines
BA, MC

VALLEY OF THE MOON

Valley Of The Moon winery, founded in the 1880's by Eliot Sheppard, was once part of a ranch occupied by three famous Generals and a Senator: William Sherman, Fighting Joe Hooker, and Charles P. Stone, and George Hearst; it was purchased by Enrico Parducci in 1945.

Enrico and his son Harry now operate this winery. Harry, who functions as winemaker, manages to turn out some 200,000 gallons of wine annually. All of the grapes which go into making the wine are either picked from the Parducci's 200 acre vineyard or purchased from surrounding vineyards. The emphasis is upon quality bulk wine, but fifth bottles are also available. The tasty and reasonably priced estate bottled wines are: Zinfandel, Semillon, and French Colombard. Burgundy, Claret, and Rose are also available at Valley of the Moon.

VALLEY OF THE MOON WINERY
777 Madrone Rd., Glen Ellen
(707) 996-6941, 9am-5pm daily except Thurs.
Tasting
Generic & Varietal Wines
BA

KENWOOD VINEYARDS

Kenwood Winery is located in the historic Sonoma Valley. This region is recognized as one of the worlds finest for growing varietal grapes.

We invite you to experience Kenwood wines and to visit us at the winery. Tasting hours are from 9am to 5pm daily, for information call (707) 833-5891, or write P.O. Box 447, Kenwood, CA 95452.

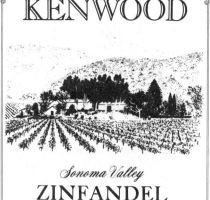

KENWOOD

Sonoma Valley
ZINFANDEL
1972

PRODUCED & BOTTLED BY KENWOOD VINEYARDS
KENWOOD, CALIFORNIA

ALCOHOL 12% BY VOLUME

KENWOOD VINEYARDS
9592 Sonoma Hwy., Kenwood
(707) 833-5891, 9am-5pm daily
tasting, informal tours
generic and varietal wines

Sonoma County Wineries

LANDMARK VINEYARDS

A long row of cypress clearly marks the entrance leading to the Spanish Hacienda at Landmark Vineyards. The destiny of the winery is being thoughtfully guided by Bill and Michelle Mabry. With a pleasant smile Michelle handles the marketing of the premium wines, while Bill enthusiastically perfects vintages in his centrally located new second story laboratory which overlooks vineyards of Johannisbery Reisling and Gewurztraminer, as well as the beautiful century old estate.

Currently marketed under the Landmark label is Cabernet Sauvignon, Pinot Noir, Chardonnay, Gewurztraminer, Chenin Blanc and Johannisburg Riesling. You can begin your tour of the winery or purchase premium Landmark wines at the Hacienda and then picnic in the pleasant surroundings of the cypress grove and adjoining reflecting ponds and waterway. The Mabry's youthful enthusiasm, premium wines, pastoral setting, and "Molly my Collie", Bill and Michelle's beautiful pet collie Molly, makes this century old estate a delightful place to visit.

LANDMARK VINEYARDS
9150 Los Amigos Rd, Windsor
Tours & Retail sales Wed-Fri 1pm-5pm
and Sat & Sun 10am-5pm or by appt,
Varietal wines
MC, Visa
(707) 838-9466

Wed-Fri 1 to 5pm
S-Sun 10am-5pm or by appt.

KORBEL CHAMPAGNE CELLARS

Picture in your mind a beautiful, ivy covered, 110 year old building; surrounded by redwood trees and a river; producing outstanding premium wines, champagnes, and brandy. This is F. Korbel and Bros. Winery in Guerneville, California.

Some new estate-bottled and vintage wines available from Korbel, this year, a Johannisberg Riesling, Pinot Chardonnay, Gewurztraminer, Zinfandel, and Gamey Rose.

As new vineyards develop over the next two years, the superior Cabernet Sauvignons and Pinot Noirs from Korbel will be estate-bottled and vintaged along with generic wines such as Burgundy, Chablis, and Vin Rose.

Korbel Winery is open to the public daily for tours and tastings. Tours are conducted from 10:30am to 3:00pm (every 45 minutes), and the tasting and sales room is open from 10:30am to 4:30pm.

KORBEL CHAMPAGNE CELLARS
13250 River R, Guerneville
(707) 887-2294, 10am-4:30pm daily
tastings and tours
generic and varietal wines

DAVIS BYNUM

When in 1973 Davis Bynum Winery moved from Albany, California, where it was founded in 1965, to its present location at 8075 Westside Road, Healdsburg, production and storage capacity was increased from 16,000 to 80,000 gallons. Coincidentally, its marketing emphasis was changed to increase the production of varietal wines and reduce the volume of generics which had long been marketed under its unique "Barefoot" label. Located about eight miles down the Russian River from Healdsburg, the winery lies in a Region I growing district, which is ideal for the growing of Pinot Noir and Chardonnay — two wines which it will feature. Its labels include Davis Bynum, River Bend, and Barefoot Bynum.

DAVIS BYNUM
8075 Westside Rd., Healdsburg
(707) 433-5852 9am-5pm M-F,
10am-4pm Sat & Sun. Retail sales
Varietal wines. MC & Visa

HOP KILN WINERY

The Hop Kiln Winery is one of the most charming wineries you can visit in Sonoma County. This relatively new winery, owned by Dr. L. Martin Griffin, Jr. is housed in a 1905 stone and redwood hop kiln overlooking the Russian River, It was recently declared both a county and state landmark. There is a picnic area and trails for nature walks.

The Griffin's premium wines, produced from their surrounding vineyards, are of excellent quality. Current releases include four Rieslings, among them a Weihnachten (German for Christmas), which is a late harvest Riesling, French Colombard, Gewurztraminer, Petite Sirah, Gamay Beaujolais, Zinfandel, and two blends.

The winery is open daily (week days/12am-5pm, week ends/10am-5pm) for tours and tasting. By prior arrangement, large groups can be accomodated for tours, tastings, picnics, and nature walks. There is a $2.oo per person service charge for special arrangements. The motion picture "Magic of Lassie" staring Jimmy Stewart was filmed here. Jimmy became a real fan of Hop Kiln's "77" French Colombard. A visit to the Hop Kiln Winery is truly a delightful experience.

HOP KILN WINERY
6050 Westside Road, Healdsburg
(707) 433-6491. Open for tastings,

tours, picnics, & nature walks from
12am-5pm weekdays, 10am-5pm
weekends. Generic & varietal wines.

DRY CREEK VINEYARDS

Resting proudly in the midst of the Dry Creek Valley stands David Stare's Dry Creek Vineyard, recognized for its high standards for producing fine premium wines for your table. Beginning with the production in 1972 of three varietal wines, Chenin Blanc, Fume Blanc and Chardonnay, the winery has gone onto win more gold medals during 1977 and 1978 than any other Sonoma County winery. Special attention is paid to every detail of the winemaking process at Dry Creek in order to maintain this standard of excellence. To retain the rich fruity character of the grape noted in wines such as Chenin Blanc, a slow, cold fermentqation process is emphasized. The big "Burgundy style" of the Chardonnay is produced by partial fermentation in French Limousin oak barrels. Every aspect of the process is designed to deliver to you all the joy and full flavor of the wine which is the signature of Dry Creek Winery. Visitors are welcome to visit the recently added tasting room.

DRY CREEK VINEYARD   tasting, tours, picnic
3770 Lambert Bridge Rd, Healdsburg   varietal wines
(707) 433-1000 10:30-4:30 pm Daily   BA,MC

JOHNSON'S ALEXANDER VALLEY WINES

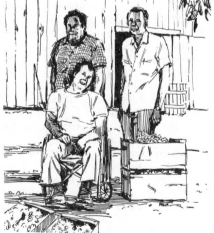

Johnson's Alexander Valley wines is a young winery owned by three brothers: Tom, Jay, and Will. The family previously sold their grapes to surrounding wineries. But in 1966, they decided to make their own wine, and replanted their land to the grape varieties they wanted to make. They released their first wine, a Pinot Noir, in 1975.

Johnson's will concentrate on the production of four white wines and three reds. All of the grapes used in their wines will be their own.

The atmosphere at the winery is friendly and relaxing. You'll have a chance to speak with the winemakers themselves. While visiting with the Johnson's and sampling their wine — you won't want to miss a look at the 1924 theatre pipe organ in the tasting room! *JOHNSON'S ALEXANDER VALLEY WINES*
8333 Hwy. 128, Healdsburg   *(707) 433-2319, 10-5pm*
Tours, Tasting, Retail Sales, Picnics

FOPPIANO VINEYARDS

A new Redwood tasting room awaits visitors to Foppiano Vineyards. Completed in fall of 1979 the rustic interior with its wood burning stove graciously accomodates wine tasters during summer and winter months who wish to savor and purchase premium Foppiano wines at the winery.

The vibrant presence of the Russian River provides the ideal climactic conditions for producing the famous Foppiano wines. For four generations the Foppiano family has been making quality wine for your table from the Russian River grapes so perfectly warmed by the sun. The passage of this river through the Foppiano vineyards allows the ocean fogs to enter the area and serve as a natural cooling system. The result is that the vineyards are able to cool off at night from the intense eighty-five to ninety degree heat of the Valley's growing season.

The Foppiano winery and vineyard covers two hundred acres of superior grape plantings which include the varietals of Cabernet Sauvignon, Pinot Noir, Petite Sirah, Pinot Chardonnay, Sauvignon Blanc, Gamay Beaujolais, and Zinfandel. All of the Foppiano wines are aged in wood, with the emphasis on flavor beginning in the vineyard, not in the laboratory. The grapes are blended in the vineyard, not in the winery, a tradition in Foppiano winemaking which dates back to 1864 when great-grandfather John Foppiano came to the Russian River Valley from Italy.

The Foppianos firmly believe that it is the winemaker's own experience and knowledge of his grapes which produce the unique taste of the wine. Louis Joseph Foppiano, and his sons Lou and Rod prefer to limit the amount yearly of each varietal in order to assure a high degree of quality in the wine. The philosophy of the Foppiano family is to produce a limited amount of superb wine, rather than lose quality by competing with the larger wineries for quantity.

Louis Joseph and his sons warmly invite you to visit them at the Foppiano Winery and see for yourself the difference the Foppiano tradition of winemaking produces in the distinctive taste and quality of their wines.

FOPPIANO WINERY CO.
12781 Old Redwood Hwy., Healdsburg
(707) 433-1937, 9:30am-4:30pm daily
tours by apt., tasting, retail sales
generic and varietal wines

TRENTADUE

"Par Excellence" is the only term applicable to describe the quality of the wines produced at the Trentadue winery. Trentadue, meaning "thirty-two" in its native Italian, is a small, yet influential winery founded in 1969. The Trentadue family own and operate the winery as well as the vineyards, and are responsible for the precise attention paid to the production of quality wines. The goal of the Trentadue family is to produce wines which reflect the mellow warmth and flavor of the beautiful Sonoma County in which they are grown. Located 65 miles North of San Francisco, the Trentadue winery and vineyards are presented in the midst of rich farmland and vineyards, framed by an idyllic setting of rolling hills and clear sea-blue skies. This is the setting in which the superb Trentadue wines are produced.

Leo Trentadue, the leader of the Trentadue family, is reknown throughout Sonoma County as one of the first innovative growers in the area to plant Vitis-Vinifera Varietals in any significant amount. Aged in 50 gallon American and French oak barrels, the Trentadue red and white wines are thus allowed to reach their full distinct flavor. The remaining bulk of wines produced at Trentadue, other than the Burgundy, are a full hundred percent Varietals, all well Vintaged and carefully Estate bottled. Keeping in the tradition of producing wines retaining the fullest natural flavor, the wines of Trentadue have relatively little or no filtering, and remarkably few chemicals.

Come to Trentadue, browse among the treasures of the gift shop - imported crystal, wine glasses, Black Hills gold, Capo dimonte vases (from Italy), books, maps and you can order personalized labels. Sip and savor the wide variety of superb wines before making your purchase. Trentadue wine, in an environment of rolling hills and carefully cared for vineyards is an experience you will not soon forget.

TRENTADUE WINERY
19170 Redwood Hwy., Geyserville
(707) 433-3104, 10am-5pm daily
tasting , no tours
varietal wines
MC BA

GEYSER PEAK WINERY

Auguştus Quitzow, one of Sonoma's pioneer winemakers, was first drawn to the Geyserville area by the warm mineral baths and spectacular geysers. As he observed the evening fog spilling in from the ocean, rolling down into the valley with its natural cooling effect, and saw the temperatures climb in the long days of July and August, he pictured the hillsides filled with vineyards and knew he had found the spot he had been seeking. On that spot, he established the Geyser Peak Winery.

Today, nearly a hundred years later, the winery still flourishes. In fact, in the past few years two magnificent fieldstone and redwood buildings have joined the old 1880's structures of Geyser Peak Winery. Now, inside those imposing buildings, winemaster Al Huntsinger watches like a patient father over the sleeping wines. In September, 1974, the first wines under Geyser Peak's Voltaire and Summit labels entered the market.

In the tasting room, with light pouring rainbows through the stained glass windows, visitors may taste the results of patient aging. Now, Vintage dated wines under the Geyser Peak label are joining the product line, and winning medals in prestigious judgings.

Geyser Peak Winery's President, George Vare and Vice-President, Dante Bagnani, are proud that the winery still carries on its century old tradition of fine winemaking. From its own vineyards the grapes climb the hill to be pressed into splendid table wines, and somewhere, surely, the ghost of Augustus Quitzow is smiling with satisfaction.

GEYSER PEAK WINERY
1 Mile North of Geyserville
Canyon Rd. exit from Hwy. 101
PO Box 25, (707) 433-6585
10am-5pm daily
Tasting, tours, retail sales, gift shop
Generic and varietal wines

ALEXANDER VALLEY VINEYARDS

Alexander Valley Vineyards is one of the most enthusiastic young wineries in Sonoma County. This family operation, established just last year, is owned by Harry Wetzel, Jr., and Hank Wetzel, winemaker, with Dale Good as vineyard manager. Hank is concentrating on the production of four premium wines: a Chardonnay, Cabernet, Riesling and Gewurztraminer.

A visit to Alexander Valley Vineyards is well worth the trip - you will see the winemaking process first hand, talk with the winemakers themselves, and view the attractive-modern winery which rests atop a small knoll in beautiful Alexander Valley.

ALEXANDER VALLEY VINEHARDS
8644 Hwy 128, Healdsburg
(707) 433-6293, 8-5pm daily
tours, tasting, retail sales

PASTORI VINEYARDS

Constante Pastori emigrated from Italy and began producing wine in Sonoma County in 1914. Since then the Pastori's business has been closed twice, once during prohibition and again during World War II. A winery bearing the Pastori name was opened for the first time in thirty years in March of 1975. Constante's son Frank now owns and operates a fifty acre vineyard and winery. The Pastori's wine is exceptionally fine because it is completely processed from vine to bottle by the family. Once again Californians may enjoy fine Pastori wine by stopping at the conveniently located sales room on Geyserville Avenue in Geyserville.

PASTORI WINERY
23189 Geyserville Avenue, Geyserville
(707) 857-3418, 9am-5pm daily
tasting, no tours, retail sales
generic and varietal wines

SOUVERAIN CELLARS

The Souverain winery, built in 1973, was designed by the well-known St. Helena architect, John Marsh Davis. Its two distinctive towers are reminiscent of the old hop-drying kilns which still dot the Sonoma County countryside.

Souverain winery produces a full range of varietal wines, as well as a generic chablis and burgundy. All Souverain wines are made from premium grapes grown in Napa, Sonoma and Mendocino Counties. Tours and tastings are given seven days a week except on Easter, Thanksgiving, Christmas, and New Year's Day.

The charming Souverain restaurant with its beautiful view overlooking the Alexander Valley and Mt. St. Helena, serves light lunches. The menu features egg dishes, a variety of salads, and one or two heavier dishes. Elegant dinners are also served at the winery. Prices range from $6.75 for filet of sole to $9.85 for tournedos Bearnaise. Hours vary by season and reservations are recommended.

From time to time the winery sponsors art exhibits, concerts, country fairs, and other special events. In the summer there are performances in the winery courtyard by actors from the American Conservatory Theater in San Francisco. These events are usually combined with a special dinner at the Souverain restaurant, making an "Evening at the Winery" a truly memorable experience.

SOUVERAIN CELLARS
Hwy. 101, 5 Mi. N. of Healdsburg
Independence Lane exit
(707) 433-6918 Winery
(707) 857-3789 Restaurant

Restaurant - tasting - tours
Varietal and generic wines
BA, MC
10am-5pm daily

Tom Byrne '75

J. PEDRONCELLI VINEYARDS

Some old time wine growers believe that it is the struggle to survive which has produced the strikingly distinctive flavor of the grapes which produce the famous J. Pedroncelli wines. Climbing along the hillsides of Canyon Road, the Pedroncelli grape vines battle the rugged slopes of the hills to produce a small but potent crop of grapes rich in nutrients, flavors, and potential esters which are the significant trademark of the Pedroncelli wines. The distinctive flavor of their wines comes from these mountain grown grapes, and the table wines bearing the Pedroncelli label all carry this hardy flavor and legacy of merit.

Grape vines are rarely planted on hillsides anymore because the crop yield, though far richer in quality, is less in quantity, than that of the flatlands. Yet John Pedroncelli Sr. was determined in 1927, to found his winery on a site reminiscent of his native Lombardy, and proceeded to develop quality table wines which proudly bear the fact that it was well worth the effort.

Jim and John Pedroncelli Jr. run the winery today, and they carry on the family tradition of respect for the hardy grape which has so steadfastly proven that quality far exceeds quantity when it comes to producing fine wine. The Pedroncelli, Pinot Noir, is considered a classic example of a high quality California Red Burgundy; its rotund flavor proves the worth of the hill-grown grape. The Pedroncelli Sonoma Red wine is distinctively a Northern Sonoma wine, rich with depth.

Come to the Pedroncelli tasting room and let John Soule, the colorful Wine-tasting Room host, offer to you samplings of the hardy hill-grown Pedroncelli wine. It is a wine-tasting experience you won't easily forget.

J. PEDRONCELLI WINERY
1220 Canyon Rd., Geyserville
(707) 857-3619, 9am-5pm daily
tasting, no tours
varietal wines
BA

The old Hopland schoolhouse has been rennovated into a new tasting room fo
Fetzer Vineyards. Besides tasting premium Fetzer wines, you can shop for uniqu
wine related gifts, books, local art, antiques, and there is a deli for picnickers.

The Wineries of Mendocino County

VINEYARDS AND WINERIES
OF MENDOCINO COUNTY
by Greg Graziano

Mendocino County grape growing
and winemaking dates back as early
as the 1840's. For lack of quality
grape varieties and wineries, Mendocino
County has been know as a bulk wine
producer. Though she has had to take
a back seat to her two sister counties,
Sonoma and Napa, non the less the
character and history of her early
years was just as colorful. It wasn't
until the wine boom of the 60's &
70's that vineyardists and winemakers
tapped the soil and grapes to produce
premium wines that could compete
with the international wine market.

Even with all the new plantings
and new wineries that have occurred
in the last two decades, there still
exists many acres of traditional
wine varieties which are sent to the
counties of Sonoma and Napa as

well as farther south for bulk wine production. Today approximately 60%
of the total grape production is sold
outside Mendocino County. There
are close to 10,000 acres of grapes
planted to fine grape varieties such as
Cabernet Sauvignon, Zinfandel, Petite
Sirah, Gamay Beaujolais, Pinot Noir,
Chenin Blanc, Chardonnay, Colombard,
Sauvignon Blanc, and to a large degree
Carignane. These five varieties, the
many diverse soil types and micro-
climates, plus the ability of skilled
winemakers make Mendocino Wines
among the finest in the world.

The regions of Mendocino County
are defined by the valleys in which
they occur. The largest valley in
Mendocino County is the Ukiah Valley
in which the wineries of Parducci,
Cresta Blanca, Parsons Creek and
Tyland Vineyards are located. To
the north ever-growing Fetzer Vineyards and Wiebel are located in the
Redwood Valley. Here early grape

growing and winemakeng roots run deep. To the east lies Potter Valley; one of the newer grape growing regions in Mendocino County. In the past this area has been noted for it's orchards nnd pastures. The southern section of Mendocino County is fast becoming a very important grape and wine region. Here in the Sanel Valley (Hopland) Milano Winery and the new Fetzer tasting room are located. The town of Hopland got its name from the extensive plantings of hops grown here in the early part of the century. Still today many picturesque Hop Kilns dot the landscape. To the east of Hopland, the plateau-like McDowell Valley has it's only winerv - the newly founded McDowell Valley Cellars.

The coolest and newest of Mendocino Counties grape growing and winemaking regions is the beautifully wooded Anderson Valley. Located near the coast, this area is fed by cool sea breezes and morning fog which makes it ideal to grow varieties like Pinot Noir, Chardonnay and Gewurztraminer. Once known as a famous apple growing area, apple trees now share the landscape with the grape vine. Here the small family operated vineyards and wineries of Navarro, Husch, and Edmeades prosper.

We in Mendocino County are at last experiencing a fine wine revolution. All who produce or drink these wines will agree, we live in one of the finest wine regions of the world and our premium wines share shelf-space with the finest wines produced in the world.

PARDUCCI WINE CELLARS

Parducci Wine Cellars just north of Ukiah is the oldest winery in Mendocino County. It was founded by Adolph Parducci at the close of prohibition in 1931. In 1961 two of Adolphs sons, John and George Parducci took over control of the winery. It was then that the philosophy of Parducci Wine Cellars changed from bulk wine production to varietal table wine.

In 1974 the Parducci's got a third partner and production of their winery was expanded. Parducci of their winery was expanded. Parducci produces about 200,000 cases annually from large holdings of their own vineyards and also from local farmers in Mendocino County.

The major wine types are Cabernet Sauvignon, Petite Sirah, Zinfandel, Gamay Beaujolais, Pinot Noir, Burgundy, Chardonnay, Chenin Blanc, Sauvignon Blanc, Riesling, Colombard and Chablis.

The winemakers at Parducci are John Parducci and Joe Montesori. Their philosophy on winemaking is that the white wines are fermented cold with no wood aging and the red wines are naturally made with Redwood Tank aging and little or no oak aging.

John Parducci has always maintained that Mendocino County is a great wine growing region and that to make great wines you must grow the right grapes in the proper region.

John Parducci with vineyard worker and right hand man Willy Ramerez in the vineyards adjacent Parducci Winery.

CRESTA BLANCA

The first Cresta Blanca Winery was founded in 1872 by Charles A. Wetmore, a San Francisco journalist. In 1971 the name was bought by Guild Wineries and Distilleries of Lodi and the old Mendocino Grape Growers Co-op Winery in Ukiah was purchased to house the finest of Guild's many wineries. In 1980 a new aging cellar and bottling plant was completed to improve the quality of their fine wines.

The grapes Cresta Blanca uses come from many local traditional grape growers and from new Southern California viticultural areas. The winemaker and manager is Gerald Furman, a graduate of Fresno State and winemaker from one of Guild's many wineries.

Many of the wines are of Mendocino appelation and the following wines are produced: Chardonnay, Chenin Blanc, Riesling, Colombard, Gewurztraminer, Muscato di Canelli, Chablis, Cabernet Sauvignon, Petite Sirah, Gamay Beaujolais, Zinfandel, Pinot Noir, Burgundy, Sparkling Wines, Brandy and fortified wines. Capacity in the near future will be 2.5 million gallons.

FETZER VINEYARDS

Tucked away in a mountain canyon in Redwood Valley, the wood and fieldstone winery of Fetzer Vineyards is an ideal place to produce fine table wine.

In 1955 Bernard Fetzer and his large family settled and since have planted vines of Cabernet Sauvignon, Zinfandel, Gamay Beaujolais, and Sauvignon Blanc. The winery was established in 1968 when they produced 6,000 cases of table wine.

Today because of the wide appeal for fine Fetzer Red wines (Cabernet Sauvignon, Zinfandel, & Petite Sirah), they are producing close to 200,000 cases per year with more growth in the future. In the latter past of the 1970's a new winery was built to produce fine white wines.

Fetzer Vineyards is a true example of a family operation for 8 of the 11 in the family work there. John Fetzer is the manager and Fresno graduate Paul Dolan is the winemaker. Fetzer winemaking philosophy includes fresh and fruity low alcohol wines such as Riesling, Muscat, Gewurztraminer and banel fermented Chardonnays and Sauvignon Blanc. Red wines shall be as always, heavy and rich, being of high quality at reasonable prices.

Recently the Fetzers bought the old school and gymnasium in the village of Hopland between Cloverdale and Ukiah. They have beautifully restored the building for their tasting room, deli gift shop, antique shop, and a potential restaurant. All visitors are asked to visit the tasting room first, before a appointment can be made to visit the winery.

WEIBEL WINERY

Redwood Valley is the newest location for the latest expansion of Weibel Champagne Cellar of Mission San Jose. It is here that Weibel still wines are produced with the possibility of moving their entire operation in the future due to development in the San Jose area. Weibel owns hundreds of acres here, but still buys many grapes from local farmers.

Fred Weibel Jr., grandson of founder Adolph and son of owner Fred Weibel is the winemaker. There is a long list of wines available such as their famous Green Hungarian, Chenin Blanc, Gamay Beaujolias, Zinfandel, Pinot Noir, Cabernet Sauvignon, and Petite Sirah. Their beautiful tasting room, shaped like an inverted champagne glass also sells a large variety of sparkling wines. A nice picnic area is also available for visitors.

EDMEADES VINEYARDS

Located near the small town of Philo in the Anderson Valley, Edmeade

MILANO WINERY

The most youthful example of Mendocino County's wine reniassance can be found at Milano Winery, which is located one mile south of the tiny community of Hopland. The owners, Greg Graziano and Lori and Jim Milone, carefully tend vineyards of Cabarnet, Gamay Beaujolais, and Chenin Blanc around an ancient Hop Kiln they have restored into a rustic winery, offices, and tasting room. Printed on the Milano label are the words, "We blend tradition, technology, and Mendocino County grapes to produce wines that are true extensions of the grape".

Their spirited dealings with mother nature and wine technology have produced vintages that are surprizingly full bodied and distinctively unique in taste. Releases of Cabernet, Gamay Beaujolais, Zinfandel, Petite Sirah, Sauvignon Blanc, Chenin Blanc and Chardonnay are available at finer restaurants and wine shops in Northern California. Do plan a visit to this winery, but be sure to call in advance. A taste of properly served Milano wines will put a twinkle in your eye and a smile on your face.

MILANO WINERY
14594 South Hwy 101, Hopland
(707) 744-1396
Open 10am - 5pm Sat - Wed

Thurs & Fri by appointment only
Retail sales and tasting
generic and varietal wines

In the village of Hopland, half way between Cloverdale and Ukiah, you will find the new Fetzer Vineyards tasting room lodged in Hopland's old schoolhouse. Here is a warm, friendly atmosphere within which to buy, taste, and talk wine. There is also a unique selection of gifts and local art, an antique shop, and a deli for picnickers.

FETZER VINEYARDS

Fetzer Vineyards is the northermost of the famous Mendocino County wineries . . . .tucked into the remote slopes of the Coast Range mountains north of Ukiah. If you wish to visit the winery you may make arrangements at the Tasting Room. The Fetzer family founded their vineyards and wine operations about 20 years ago and today their Zinfandels, Cabernet Sauvignons and Petite Sirahs are found wherever premium wines are sold.

FETZER TASTING ROOM
Hwy 101 in Hopland
(707) 744-1737

FETZER WINERY
1150 Bel Arbres Rd.
Redwood Valley
(707) 485-8998

EDMEADES VINEYARDS
5500 California State Hwy 128
P.O. Box 177, Philo, Ca. 95466
Open daily 10am - 6pm Summer
11am - 5pm Winters. Tours, tas
ings & retail sales. generic & vari
wines, MC, Visa (707) 895-3232

EDMEADES VINEYARDS

Rows and rows of grapevines obediently march up the Navarro River Bluff toward the winery. Their grapes, as if by magic are transformed into Rain Wine, Ice Wine, and Whale Wine. Could this be the work of a socceror's apprentise who casts spells over these Mendocino Vineyards? Anything is possible in this region of Northern California.

The fine Edmeades wines are produced through the inspiration of Deron Edmeades and winemaker Jed Steele who have taken the sacred oath to "make only the best wines the grapes will allow." In 1977 nature set the stage for a unique experiment in the Edmeades Vineyards which resulted in the creation of the first "Eiswein" (Ice Wine) ever produced in America.

Vintages of Edmeade's Chardonnay, Gewurztraminer, Cabernet, Zinfandel, Apple Wine, and the famous Rain Wine are served in restaurants and sold at wine shops across the country.

You are invited to visit Edmeades Vineyards to sample their fine wines. Tasting room host Earlene Merriman states "An informal and friendly country atmosphere prevails here, where cattle and sheep graze, apples blossom, and grapes grow."

NAVARRO WINERY

Miles of aged redwood picket fences race up hillsides dotted with sheep and rows of vineyards. An occassional hawk cries out as it slowly circles the valley. This is the setting at Navarro Winery, one of the newest editions to Mendocino County's wine industry.

Ted Bennett, one of the founders of Pacific Stero, left the city with Deborah Cahn so they could move here to make premium wine. They choose a knoll just north of Philo in the Anderson Valley for their site. "Here cool Ocean breezes, combined with the valleys Rocky soil, heavy autumn rains and a short growing season, produce a somewhat lower yield than most other viticultural areas, but the end result is a higher concentration of flavor per berry, and better wine", states Deborah. Their Cabarnet Sauvignon, Gewurztraminer, White Riesling, and Vin Blanc speak for themselves.

Down the knoll and to the west sits a new tasting room - an overt invitation for you and your friends to drop by the winery for a taste of the premium wine made at Navarro Vineyards.

NAVARRO WINERY
5751 Hwy 128 (between Philo & Navarro)   *Summer: Thur-Mon 10am - 5pm*
(707) 895-3686   *Winter: Fri-Mon 10am - 5pm*
Tours by appointment, tastings, retail sales   *Varietal and Generic Wines*

PARDUCCI WINE CELLARS

The reputation of Parducci Wine Cellars, located in California's northern most wine producing district rests on three generations of one winemaking family and more than half a century of experience. The firm was founded in 1916 by Adolph Parducci, who learned his trade in Italy. In 1921 he established the present vineyard at Ukiah and began building his winery in a cool, wooded canyon.

Today management is in the hands of Adolph's sons, John and George, assisted by a third generation of Parduccis.

Until recently Mendocino County vineyards were planted exclusively with Zinfandel, Carignane, Burger, French Colombard, and lesser varietals. And almost all wines were sold to Napa or Sonoma County wineries. Mendocino County wines had no identity of their own. The Parducci family has been working hard to change that image of Mendocino wines, and they are succeeding. This is a family of pioneers in the wine field. John Parducci was the first to plant and produce premium wine from the grape varietals of French Colombard, Sylvaner Riesling, Pinot Chardonnay, Gamay Beaujolais, Pinot Noir, and Cabarnet Sauvignon in Mendocino County.

Parducci wines are under strict scientific controls. This enables the winemaker, Joe Monostori, to select the right fermentation time and temperature for each individual variety, preserving the distinct characteristics and aroma of each wine. Only the free-run juice, crushed but not pressed, is used for Parducci white wines, which captures the varietal character and fermentation bouquet.

Parducci has no plan of becoming a large winery. Stress is still put on painstaking production and sound technology. Along with the pioneering of new wine growing regions.

PARDUCCI WINE CELLARS
501 Parducci Rd., Ukiah
(707) 462-3828, 9am - 5pm daily
Tours, tasting, gift shop, sales
Varietal Wines
BA, MC, Visa

Vineyards was established in 1964 by Dr. Donald Edmeades. The winery was started in an old apple dryer by son Deron Edmeades in 1972.

Today a small corporation with several partners, Edmeades produces around 12,000 cases per year of Cabernet Sauvignon, Zinfandel, Rain Wine (Colombard), Chardonnay, Gewurztraminer, and Pinot Noir. Most of the grapes come from the Anderson Valley. The winemaker is U.C. Davis trained enologist Jed Steele. Both Deron and Jed have taken the sacred oath to "make only the best wines the grapes will allow."

In 1977 nature set the stage for a unique experiment in the Edmeades vineyards. Excitment shot through the vineyards as unwilling workers "were enticed" into the 18 degree fahrenheit weather to pick frozen clusters of French Colombard grapes in the pre-dawn hours. As the "rosy fingers of sunrise" spread over the tiny valley a light snowfall further chilled the grapes. Natures spell was captured beautifully by Jed Steele and the first "Eswein" (Ice Wine) ever produced in America had been created. Was it Mendocino magic that had made possible this spellbinding event?

NAVARRO VINEYARDS

Navarro Vineyards was established in 1974 by Ted Bennett and Deborah Cahn when they purchased 900 acres of wooded Anderson Valley. They planted their vineyards to Pinot Noir, Chardonnay, and Gewurztraminer. To produce estate bottled wines a beautiful redwood winery was built along with a new tasting room and case storage facility which was completed in 1980.

Navarro is growing their own Gewurztraminer and Pinot Noir, while buying varieties such as Cabernet Sauvignon and Riesling from local farmers. Ted Bennett is the winemaker along with U.C. Davis graduate Tex Sawyer.

Whale Wine: The inspiration of whale war crusader Byrd Baker and Deron Edmeades.

Eiswein Wine in Germany; Ice Wine in Mendocino. In 1977 Edmeades wine maker Jed Steele created the first Eswein ever produced in the U.S.A.

A brand new tasting room and premium wine await you at youthful Navarro Vineyards.

IUSCH VINEYARDS

In the late 60's Tony and Gretchen Iusch planted their vineyard in the Anderson Valley with Chardonnay, Gewurztraminer, and Pinot Noir.

Winemaking began in 1971 with Tony s winemaker. In 1973 Al White joined Tony as assistant winemaker. By the late 70's growth brought them to around ,500 cases per year with the addition of Cabernet Sauvignon and Riesling. Winemaking style is traditiinal with aging done in oak. As the 70's came to a close the Iusch's sold their winery to Hugo Oswald, Ukiah grape grower. Al White will stay on as winemaker with help from the Oswald family.

McDOWELL VALLEY VINEYARD

A few miles east of Hopland in the McDowell Valley, Richard and Karen Keehn have built a winery surrounded by their vineyards of Cabernet Sauvignon, Petite Sirah, Zinfandel, Grenachi, Carignane, Chenin Blanc, and Riesling. The first crush took place in 1979 with winemaker George Bursich at the helm. A total of 15,000 to 25,000 cases will be produced.

TYLAND VINEYARDS

Tyland Vineyards are located south f Ukiah in a narrow canyon west of Hwy 101. Owner and winemaker Dick Tijsseling has planted his vineyard to fine wine varieties such as Cabernet Sauvignon, Chardonnay, Chenin Blanc, Gamay Beaujolais, Zinfandel, Pinot Noir, and Petite Sirah. A beautiful redwood winery was built in the late 70's and in 1979 a small amount of Cabernet Sauvignon, Zinfandel, Gamay Beaujolais, and Chardonnay was produced.

PARSON'S CREEK

Another new winery, Parson's Creek was established in 1979 in the Ukiah Valley. Here owners Jess Tidwell and Hal Doran produce their wines from grapes that are field crushed and pressed.

Three white wines were produced in 1979 totaling 4,000 cases of Riesling, Chardonnay, and Gewruztraminer. Winemaker Jess Tidwell has chosen to cold ferment all wines in stainless steel tanks.

MILANO WINERY

The most youthful example of Mendocino County's wine reniassance can be found at Milano Winery, which is located one mile south of tiny Hopland. The owners, Greg Graziano and Jim Milone carefully tend vineyards of Cabernet Sauvignon, Gamay Beaujolais, and Chenin Blanc. The winery was built in a ancient Hop Kiln where a tasting room and offices are also located.

Printed on the Milano label are the words "We blend tradition, technology, and Mendocino County grapes to produce wines that are true extensions of the grape." Their spirited dealings with mother nature and wine technology have produced vintages that are suprizingly full bodied and distinctively unique in taste. Releases of Cabernet, Gamay Beaujolais, Zinfandel, Petite Sirah, Sauvignon Blanc, Chenin Blanc and Chardonnay are available at finer restaurants and wine shops in California. A taste of properly served Milano wine will put a twinkle in your eye and a smile on your face.

Milano

1978
M & M Vineyards
Redwood Valley Mendocino
GAMAY BEAUJOLAIS
ALCOHOL 12.5% BY VOLUME
PRODUCED AND BOTTLED BY Milano Winery
HOPLAND MENDOCINO COUNTY CALIFORNIA

At Milano Winery tradition and technology are blended together.

Whether you reside in Mendocino County or plan a trip there, be sure to stop in at some of the wineries. You will be able to view the winemaking process, talk with the winemakers, and then taste their finished product. Your visit will be both informative and enjoyable.

plimentary wine and warm glow of the evening fire in the parlor soothes your soul. Next door to the Victorian Farmhouse is one of the best restaurants in Northern California. I can't rave enough about the food served at Ledford House. The atmosphere and cuisine are reverent. The five consistently superb entrees start at $12 and are worth every penny. The nightly special ranges from Pork Normande to Salmon Kouliback - with regular entrees of shrimp cannelloni, baby lamb chops, and filet of beef. The Little River Inn is a lively social center. The spacious restaurant, full bar, and rooms are located in a large victorian on a knoll adjacent the Little River Golf Course. Across the street is the Little River Market and Post Office with it's gas pumps out front. In the northwest corner of the building is the Little River Cafe. With only two seatings nightly (at 6:30pm & 8:30pm), the tiny restaurant is usually packed. The new owners, Nancy Alford and Robert Rutley serve excellent cuisine. Call (707) 937-0404 for res.

Around the sharp bend and in the hollow is Van Damme State Park. Campers from all over the United States favor this park with its fresh water creek, fern forests, secluded camping spots in the evergreen forested hills, ocean beach, and close proximity to the many gourmet restaurants in Mendocino. Another sharp S turn past Van Damme State Park and up the hill on the right you'll spot Glendeven. Glendeven, with it's six antique furnished rooms and large living/dining room with fireplace turn foggy winter e evenings on the Pacific into a real pleasure.

Across Big River and on the left of Hwy 1 is Mendocino - the country inn capitol of the West Coast. Located here is my favorite country inn - 1021 Main Street Guest House. Owner Marilyn Solomon and her two sons operate one of the more interesting country inns in Northern California. 1021 Main captures the Mendocino Mystic well. It hugs the coastline, has a view of Big River where it flows into

the sea. Each day the landscape change as river and sea interact to resculpt the driftwood scattered sandy beaches. The interior of the inn is a showplace of contemproary & ancient art from both Eastern & Western Civilizations dating back centuries. The environmen is like being inside a time machine. Your imagination is the control lever. The cloak of formality is shed at the door. You can go forward or backward as far as you want. Its always up to you. Each inn has that potenti whether obvious or latent. Each person has their own perspective of how the world should be. Each will find his or her special retreat in Northern California. 1021 Main Street Guest House is mine - a home away from home, in the truest sense of what a country inn should be. You can sit for hours on upstairs deck or at the table where breakfast is served in the morning, and watch the tides come and go, with the waves swallowing a little more or little less of the beach each time. Occassionally a tornado of excited gulls will descend on the river mouth to feed on the fish swimming up and down the Big River.

Across the street is Sip & Sup Soup House. Here hearty bowls of soup, homemade bread and gourmet appetizers are served. The social heartbeat for locals in Mendocino is focused on the Sea Gull Restaurant & Bar. Here you can dine on the first floor and drink in the cellar bar upstairs. Behind the Sea Gull Restaurant is the Sea Gull Inn, one of the first of 10 lodging facilities currently open in Mendocino. There are more in the works.

The very first country inn in Mendocino was the Randall/Packard Art Gallery and Guest House. Famous artists and humanitarians Byron Randall and Emy Lou Packard founded the inn in the late 1950's. In the late 1960's they sold the art gallery and guest house. It is now called the Mendocino Village Inn. Byron operates a guest house in Tomales, California, which is a sleepy community in northwestern Marin County. Tomales today, is much the same as

When its foggy elsewhere, the sun ten shines at the Holly Tree Inn in int Reyes.

Steeped in Old World superstitions & legends from the 16th century, the Pelican Inn is one of the more adventurous bed & breakfast inns.

"Happy birthday to you!" A little nera shy birthday girl is one year l today at Cafe Beaujolais.

The elegant Victorian Farm House occupies a setting just south of Little River overlooking the Pacific.

ome of the finest cuisine in North-California is served at Ledford House.

Ann Samas waits in front of her inn, the Blue Rose Guest House in Fort Bragg.

Mendocino was 20 years ago; but it too has started to grow. The 3 story Mendocino Village Inn has 13 antique furnished guest rooms - 7 have fireplaces and 88 private baths. The two attic rooms, one with a breathtaking ocean view, are very conducive to pleasant dreams.

The Mendocino Hotel is the central structure in the historically preserved portion of Mendocino. It was built in 1878. Guests will find the 26 rooms, 2 bars, cozy lounge, and restaurant have been graciously remodeled. MacCallum House, like 1021 Main Street Guest House, captures the Mendocino Mystic well. It was built in 1882 by William H. Kelly for his newlywed daughter, Daisy MacCallum. The buildings and grounds reminds one of a miniature Mendocino within Mendocino. The proprietor is Sue Norris. There is lodging in the main house, the Carriage House, the Greenhouse, Gazebo, and Water Tower. An elegant gourmet restaurant is housed on the first floor of the main house as well as the Grey Whale Bar. On certain days you can hear the faint roar of Byrd Baker's buss saw behind the Mac Callum House. Baker is one of several famous Mendocino artists. He carves whales & birds out of huge blocks of wood with a buzz saw. One of his whales sits at the entrance of MacCallum House.

On a corner across from Mendosa's Market in downtown Mendocino is The Cheese Shop. Here you can purchase picnic baskets full of fine cheeses, premium wine, French Baguettes, & gourmet delights. The Cheese Shop has a large selection of premium wine and cheese to choose from. If you are interested in some good reading material to take to your room with you, then I recommend the Gallery Bookstore near the Mendocino Hotel.

On a Hill north of town is Hill House of Mendocino. Hill House is a luxurious half breed between the old and new. Everything about it is very new, but it looks very old. The inn is very popular among celebraties as well as motion picture crews who are filming the Mendocino landscape. In the beginning of this year

there was a crew filming a full length motion picture called "Dead and Buried". Where were the stars staying? On the "Hill" - of course! Mendocino has always been a favorite for Holiywood. The "Russians are Coming," "East of Eden," "Same Time Next Year," "Summer of 42," and "Johnny Belinda" are a few of the films in which producers and directo used scenic Mendocino as a backdrop.

Locals have started to complain about being unable to find parking spaces and waiting in line at service stations, stores, and restaurants; not only because of the large tourist population the town attracts, but also because of the confusion the film crews cause. Wasn't there a TV commercial with the line "You asked for it, you got it. . . . . ." Seems the free-wheelin' generation of the 50's and 60's is getting family orientated and thats all and well, but let remember who makes it possible to pay the bills. If the town is too conjest to raise a family in, then why not turn the tourist orientated parts into a walking community like Yountville in the Napa Valley? Small parking lots could dot the periphery of the tourist orientated sections (which could be open to residents for permit parking) and the downtown market area could be open to residents and tourists alike. Unfortunately many of the chronic complainers intellectualize their existence and are more interested in psychoanalyzing each other and asking questions like "How (pause) do (pause you (pause) feel (big pause)?" rather tha logically and quickly dealing with the problems at hand.

At the Headlands Inn, host George Webb is a match-maker. He tries to book the inn full of couples who have something in common each night. "Guests get along phenomenolly well," he points out. One block south of the Mendocino Art Center on Kasten Street another old homé is being restored by Curt Acker and Bill Pound. They hope to provide a turn of the century boarding house to accomodate residents of Mendocino or tourists; depending upon what is passed down when the general plan for Mendocino is formalized. To find out more infor-nation call (707) 937-4903 or (707) 937-0697.

On Little Lake Street is Joshua Grindle, a victorian with 5 rooms furnished with early American antiques. North of town on the original Hwy 1 is Sea Rock, a refurbished lodging facility with private cabins that overlook the ocean; some have kitchenettes & fireplaces. A steep trail jags down the cliff to a small private beach. A few miles down Little Lake Road to the east is the secluded Ames Lodge. The setting is isolated and ideal for group seminars or family outings. You can also stay at the Mendocino Woodlands in one of several redwood cabins with massive stone fireplaces and balconies from which you can gaze out into the silence of a virgin Douglas Fir & Redwood Forest. The Big River is nearby. The Old Mill Farm is a must. The 340 acre farm is isolated on a mountaintop and surrounded by the 63,000 acre Jackson State Forest. I spent three delightful days there and wrote by kerosene lantern light and cooked on a wood burning stove. Though still very primitive (there are no power lines or phones), it will be quite comfortable once all the alternative energy systems are hooked up and the water tower and log cabin is finished. Delicious farm fresh meals are served. You have to write Box 463, Mendocino, California, 95460. Enclose a self addressed stamped envelope for a free brochure Two miles south of Fort Bragg and on the west side of Route 1 is the Mendocino Coast Gardens. An unbelievable number of plants flourish in several micro-climates on the 47 acres of creeks, valleys, meadows & Pacific Coastline. New owners host outdoor concerts and have opened a restaurant for guests. The Mendocino Coast Gardens is a must see!

In Fort Bragg you can stay at the Grey Whale Inn, Blue Rose Guest House, Colonial Inn, Casa Del Noyo, Harbor Lite or Vista Manor. A favorite of many travelers is the Pine Beach Inn with its modern rooms & private beach full of storm tossed driftwood. You can whale watch (December - March) through binoculars at the Grey Whale Inn. Once the Redwood Coast Hospital and now the largest country inn on the coast, the Grey Whale Inn has 12 antique furnished rooms and wheel chair ramps. Across the street is the Blue Rose Guest House. Your host, Ann Samas, is as charming as the buue victorian country inn she has created. A beautiful garden with every color of the rainbow embrace this old victorian. Ann and her daughter, Christine, lovingly brought the old home back to life. The five rooms are tastefully appointed (two rooms upstairs have a shared bath and the rooms downstairs have private baths). Special breakfast items stock the kitchen. You can cook yourself a delicious breakfast at the hour most convenient for you during the morning. Hows that for convenience? The famous skunk train depot and several gourmet restaurants are nearby such as the Paradise Cafe, Egghead Omelette, and The Restaurant.

Just south of Fort Bragg is picturesque Noyo Harbor. Both the Harbor Lite Lodge and the elegant Casa del Noyo overlook the harbor and moored fishing fleet. Casa del Noyo has four comfortable antique furnished rooms. It sits semi-secluded on a hill that borders the river front. A delightful place to stay. Just down the road is Carine's Fish Grotto. The owners have their own fishing boat and serve hearty fisherman lunches and dinners (Italian style). The fresh Salmon (in season), sole, red snapper, ling cod, crab & shrimp louis lunch & dinners are very filling and delicious. Also nearby is the Warf and Captain Flints. Both are very popular restaurants with residents and tourists.

North of Fort Bragg is the Vista Manor. Recently the 54 rooms were remodeled with natural wood, bright colored carpets, drapes and bedspreads and the bathrooms modernized. Telephones equip each room and a comfortable two bedroom cottage complete with kitchen and fireplace provides a rustic setting for small conferences or private social gatherings. Major motion picture companies traditionally stay here while filming in the area. Almost isolated on the northern leg of Hwy 1 in Mendocino County sits Westport. The now tiny community was once a booming logging town & seaport boasting 14 hotels and 17 saloons; now only one is left - the Cobweb Inn. Delicious home cooked meals, fresh seafood and a full bar compliments the 6 homey rooms on the second floor. The Pacific is only 100 yards away. Just outside Westport and before Hwy 1 turns east to rendezvous with Hwy 101 at Leggett is Dehaven Valley Farm. The Dehaven Creek cuts across the pastures of the once 7,000 acre ranch. A six course country dinner is served in the dining room at 7pm. Appetizer, home made soup, entree, salad, fruit and cheese and dessert make up the evenings offerings. A continental breakfast is served from 9am to 10am the following day. The six rooms are named after colors and there is the Dehaven Suite. The owners hope to turn the remaining 40 acres the country inn sits on into a working farm. Perhaps someday the sweetwater creek will ripple to the nearby thud of hoofs and the cut of the plowshare into the fertile soil. . . . . and reflect the sunlite golden tassels of wheat waving in the late autumn breeze at harvest time. The seeds of the 80's have been planted . . . . .

At 1021 Main Street Guest Hous you can go forward or backward as far as you want. The creative environment fires your imagination and triggers the time levers of the subconscious mind. 1021 Main is poise on a cliff overlooking the Big River where it empties into the Pacific.

Harbor House in Elk is poised on a cliff overlooking a spectacular ocean grotto of rugged outcroppings and sea caves from which breakers surge through. The setting can only be described as Magic.

Mildred Gomer is one of the mor gracious hosts to be found in Northe California. The old fashioned gift sh she is standing in is located next do to the Cobweb Palace Inn in Westpo Both the Inn and nearby Dehaven V Farm are excellent places to stay.

RUSSIAN RIVER REGION
HAS MADE A COMEBACK

For years the Russian River Region layed dormat. The hay-day years of the 30's & 40's when it was a booming resort area were all but forgotten. Then within the past few years it started to make a comeback. Statistically speaking, 70% of the lodging facilities of Sonoma County I endorse lie in this region as well as many of the 1980 recommended restaurants of Northern California. Couple this with the majestic redwood forests, clear creeks, meandering Russian River, Pacific Ocean, summertime bikinied swimmers, hot tubs, and intimate fireplace settings during those fierce winter storms and you'll begin to understand why this region is so desirable. The area I'll cover in this story has for it's Western boundary Hwy 1 from Valley Ford to the South and Sea Ranch to the North with the Northern boundary being Skaggs Springs Road and the Southern boundary being Bodega Hwy into Sebastopol and the Gravenstein Hwy into Hwy 101 at the Cotati Exit.

On Hwy 101, roughly 42 miles from the Golden Gate Bridge between the cities of Petaluma nnd Santa Rosa, you'll come to the Cotati-Rohnert Park Exit. Turn off Hwy 101 and head West on the Gravenstein Hwy (Hwy 116) into the heart of Sonoma Counties prime farmland (do yourself a favor and pick up Farm Trails Map - your guide to farm fresh produce). Luther Burbank, the "Plant Wizard", called this region an agricultural choosen spot. Restaurants in this area have a tremendous advantage if they choose too. They can acquire the freshest seasonal vegetables, dairy products, and fresh catches from the Pacific. Some fishermen and small farmers will even bring their fresh produce right to the chefs doorstep.

Vast's Garden Dining, a small family run restaurant on Hwy 116 had a reputation for not only using fresh farm produce, but growing much of it right on their farm adjacent the restaurant. Unfortunately, Fred & Silvie Vast recently retired and eager diners will have to wait until the restaurant is re-opened (call 823-1980). I'd give them a star rating anytime. A few miles down Hwy 116 is Chez Peyo, a casual restaurant where Country French entrees (family style) are served for extremely reasonable prices. Just south of Sebastopol is Le Pommier, another excellent French restaurant, (a brother runs A Chez Nous in Cotati).

From downtown Sebastopol turn left (at the stop light) and drive West on Bodega Hwy to Freestone (Sonoma Countie's first Historic District). Just outside of Sebastopol you can dine on good Mexican food at Taco Ed's. Freestone is a crossroads. Thanks to the thoughtful efforts of men like Tom Golden (Wishing Well Nursery) and Gene Walker (Gene Walker Realestate), Freestone will remain a small historic community. You can travel through this Historic community into Occidental which is famous for generous family style servings at it's three Italian restaurants: Firoi's, Negris, and the Union Hotel; or you can continue down Bodega Hwy to the tiny community of Bodega and dine at the Bodega Art Gallery and Restaurant. It was here (the Potter School House) where Alfred Hitchcock directed one of his most classic films, "The Birds."

Past Bodega is the T-junction of Bodega Hwy and Coast Hwy 1. A few miles to the left on Hwy 1 is Valley Ford and Dinucci's, a popular Italian restaurant known for generous servings of hearty food and the colorful personalities of it's owners Gene and Betty Dinucci. To the right on Hwy 1 is Bodega Bay. Here you can stay at the Bodega Bay Lodge (south of town) or at the Tides Restaurant & Motel (downtown). Through the dining room windows of the Tides you can watch the Fishermen dock and carefully weigh in their daily fresh catch's as alley cats hide in the shadows and beedy eyed seagulls, perched on mooring posts, wait for the opportunity to pounce on any scraps the fishermen leave behind.

North of Bodega Bay, Hwy 1 snakes its way toward Jenner where you can enjoy the fine cuisine and festive atmosphere of Murphy's Jenner by the Sea. Before Jenner you might stop at Bodega Bay Gifts and Gallery. There are few truly unique gift shops along the coast, but this is one. The proprietor is Helen Bonfigli. The Whale Cups she helped a local artist design are a must. At Chanselor Ranch you can relax and enjoy some fine cuisine. Your hosts are Bonnie and Bob Hardenbrook. There is one seating for the country cuisine errved at 7:30pm and guests can dine family style on anything from poached salmon to stuffed rack of lamb.

Across from Murphy's Jenner by the Sea is the Seagull Giftshop, another unique souvenier shop on the coast. The proprietor, Jackie Robins, is quick to answer any questions you may have about the area.

There is another route to drive to get to Jenner from inland, which I'll trace before I take you any farther north on Coast Hwy 1. It starts at the Russian River Resort Area Exit on Hwy 101 just north of Santa Rosa. This is River Road and it winds it's way past orchards and vineyards until it arrives at Mirabel Park where the redwood forests begin and then continues past Hacienda Bridge, Guerneville, Northwood, Monte Rio, Duncan Mills, and finally arrives at Jenner.

At Mirabel Park there is a T-junction where Mirabel Road dead-ends into River Road. Here you can rent a canoe from Burke's Canoe Rentals and paddle down the Russian River. A noteworthy side trip is to drive into Forestville and dine at

L'Omelette restaurant - the delicious French cuisine has been one of the best kept secrets in the Russian River area. Just two miles past Forestville and on the right is Russian River Vineyards. Here you can wine taste or enjoy the seasonal offerings served in the restaurant or on the outdoor patio (weather permitting). Now, lets get back on River Road.

Just past Hacienda Bridge you'll spot Sebastians of Hacienda, a friendly neighborhood bar, where you can feast on some of the best pizza to be found anywhere in Northern California. The proprietor is Joel Hale and the chef is Stephen Rebozo, pizza can be ordered to go by calling (707) 887-7821. Just before Guerneville is the historic Korbel Winery & Champagne Cellars, with its new outdoor gardens and wine tasting center and just before Korbel Winery and above River Road and to the right is an old-fashioned ranch house that has been converted to a elegant bed & breakfast inn. It is called the Ridenhour Ranch House Inn and is definitely worthy of checking out. Just east of Guerneville is Burdon's Restaurant. The chef serves French-American entrees such as Steak Au Povier Hotel Paris, Mahi Mahi Dore, or Veal California. In Guerneville there are several fine restaurants and excellent lodging facilities.

A good place to stop for current recreational data and a calendar of events is the downtown Guerneville Information Center or just south of main street and over the steel bridge to Hwy 116 is Southside Resort (869-2690), where Pete Sheridan (1980 President of the Russian River Region) keeps information on hand. Past Southside Resort Hwy 116 turns sharply to the left and into Pocket Canyon; just before this turn (where the Tyranisaurus Rex is), head to the right and down Neely Road to Riverwood Resort. Riverwood is a multi-functional lodge with facilities ranging from hook-ups for RV campers to elegant antique furnished rooms in the bed &

RENAISSANCE ON
THE RUSSIAN RIVER

New owner, Kurt Visser, and his staff have completely rennovated the menu, lounge, and many of the rooms at the rustic Village Inn near Monte Rio. You'll find your stay peaceful & serene.

Fresh trout from the waterfall fed nd to your table in minutes adds to ℮ pleasure of secluded Cazanoma Lodge.

The newest bed & breakfast addition to the Russian River Area is Ridenhour Ranch House Inn. It is located near Korbel Winery.

Left: Riverwood Resort owner Bob Hope takes time out to pose with daughter Kerri & Jason in their kitchen. Kerri & mother Rosalie own a gourmet catering service called Oui Cater. Above: The entrance to Riverwood Resort is clearly very inviting.

breakfast country inn created by Bob & Rosalie Hope. Rosalie and daughter Kerri also have a catering service called OUI Cater at Windsor Vineyards (Sonoma Vineyards) near Healdsburg. Consistently, the best Mexican food served in Northern California is at Casa de Joanna. Unfortunately, Casa de Joanna is as hard to find as the food is good. Drive a few miles farther down Neely Road and turn right on River Lane. Where River Lane ends you'll see a high wooden fence and on the other side through the gate and overlooking the Russian River is Casa de Joanna. From the main intersection in downtown Guerneville you can drive 2 miles north along Armstrong Woods Road to the Hexagon House, an elegant facility whose restaurant and lodge is very popular, especially for Bohemian Grove Club members during their annual summer encampments. It is not uncommon for celebrities like Betty Hutton to entertain there. West of town and across Fife Creek is Fife's Resort. Fourteen acres of grounds bordered by the Russian River have a gourmet restaurant, rustic cabins & suites, outdoor stage & patio, swimming pool, private beach and vegetable garden, making Fife's one of the most complete resorts in the Russian River Region. Across from Fife's is Ferngrove, a remodeled resort with 18 cozy cottages privately set next to a stand of redwoods. Some of the cottages are equipped with fireplaces and kitchenettes and there is a heated swimming pool flanked by well tended grounds. Next door, at Le Chalet restaurant, Gerard and Josiane Moser serve excellent Country French cuisine as well as host special parties and wedding receptions.

A few miles to the west on River Road, roughly half way between Guerneville and Monte Rio are the rolling meadows and redwood corridors of Northwood Golf Course. At Northwood Restaurant you can enjoy one of the finest salad bars (a meal in itself) in Northern California, and during Crab season - special Friday nite feeds of fresh Dungeness Crab, which is a big hit with the locals. Next door is modern Northwood Lodge with a choice between rustic cabins or modern rooms; some furnished with water beds, and isolated outside by a small grove of towering redwoods is the Northwood Lodge hot tub.

In Monte Rio on quiet River Boulevard is the three story Village Inn. Peacefully shielded by a grove of redwoods; lodging at the Village Inn is very calming in the family style atmosphere new owner Kurt Visser and his staff have created. An international selection of gourmet entree's awaits you in the downstairs dining room. A little farther down River Boulevard is Angelo's Restaurant. Here you can enjoy excellent Italian cuisine served by father and son hosts, Angelo Sr. & Angelo Jr. Angelo Sr. has served fine food in the Russian River Resort Area for over 37 years. Of special note is the Racoon Comedy Show. About 7:00pm wintertime or 9:00pm summertime a rag-tag band of adult and baby racoons show up to be further fattened on Italian spagetti which is served to them on a private platform in the trees just outside the picture windows of the bar. Across the street are 10 cabins that can be rented by the night or by the week. Just west of Monte Rio and secluded off River Road to the left is River View Lodge with its private sauna and unique rooms. West of Monte Rio the Russian River closely parallels the sharp turns in River Road. Just before Duncans Mills is the Cazadero Highway. Turn right off River Road and drive thr three miles to Kidd Creek Road (on your left) and drive another 1.1 miles to the isolated Cazanoma Lodge. Clean air, a water fall, trout farm, and redwood covered hillsides create the perfect setting. Inside the lodge a full bar and exquisite German and American entrees await you. You can also catch a fresh trout (yourself) and have it expertly prepared and served within minutes. Your hosts, Randy and Gretchin Neuman, also offer comfortabe accomodations in the lodge or in secluded cabins. Nearby is Elim Grove, a old resort that has been taken over by

Jack & Pam Evans and Don & Niki Bauer. They are in the process of whipping it into shape and will be serving some delicious gourmet meals (year - round) in the very near future. They also have started to put together a excellent wine list and hope to rennovate some of the cabins.

In Duncans Mills you can purvey a variety of interesting shops in a old-fashioned late 1890's town setting complete with wooden board walks. Here beer, wine, and deli items may be purchased from the Cheese Merchant. Across the highway is the Blue Heron Inn, where wholesome vegetarian cuisine is perfectly complimented by fresh squeezed juices and drinks from the full bar. Along the banks of the Russian River you might spot a majestic Blue Heron or a doe with her fawn foraging through the undergrowth. After a few more turns you can smell the salt air of the Pacific . That brings us back into Jenner. At the west end of town overlooking the Russian River where it flows into the Pacific is River's End Restaurant. Herr Wolfgang Gramitsky is famous for the internationa selection of gourmet dinners he and his fine staff prepare and serve. There are also three cabins and a large house you can rent daily or weekly. To find out what lies between Jenner and Gualala then turn to the travelog on Coast Highway One.

A quote from the menu of Murphy's Jenner by the Sea sums up the feeling of dining in this tiny town that precariously hugs the western fringe of North America: "of a peaceful nature. . . where the northern sun dances silver on a Pacific Sea. Welcome. . . . into communication of trust in the movement of life. . . . be tranquil in beauty to the eye, the palate, and the spirit."

Top: Herr Wolfgang Gramitsky (right) poses with is charming staff at Rivers End Restaurant. ottom: Colorful entrepeneur, Richard Murphy, is at he helm of his restaurant, Murphy's Jenner by the Sea.

The "Expanding Universe," a sculpture by Benjamin Bufano, which is dedicated to World Peace, stands at Timber Cove Inn.

Two Worlds Apart - Deep in the forest an Indian grips his rifle and trap and poses beside his redwood tree house. His main concern is survival. The Carson Mansion was built as a monument to the Redwood Empire lumber industry. It is now owned by the Inglemar Club who throw lavish parties and thoughtfully preserve their "clubhouse" with monthly dues. The craftsmenship that went into the building of the Carson Mansion could never be repeated on such a scale.

HIGHWAY 101 - THE REDWOOD HIGHWAY
THE GOLDEN GATE BRIDGE TO THE OREGON BORDER

The Redwood Highway winds its way 392 miles through the five coastal counties of Marin, Sonoma, Mendocino, Humbolt, and Del Norte; intersecting the county seat of each. In between these cities you'll travel through lush farmland, orchards, vineyards, redwood forests and past coastal beaches. You'll cross the seasonally tempermental Russian, Eel, Klamath, and Smith Rivers and their numerous tributaries and creeks.

Sausalito hosts three elegant hotels, which I've already mentioned - the Alta Mira, Sausalito, and Casa Madrona. Marin county is blessed with an abundance of excellent restaurants, but few lodging facilities in the country inn class. Most are scattered along Coast Highway 1. There are a number of excellent motels and inn chains (Holiday Inn, Best Western, etc); most of which are located inland and this addition of North of San Francisco does not cover that region. Consequently the restaurants and lodging facilities of Marin county proper have been left out.

Past San Rafael and just before Novato, you can take Hwy 37 east into Sonoma County to historic Sonoma. It was here that the Bear Flag

Revolt occured in 1846. On one corner of the tree shaded plaza is the three story Sonoma Hotel. The Vallejo Room is furnished with pieces from the General Vallejo family. Private and shared baths are available. Nearby you can dine at several excellent restaurants, purvey unique shops around the plaza, as well as wine taste at local wineries.

Take Hwy 12 into Glen Ellen and be sure to visit the Jack London Museum and Bookstore. Russ and Winnie Kingman are the worlds foremost experts on Jack London. Nearby you can tour the Wolf House Ruins at Jack London State Park. Lodging is available at the London Lodge in Glen Ellen and you can enjoy excellent provisions at the Glen Ellen Inn or the Hungry Wolf Cafe.

On the way to Santa Rosa you'll pass Bunny's Kountry Kitchen, the little town of Kenwood, Kenwood Vineyards and Chateau St Jean Winery. Just past Chateau St Jean turn right, and drive down Adobe Canyon Road to the secluded Golden Bear Lodge. Here you can enjoy creekside dining on dinners ranging from succulent steaks to squab. Continue on Hwy 12 and into Santa Rosa. At the junction of Hwy 12 & Farmers Lane (roughly he 5th stop light from Chateau St Jean) look to your right and you'll spot the Flamingo Resort Hotel. The Flamingo is a large recreational facility with two restaurants, a solar heated swimming pool, tennis courts, luxurious rooms and suites and banquet facilities for 600. The crews of major motion picture companies hang their hats here while filming the beautiful landscape of Sonoma County. At this junction Hwy 12 becomes 4th Street, the main thoroughfare of Santa Rosa.

If you are a golfer and want some good food then turn left and onto Farmers Lane and take ti all the way till it dead ends into Bennett valley Road. Turn left on Bennett Valley Road and drive about 1½ miles. At the end of town and on your left, you'll spot the Bennett Valley Golf Course. At the Rusty Putter Restaurant you can have a good breakfast or lunch as well as play the 18 hole golf course. The chef is Joe Hogan, who used to prepare Rib eyes, Chateaubriand, Grave-Yard Stew & Oyster Stew for the Northwest Pacific Railroad execs, crews, and gandy dancers (railroad trouble shooters). Dave Wesendunk tends bar.

If you want to visit downtown Santa Rosa, then continue down 4th Street and you'll run into Courthouse Square and the new downtown shopping center. Several elegant restaurants are anxious to serve you. Among them are the La Fontana (recently remodeled), Joe Froggers, and Courthouse Cafe. Fresh produce is served at all these restaurants. La Fontana serves Italian cuisine, while Joe Froggers serves farm fresh dinners and a variety of gourmet entrees awaits you at the Courthouse Cafe. On nearby Cinema Square you can feast on the delicious Mexican food that is served at Rosie's. The owners also have another location in Cotati called Rosie's Cantina.

What used to be a race course for teenage cruisers on Friday & Saturday night is now a walking mall flanked by elegant shops and restaurants. Fourth Street used to run perpendicular and under Hwy 101. On the west side of the freeway, where 4th Street picks up again, is Santa Rosa's Historic Railroad Square. The tracks of the Northwest Pacific Railroad cut directly through here as they head north into Redwood Country and Eureka. Railroad Square is on "the quiet side of town" and I heartily recommend you spend some time there. For dining you can take your pick between Sourdough Rebos, 3rd Street Station Cafe, La Gare, or the Omelette Express. For entertainment there is old-fashioned vaudville at the Marquee Theater. Before performances you can catch dinner at 3rd Street Station or after the show you can enjoy the fine cuisine served at La Gare, a very charming French restaurant. Next door at Sourdough Rebos you can drink and frolic with the Can-Can dancers in a setting reminiscent of the Klondike Gold Rush.

If you are in a daytime hurry, yet want to dine on quality and healthy food, then I recommend you stop at the Bread Board (at the Hwy 101 Steele Lane Exit) for delicious sandwiches, vegetarian soups (hot & cold), and smoothies. A variety of beer and wine is also on hand at the Bread Board. At the Garden' of Eatin' (take the Hwy 101 Bicentennial Exit) on Piner Road you can purchase a picnic basket full of gourmet goodies, premium wines, and a map of area attractions. Owner Tom Patterson also serves the "best ground beef money can buy" on his hamburgers. You can also enjoy a delicious breakfast or lunch (call for orders to go).

North of Santa Rosa you'll cross the Russian River and to the right is Healdsburg. You are in the middle of wine country and a good place to seek lodging is at the Wine Bibbers Inn or Belle de Jour. If you phone well in advance the hosts of Belle de Jour will prepare a gourmet meal to your specifications. Your hosts at the Wine Bibbers, Jayne and Don Headley, opened in late 1979. Guests are delighted by their friendly hospitality and complementary glass of wine at the doorstep. In the truest sense of innkeeping they keep a spare gallon of gasoline for guests who might be running on empty.

I heartily recommend Giorgio's, on the south side of town, (George is famous for the pizzas he makes. Downtown on the Healdsburg Plaza is Wine Country, a delightful restaurant for dining and dancing. If you want to swim on a clean stretch of the Russian River, then visit Camp Rose Inn (on Fitch Mountain Road southeast of town). The restaurant is set majestically above the beach and delicious food and spirits are served indoors or (summertime) on the redwood sundeck. The proprietors, Jane & Ben Salvon are experienced in drama and occassionally host plays beneath the restaurant.

The heart of the Northern Sonoma County wine country is centered upon Geyserville. In this region there are over 20 wineries (called the Russian River Winery Road) with tasting facilities. In downtown Geyserville (population 1,000) you can leisurely dine at the Hoffman House or Catelli's the Rex. The best Scampi I've ever had in my life I had at Catelli's - Richard Catelli was cooking that night. Hoffman House received a national recommendation from a emminent critic who writes for a leading medical magazine. The critic is deaf and blind so his taste buds are highly developed.

A few miles to the north in Cloverdale you can gas up. Just north of town you have a decision to make. Will I turn left for the coast or will I keep on Hwy 101 for the redwoods? If you need time to make up your mind then pull over at Mama Nina's (1 mile north of Cloverdale) for a good drink and some excellent Northern Italian cuisine. If you decide to turn left onto Hwy 128 you will eventually arrive at Booneville, a rural community where two worlds recently collided and are in the process of blending together.

HIGHWAY 128:
CLOVERDALE TO NAVARRO AND COAST HIGHWAY ONE

For such a small town, Boonville has currently got to be under the influence of one of the most diversified forcefields in Northern California. At one end of town is the Boonville Hotel, which is being rennovated into a elegant elegant country inn and restaurant. The staff reflect the new breed of pioneers needed in the 80's. The menu is dedicated to indigenous foods (only local produce). Fresh vegetables come

from a beautiful Bio-Intensive Garden which raps around the dining room. In the heart of Boonville is the Boonville Lodge, a popular bar patronized by some of the biggest loggers and backwoods pioneers you've ever seen in your life. Now granted- the Boonville Hotel and Boonville Lodge are two worlds apart - but for some reason most everybody seems to get along. Mike Stanton, the head bartendar at the Boonville Lodge told me he would be happy to assist any travelors passing through Boonville. I got the feeling that if you got in a pinch, especially late at night - a phone call to Mike (895-9972) would get you all the help you'd need. That's whats so nice about a rural community - people know the area and a lot of times will drop everything to help you out.

Next door to the Boonville Lodge is Thomasson's Chevron Station. Its open everyday but Sunday from 8am to 6pm (895-3435). The proprietor, Ruben Thomasson, runs one of the few modern day "stage coach stops" between Hwy 101 and Coast Hwy 1. He even speaks Boontling, that backwoods lingo that made Boonville famous (a la Johnnie Carson show). Only someone like Ruben could come up with a unique rationing solution regarding the use of service station restrooms. If you have a social security number ending with odd numbers you can use it on odd days - even numbers on even days. However, tourists or heavy drinkers may apply for a "C" sticker which will exempt them from these procedures ; and on the 31st of any month is a free day. Jeff Short, who runs the Union 76 (895-3018) in Boonville is another character. I met he and his wife at Bear Wallow Resort, 4 miles west of Boonville. Live Main Lobster and a lesson in Boontling made the evening worthwhile. On Thursday night delicious family style dinners are served, and any other night (Fri - Sun) you can reach satisfaction on succulent cuts of top sirloin & filet mignon as well as terriyake breast of chicken. At nightime you can hear the hoot owls and wind whistling through the pines above the roof of your secluded cabin. Boonville also has a small airport and the owners at Bear Wallow well send someone down to pick you up if you so desire.

Just northwest of Boonville is Philo, a small community centered on a lumber mill. By the way, you'll see heavy chip and log trucks loaded with tons of redwood rolling up and down Hwy 128. If one gets on your tail, then the best thing to do is pull over and let him or her by. To a degree their livelihood depends on scheduling and unfortunately they can get very impatient with tourists. If you have a serious problem with one of the rigs then take the truck or trailor number and phone the parent firm and ask for the supervisor and tell him your story. Safety is a priority and the parent company can usually get in radio contact with the driver.

Just past Philo are three wineries where you can wine taste - Navarro, Edmeades, and Husch. After you encounter the first stand of redwoods you'll notice that Hwy 128 begins to parallel the Navarro River. At the Floodgate Store east of Navarro you can get gas, snack food and beer. Just before the coastline you'll spot a large green steel bridge. If you turn left you can visit Elk - home for three fabulous country inns and restaurants: the Elk Cove Inn, Greenwood Pier Cafe, and the spectacular Harbor House, which is poised on a cliff overlooking a beautiful grotto. At Harbor House a delicious gourmet dinner and continental breakfast is included with your over night accomodations. Your host is Trisha Corcoran. She and her friendly staff will see to it your stay is as pleasant as at any of the other country inns in Mendocino County. If you keep on Hwy 128 it will become Coast Hwy 1 which winds its way several hundred feet up a cliff line that parallels the Navarro River until it empties into the Pacific Surf. The scenery is spectacular. A few miles north and on the left overlooking the ocean is Gregory's restaurant, which is known for authentic German cuisine and drink. Mendocino, the country inn capitol, has already been covered in the Route 1 story. The mouth of the Navarro River is a nice spot for beach combing and just south of Mendocino is Van Damme State Park - an ideal setting for camping and hiking.

HWY 101: CLOVERDALE TO THE OREGON BORDER

Highway 101 narrows just past Cloverdale. Both the Russian River and Northwest Pacific Railroad tracks parallel the highway. Occassionally a train will play hide and seek with you as it darts in and out of the tunnels carved out of the steep rocky cliffs. Hwy 101 narrows to a single lane and then widens to freeway several times before you get to Ukiah. There are several stretches of passing lanes for large trucks and passenger cars as well as turn offs for those who want to explore the Russian River's rocky shoreline and sandy beaches. In Hopland be sure to visit the new Fetzer tasting room and tiny Milano Winery just to the south. At Milano, winemaker Greg Graziano and Jim Malone will give you a tour, time permitting, and let you taste their premium award winning wine. At Fetzer you can also shop for unique gifts and wine related items.

Ukiah is the capital of Mendocino County. Here you can stay at the elegant Palace Bar, Grill, & Hotel. The Palace is the finest hotel on Hwy 101 between Sausalito and the Oregon Border. Each of the 90 rooms is individually furnished and rates include a delicious continental breakfast. The staff will advise you about wine tours and if you fly in, they will pick you up at the Ukiah Airport. In downtown Ukiah you can dine at the Lido (Italian), the Coach House (Continental), at the Palace Hotel's restaurant or on the way out of town at the Manor Restaurant & Motel. In the past, film crews have stayed here while doing television and motion pictures. Just north of Ukiah you can wine taste at Cresta Blanca, Parducci, or Weibel wineries. In Redwood Valley, the Broiler Steak House serves up delicious char-broiled steaks and chops. The Broiler is located just to the left of Hwy 101, where it narrows from freeway into a single lane. A mile up the road is Mrs. Denson's Cookie Factory and a favorite restaurant for locals and tourists who are lucky enough to find a seat - Scotty's Old Mill Inn. Here you can savor huge "Big John" steaks, linguini with clam sauce, stuffed pork chops, and BBQ oysters as well as delicious drinks from the bar. Your host's are Scotty & Elives Fredrickson. From

From here the freeway gently climbs up a steep hill and the next town is Willits, about a ½ hour drive away. The panorama of hillsides and forests visible for miles from the highway is very relaxing. Just south of Willits you can gas up or stay at the Ridgewood Park Motel. Legend has it that the notorious highwayman - poet, Black Bart hid behind the large rock across the freeway from Ridgewood and robbed a stage coach. After he pulled a job he always left a poetic calling card behind. One read:

> Here I lay me down to sleep
> To await the coming morrow
> Perhaps success, perhaps defeat
> And everlasting sorrow.
>
> I've labored long and hard for bred
> For Honor and for riches,
> But on my corns too long you've tred
> You fine haired Sons of Bitches.
>
> Let come what will, I'll try it on
> My condition can't be worse
> And if there's money in that box
> 'Tis munny in my purse.

Like Mendocino, Willits is a small town supply center where the many back-woods people and farmers drive to for tools and produce. At one of the general stores, the "Happy Belly", tourists can purchase delicious organic snack food and juices for the road. The Happy Belly is located just south of downtown Willits on the left side of Hwy 101. Next door is the Blue Whale Restaurant. One of Byrd Baker's famous whales,,which are carved out of huge slabs of wood, sits on the patio. Not only is the food delicious at the Blue Whale (fresh fish & farm produce), but it's very nutritional as well.

The highway is single lane most of the way to Laytonville. The Laytonville Inn is a nice stop for fresh baked pie and coffee. Just north of town you can peek into the future. At Wilderness Power Systems Inc. very efficient, low cost, energy systems for homes are displayed and sold. Energy is the name of the game in the 80's. Fourteen miles north of Laytonville

on a hillside to the left, is the isolated Mad Creek Inn. In the side bar delicious ice cream sundaes and cones make a great cure for those sweltering summer days. Premium wine and imported beer is also served. Mary Cefalu and staff serve exciting full course dinners complete with fresh veggies and curry dip, homemade soup, garden salad cinamon coffee, entree, and choice of ice cream or homemade cake.

At the Cummings exit I recommend you turn off the freeway and trace the meandering Drive-Thru-Tree-Road, (the original Redwood Highway), approxiametly 3 miles, and then turn left at the Big Bend Lodge mailbox and drive down the mile long gravel road. At the base of the ridge is Big Bend Lodge. The proprietors, Jack & Ken, state that some families have been coming here for over 20 years. The south fork of the Eel River makes a sharp turn here and the sandy beaches and summertime emerald-blue swimming holes are like heaven. Evenings at the lodge can be a lot of fun as couples & families, having feasted on fresh caught salmon or BBQ'd steaks, meander in to set in front of the fire. Someone nostalgically strikes up an old time tune on the piano and everybody starts singing along. Suddenly, Jack appears in a tuxedo, top hat and cain to host the evening; adding to the sponenaity that occurs at days end. Just before Leggett on the Drive-Thru-Tree-Road and off to the left is, (you guessed it), the Drive-Thru-Tree, a huge living redwood that has been hollowed out so that a large car can squeeze through.

Past Leggett on Hwy 101 is the Howling Wolf Lodge. Owner Pat Derby serves a delicious breakfast, lunch, or dinner. On evenings you can feast chuck wagon style on generous portions of potatos, vegetables, lasagna, BBQ chicken or steak. Don't set too close to the south wall of the dining room. One evening I was enjoying some BBQ chicken, and all of a sudden a tremendous roar shook the wall. I said to myself, "What the hell is going on and wondered if I should start runnin!" The waitress said, "Don't worry, it just Pat's pet

Photo by William A. Porter

The Palace Bar, Grill & Hotel in Ukiah is the finest hotel on Hwy 101 between the Golden Gate Bridge and the Oregon Border. Nothing was spared during the rennovation process. An excellent staff await your visit.

Scotty & Elives Fredrickson pause for a quick photo on a busy Friday night at Scotty's Old Mill Inn.

Ken Gosting

Jayne & Don Headley stand proudly in front of their country inn near Healdsburg and toast you - their potential guest.

Pat Derby and her 1,000 lb pet grizzly - Seymor. Pat owns the Howling Wolf Cafe north of Leggetts.

People drive from 100 miles away to dine at the Miranda Manor, which is located in the Ave. of the Giants.

African lion." Pat is a famous Hollywood animal trainer. She owns the Lincoln-Mercury Cougar (Christopher), "Love that Bobcat" (Rick-o-Shay), Rujo- a 700lb Siberian Tiger, Seymor- a 1,000lb Grizzly, and Stanley - a North American Wolf as well as other wild animals. That same night I overheard an interesting comment Pat made in the bar. A patron sitting at the counter asked her, "What is the most difficult animal to train?" Pat thought a minute and then replied, "MAN!"

Near Piercy is the Woodsmen's R.V. Park (247-3380), a very popular stop for the truckers. All day and night they pull in for coffee and a bite to eat. Inside the restaurant is a display board with the call signs and pictures of truckers poised in front of their rigs. There are almost 400 members in the 101 Club with CB handles (call signs) like Squeakin-Deacon, Susie Q, Chicken George, Hole Wizard, Fire Ball, Golden Rod, Screw Driver, Waste King, Molly, One Armed Bandit, Turd, Gladiator, Free Spirit, Timber Wolf, and Space Cowboy. They are the last of the American Cowboys. Instead of riding a horse, they saddle up in a 18 wheeler carrying 40 tons. They know Hwy 101 like the back of their hands and get impatient when tourists are poking down the single lane stretches of the Redwood Highway. The scenery is spectacular and you can't get a good look at it going 70 miles per hour - so do yourself a favor and pull over once in a while if you notice traffic building up behind you. You'll keep the highways a lot safer and instead of getting flipped off, you'll probably get a friendly wave and horn-honking thank you! Usually each truck has a two-way radio and if your car breaks down on a isolated stretch, flag a trucker, and chances are he'll help you on the spot or even radio help for you. Let's all try to work together in this country, enjoy the natural environment and keep those K-Sans rollin - thats a BIG 10-4!

Just north of the Woodsmen's and on the left is the world famous Hartsook Inn. Have you ever hugged a redwood tree? Julie Willows, who owns the Hartsook Inn, does. She encourages her guests to do the same thing and every once in a while sees one doing it. They keep coming back every year and keep hugging those redwood trees.

Go ahead - put your spine up against one of those century old giants and stretch your arms out above your head. Be patient now, and wait to feel this huge living creation slowly move back and forth - it's growing! Just up from the Hartsook Inn is the Singing Trees Resort and Restaurant. It borders one of the most majestic stands of redwoods in Northern California - Richardson's Grove. The cabins of Singing Trees are scattered on a hillside and down the river bank on the opposite side of the freeway overlooking the Eel River. The setting, like at Hartsook Inn, is ideal for long hikes in the redwoods or swims in the river's crystal clear water. I want to caution you about this stretch of the Redwood Highway. It narrows considerably through Richardson's Grove and there is a hairpin turn between the Hartsook Inn and the Singing Trees Resort. This area is very conjested during the peak tourist season, so use extra caution.

The stately 70 room Benbow Inn sits majestically off to the left one mile south of Garberville. Under the direction of Chuck and Patsy Watts, the historic landmark is going through several pleasant changes. For one, a theater has been added where you can view old time classic movies. Your admission ticket is your room key. Two tennis courts are finished and the 2nd & 3rd floors have been remodeled and furnished with antiques and very comfortable beds. Nearby in Garberville are several gas stations & motels. At the Woodrose Cafe in Garberville, you can eat some of the best whole wheat pancakes in Northern California. The tiny cafe is often packed by locals who thouroughly enjoy the organic and farm fresh produce.

Across the freeway in Redway are two excellent restaurants - the Brass Rail and the Shelter Cove Grotto. There is singing around the piano bar, dancing, meeting old friends or making new ones after a delicious steak dinner at the Brass Rail. Fresh seafood and chicken or steak dinners come with chowder, salad, baked potato, French bread, dessert, coffee or tea and wine at the Shelter Cove Grotto. You can stay across the street from the Brass Rail at the 40 Winks Motel. There is also a service station next door. Also in Redway is Redway Liquors, one of the finest wine shops in Northern California. The owner states that winters are hard in this area and a lot of the local folks appreciate the taste of premium wine while sitting around their fireplace or wood stove at night. A lot of the locals also have a lot of money to spend just before winter hits - for late fall is Marijuana Harvest Time. "You can just feel the money," remarked a local business person, "a lot of the marijuana farmers come into town with rolls of $100 bills stuffed in their pockets." They whoop it up for a few weeks and then head back up to their homesteads. All of San Francisco anxiously awaits word on when the first shipments of Humbolt County weed will be hitting the streets. After all, the best dope in the country is grown in Humbolt County.

The most spectacular grove of redwoods in Northern California is just north of Garberville. A 33 mile stretch of paved road by-passes Hwy 101 and runs right through the middle of the Avenue of the Giants. The road parallels the Eel River as it cuts through thousands of acres of virgin redwood trees - some towering over 300 feet. At the south end of the Avenue of the Giants is the tiny town of Phillipsville (population 250). You can eat, drink, and dance at the Riverwood Inn Restaurant. Next door is the Hobbit, a shrine to J.R.R. Tolkien, which is a rambling flower and rock garden complete with waterfalls, hanging bridges, caves, and castles as well as the mythical charactors Tolkien wrote about in Lord of the Rings. The proprietor, Dick Lester, also operates a small gift shop.

In Miranda you can have delicious homemade pizza with over 40 types of domestic and imported beers to choose from. Lodging is available at the Miranda Gardens or the Whispering Pines. Across the street from the Whispering Pines is the Miranda Manor, the best restaurant to eat at in the Avenue of the Giants. Fresh seafood (when available), steak and quail, and roast leg of lamb are a few of the entrees to choose from. At the north end of the Avenue of the Giants road (at the Pepperwood Exit), just before you get back on Hwy 101, there is a small park. You can see where the Old Redwood Highway was washed out by the great flood of 1964. There are several huge redwoods laying across the old highway. Pull over and walk down to where the first redwood blocks the road. Just to the northeast is a hollowed out redwood that was once a living quarters for a logger. Everyday he used to run an American Flag up over the highway until so many people came to visit him that he moved on.

Lumber is very important to the Northwest. At Scotia is the world's largest lumber mill of its kind. I recommend you tour the plant and watch the huge redwood trunks thunder down the tracks and against stops to be cut into slabs weighing tons. Also in Scotia is a museum and at the Scotia Inn you can dine. The Mendocino County historical society even documents the story of a man with a wooden family. He became so carried away when his fiance deserted him that he built his own family of wood and was highly respected. Women would even go so far as to call on his family and leave cards or attend birthday parties for his children. When the "husband", William Bennett, died, he ordered his loved ones destroyed, and so they were burned shortly after his death.

In Eureka stand several monuments to the lumber industry. Among the most famous are the Carson Mansion, Samoa Cookhouse, and the Eureka Inn. The lumber barons knew the timber industry wouldn't last forever, so they built these monuments for all to see. The Carson Mansion is the most famous Victorian in the United States. Words cannot describe the thoughtful care that was used to create this masterpiece. A private organization, the Inglemar Club, owns the Carson Mansion and they use their club dues to maintain the grand old victorian. There are no tours of the house available. At the Samoa Cookhouse you can feast on lumberjack breakfasts and dinners. You and your family can dine on steak or baked ham with all the trimmings followed by fresh baked pie.

There is also a museum at the Cookhouse. In downtown Eureka is the newly remodeled Eureka Inn. Built in 1922, the 150 room inn refuses to grow old. The Eureka Inn is the largest motor hotel in Northern California and hosts many conventions, sporting events, and crews of major motion picture companies each year.

The general manager, John Porter, and his fine staff, provide excellent accomodations. There is also the Rib room, coffee shop, heated swimming pool, beauty parlor, cocktail lounge, and room service. I like to sit in front of the huge lobby fireplace on the sofas and savor a glass of premium wine & write.

A visit to Eureka wouldn't be complete without a visit to Old Town Eureka, which is scarcely 4 blocks away from the Eureka Inn. The Carson Mansion sets on a knoll at the north end of Old Town Eureka. Bonnie Gool, the honorary mayor of Old Town Eureka, and others, worked tirelessly and with little compensation to preserve the many old commercial buildings and Victorians along the waterfront. If you havn't been to Eureka lately, you would be amazed at the number of quality restaurants and unique shops awaiting you. Eureka is only a 5 hour drive from San Francisco (4 hours from Santa Rosa) and there is plenty of gas once you get north of Ukiah. There never has been a gas shortage in this region; as a matter of fact the service stations in the south at Garberville were closing during the last "gas pinch" not because they didn't have enough gas - THEY DIDN'T HAVE ENOUGH CUSTOMERS! Also there is currently no odd/even license plate rationing of has exercised in Humboldt County, of which, Eureka is the county seat.

In Old Town Eureka you can dine on fresh fish at Lazio's, enjoy lunch and dinner specialties at the Waterfront Restaurant, feast on delicious Sicilian style pizzas & spinach pies at Tomaso's Tomato Pies, go south of the border at Reyes Y Casas Viejas, have Italian dinners at Fat Alberts, or soup and spirits at Fogs. At Maxwells Bistro (at 527 West Wabash Avenue) you can choose between a international selection of gourmet dinners and premium wines. South of Eureka you can dine on delicious cuts of Prime Rib at the Embers and at Volpis take your pick between Italian and seafood entrees. Other restaurants worth dining at include the Eureka Seafood Grotto, Weatherbys, the Red Lion Motor Inn & Shanghai Low. Also I understand the Old Town Bar and Grill is reopening. My favorite restaurant, Le Palaies de Rene, unfortunately closed this year. The chef, Rene Masvidal, and part of his staff are now in Chicago at the Patrice Restaurant. Rene hopes to eventually have his own restaurant in Northern California.

Just southwest of Eureka is the victorian community of Ferndale. Ten years ago an artist from Oklahoma with an inventive mind moved to the tiny picture-post-card community and started to perform his magic. Ferndale has never been the same. Oh, its still peaceful most everyday of the year, - even sleepy. But on the weekend thats picked to hold the kinetic car race its jam-packed with fans and participants. The creator of this yearly art event is Hobart Brown. Each year Hobart and his flock of crazies (its not unusual to find a congressman or mayor among the ranks) take to the streets to race across Humbolt Bay (with Coast Guard escort of course. In their people powered "kinetic sculptures," they ride cross-country, eventually ending up back in Ferndale. Most of the machines don't make it . Hobart himself recalls the day he almost drowned in Crab Slough. The ones that do finish the race are often greeted by cheering crowds that number in the thousands and are filmed by major television and film companies.

The crews christen their sculptures with names like "The Great Bandini Steamer," "Reliance Ball Bearing Bordello," "Pacific Lumber Wonder Blunder," "Flying Galumpkie Brothers," and "Two

Speed Kick-Back Dual Solar Roller." The races are always held on Mothers Day and Easter Weekend. This year's race (1980) was covered by a Japanese film crew doing a documentary for Japan's television audiences. I can just see the final cut now. Just as the kinetic sculptures reach the middle of Humbolt Bay, Godzilla surges forth from the depths to attack the defenseless racers. After a pitched battle with the Coast Guard and the Ferndale all volunteer obsolete air force; Mothra swoops down from out of nowhere and carries Godzilla out to sea - both never to be seen again. A suitable title might be "Godzilla and the Banana People." The July 1979 issue of Smithsonian Magazine did a cover photo and interesting story on the kinetic sculpture race. You can have a lot of fun in the Ferndale and Eureka area. Be sure to visit Hobart Gallery, where the kinetic sculptures are displayed. It's located at 393 Main Street, Ferndale.

A good place to eat in Ferndale is the Victorian, a spacious restaurant with an elegant dining room. Just past Ferndale Bridge (east of town) is the Angelina Inn. The Italian & American cuisine served here is delicious. In Fortuna, which is south of Eureka, you can dine at Parlatos (fresh seafood and American cuisine) and Youngs (Chinese food).

North of Eureka a few miles is Arcata. On the Arcata Plaza is a marvelous four story building called the Jacoby Storehouse. Built in 1857, it was completely rennovated by skilled artists and craftsmen. On the third floor is Youngberg's Restaurant, an eating establishment founded by John Young and Steve & Pattie Berg. The atmosphere, cuisine, and staff at Youngberg's is hard to beat. Go there and you'll see what I mean. Downstairs is Bret Harte's, a restaurant and

drinking establishment complimented by fine dance music. Across the Arcata Plaza and a ½ block up G Street is the Cafe Antillies. Here you can dine on exotic West Indies cuisine or enjoy the American entrees. A good wine list accompanies the dinner menu and a delicious Sunday Brunch is also served. At Northtown Park you can dine on New Zealand Rack of Lamb and succulent steaks. An array of frosted windows etched with scenes of California Parks and aquariums full of aquatic life creates an interesting dining atmosphere.

You can drive scenic Hwy 299 through primitive wilderness east of Arcata to the small community of Willow Creek. Though he has been mentioned in ancient Indian ledgends for centuries by tribes from Alaska to Mexico, it was the evidence he left behind at Willow Creek that aroused world press coverage and caused hundreds of reporters to converge there in the late 1950's to search for BIGFOOT! According to Ferndale historian Andrew Genzoli, who writes a column for the Eureka Times Standard, a woman wrote a letter of inquiry to him asking if she should be concerned about the large foot prints that had been left by a mysterious animal inhabiting the wilderness area that surrounds Willow Creek. Andrew ran a brief filler in his column after receiving the letter, and to his astonishment the wire services picked the story up. Before you could bat an eye, reporters and television crews from all over the United States and several foreign countries descended on Willow Creek to search for the creature. Andy says that 99% of the evidence and sitings are pure hoax. (Loggers were making plaster of Paris feet and walking around the forests to fire the imaginations of the investigators and freighten the residents).

Its the 1% that intrigues me. Does Bigfoot really exist? He goes by many names. He is Oh-Mah to the Hoopa Indians, Toke-Mussi to the Yurok, Dsonoqua (Timber Giant) to the Kwakiutl, Quawuchs (pronounced Sauce-Squash), and Bigfoot. He glides silently through the forest almost as if on winged feet. He can effortlessly pick up full 55 gallon drums, 250 pound truck tires, even a horse and play with it. His haunting stare has left eye witnesses hypnotized. Hunters and loggers have left the forest swearing they felt someone or something watching them for days. Something that followed their every move, yet when they looked around they saw or heard nothing, but felt a presence that made the hair stand up on their backs.

Solid sitings are few and far in between, but something is out there. In 1884 a train crew in British Columbia reported "after perilous climbing succeeded in capturing a creature which truly may be called half man and half beast." It was less than 5 feet high and weighed 127 pounds with strong black hair covering the entire body except for the hands nad feet. On December 14, 1904, a hunting party of four gave pursuit to a Dsonoqua in the Vancouver Island mountains. The wild man was apparently young, with long matted hair and a beard, and covered with a profusion of hair all over the body. He ran like a deer through the seeming impenetrable tangle of undergrowth, and pursuit was utterly impossible. In 1924 "a band of apes" threw rocks at prospectors in the hills near Kelso. One prospector is said to have gunned one of the apes which pitched backwards into the undergrowth. No trace was found. In 1957, Albert Ostman, a well known retired contractor was captured by a Quawuchs family. He was camped beside an inlet on the rugged British Columbia coast when he was carried off in his sleep. Ostman was kept in a cave and examined by each member of the Quawuch family. The stench was unbearable. He finally escaped. In his sworn statement before a British Columbia Magistrate he stated that the Quawuchs communicated with each other through gurgling and guttural sounds as well as whistling grunts.

Bigfoot's alofness and wit for survival is only equaled by the legends we have spread about him over the centuries. Perhaps one of mother natures best kept secrets will remain so forever. Who knows; perhaps some foggy moonlite night you might hear the unmistakable grunt, smell the musky scent in the breeze; and for a moment - a priceless moment,—catch the silouette of the Timber Giant on the prowl.

Just south of Trinidad you can dine at one of the gemstones of the coast,- Merryman's. Though hard to find, the cuisine chef/owner Sam Merrymen prepares is well worth it. The view of the beach and ocean at sunset is quite often unbearably beautiful. The charbroiled steaks, salmon, and pig roasts (by special arrangement) are famous to locals. For information call (707) 677-3111. In Trinidad the Eatery and the Seascape restaurants serve enjoyable fare. Just north of Trinidad on Patricks Point Drive is the Colonial Inn. The good food and 2nd floor view of the fading sun into the ocean works its magic like Merrymans. At 900 Patricks Point Drive (roughly 2 miles north of Trinidad) is Bishop Pine Lodge. Your host, Steve Kopf, is very helpful to the Northern California traveler. He shows old time movies for his guests and also freezes their fresh caught salmon until they are ready to depart for home. Steve's 13 rustic cabins are very cozy and winter or summer, there is a romantic trail that winds its way to the edge of a cliff high above the Pacific.

Northern Humbolt County and Del Norte County are pretty sparce as far as lodging facilities and restaurants, but there are some natural settings that can only be described as inspirational. At Klamath you can fish for steelhead or salmon when they are in season on the Klamath River. At Crivelli's you can dine on steaks, lobster, prime rib, and Italian food. At Tree's of Mystery, a 49 foot statue of Paul Bunyan talks back to you and waves his hand to guests entering and leaving the Tree's of Mystery Gift Shop. Questions and answers fired back & forth between the giant and tourists can be extremely humorous. One day I observed a swami clothed in a turban and robe approach the gift shop. All of a sudden the big voice in the sky spoke and the swami stopped dead in his tracks. He finally figured out that it was not Allah calling, but rather a kid a big giant having fun. Across the street is a restaurant, motel, and "the smallest bar in Northern California."

The historic Requa Inn is being carefully restored and turned into a elegant restaurant and country inn. In Crescent City you can stay at the comfortabe

The evening lights of the fishing fleet at anchor in Trinidad Bay. This historic photo is the courtesy of Steve Kopf, who owns nearby Bishop Pine Lodge. At Steve's lodge, cozy cabins and a romantic trail that winds its way to the edge of the Pacific await you.

Behind these etched swinging doors you'll discover one of the more elegant dining experiences to be found in Northern California. The restaurant is Youngberg's, which is located on the Arcata Plaza.

Parading participants of the Kinetic Sculpture Race which is held in the Ferndale/Eureka area on Easter and Mothers Day of each year. The originator of the race is world famous artist & inventor Hobart Brown, (center of picture carrying a shield) who is shown above marching through Old Town Eureka with his crew, the Banana People.

Northwood Inn and dine next door at the Northwood Restaurant. On the harbor you can enjoy seafood & American dinners at the Grotto. One of the best restaurants in Northern California sits right on the beach just south of Crescent City. Its called Jimmy's Crescent Beach House (707-464-6000). Most evenings during the summer the restaurant is packed. Jimmy Askew and his charming wife Teresa serve delicious gourmet dinners ranging from Pepper Steak of the House (entrecate au poivre Maisson) flamed with Scotch Whiskey, sour cream, onions, cream, mushrooms, and fresh vegetables to the fresh daily catch of whatever is in season, which Jim selects personally from the fishermen. From the dining room windows the Pacific waves break scarcely 100 feet away. After dinner a pleasant stroll on the beach is in order. Some of the more adventurous diners land their aircraft on the beach and walk to the Beach House to dine.

North of Crescent City is the Ship Ashore Resort. The large complex has a museum housed in an old ship, a large RV park, Best Western Lodge, and restaurant. Two miles from the Oregon Border is the Nautical Inn. The restaurant sets majestically on a cliff overlooking the Pacific. In the cozy interior with its nautical decor you can dine on fresh fish (in season), steaks and prime rib.

The most isolated lodging facility North of San Francisco is also near the Oregon Border. Patrick Creek Lodge is located 27 miles east of Crescent City. The setting is so primitive that the telephones (GTE) are still on party lines. To drive to the lodge, take Howland Hill Road out of Crescent City and drive northeast until it intersects Hwy 199. Take Hwy 199 through Gasquet, which has a small airstrip, and a few miles out of town you'll spot Patrick Creek Lodge on your left. The lodge is completely surrounded by Six Rivers National Forest. The water in the nearby Smith River is so pure you can drink right from it. Lodging is available in the motel rooms or in the lodge itself. If you desire, transportation can be arranged from the Gasquet airport. There is a restaurant where a good selection of American & International entrees are served. I suggest you try the Birchernmusli for breakfast, the Oregon Mountain for lunch, and the mouthwatering BBQ ribs for dinner. Your dinner entree includes a relish tray, homemade soup & bread, baked potato and garden fresh vegetables. Your hosts are Neal and Liz Haley. One reason why the food is so good is that Neal personally buys fresh produce from Oregon farmers and vendors. If you are a "city slicker" and want to experience comfortable lodging and excellent home cooking in the middle of wilderness, then this is the place.

I remember one night in July. The full moon struggled with fluffy wind blown clouds to bathe the lodge with light. You could see the steep forested ridgelines that hem the lodge in on all sides in the distance. The air is pure and scented with Douglas Fir and Virgin Redwood. There is a cool breeze and the rush of the turbulent waters of Patrick Creek can be faintly heard in the background. Contended guests, having feasted inside on delicious food have wandered out one by one to listen to the Dixieland Band playing on the front porch. Ladies were swinging their hips and men were tapping their feet. Up until the 30's this area was lawless, but then the highway brought the fingers of civilization in. Tonight the lodge is packed; people have driven from as far away as 100 miles to eat, drink, and listen to the music. The dixie band is playing "Bye Bye Blackbird" and a shapely curly haired blond dressed in a long white dress begins singing. From where she stands a light breeze flutters the sheet music she is holding up. The trombone player blasts a few notes in her direction. The bango music and the crowd begin to get lively - its time for "Down by the Riverside". The full moon and drink begins to weave a web of magic over the entire lodge. Several couples get up and start strutting around the small dance floor.
and the trumpet blares
and the saxaphone whails
into the starlite night . . . .
And oh how we all love it.

Robert W. Matson
March 1980

Children enjoy an old fashioned hay ride at the Old Mill Farm.

THE OLD MILL FARM

The advance guard will become the Caretakers of the future. They are the scouts and pilgrims of the 1980's who will clear the way for succeeding generations.

The Old Mill Farm is a wilderness ridge top farm at the 800 foot elevation, completely surrounded by 63,000 acres of Jackson State Forest. The nearest telephone and power lines are 8 miles away (CB communications are available for necessary needs), yet the farm runs very well on alternative energy systems - just like in the good - old - days. If you want to relive the past or learn how to become more self reliant in a world full of future uncertainty, then this is the place to do it. Come here - whether you are 70 years old or are a parent who wants your child to learn skills not usually available through standard school systems. Child group participation is encouraged. If you do not know a group which can get together and orgainize a trip to the farm, create one for your child or family or contact Caritas Creek, a non profit educational orgainization at P.O. Box 23921, Oakland, Calif. 94623 for a free brochure. The staff of Caritas Creek feel "our teaching experiences have reinforced the belief that true learning opportunities are always fun and exciting. When these learning - through - discovery experiences are shared they lead to a sense of community. Our trips to the Old Mill Farm help children learn from the land & animals and with each other and from each other, and this reinforces the feeling of community. This feeling, and the mutual respect that it cultivates, leads naturally to an inner discipline and a sense of responsibility.for oneself, for others, and for the environment which we all share."

Large groups can stay down the mountain at the Mendocino Woodlands. In Camp 1 (there are 3 camps) you can stay at one of 46 cabins with massive stone fireplaces and balconies from which you can gaze out into the silence of a virgin Douglas Fir and Redwood Forest. Their complete isolation and seclusion

Continued to page 256

Key to Understanding Listings and Maps

KEY TO THE LISTINGS: How to find your favorite Restaurant, Lodging Facility, or Winery.

At the end of many of the Listings you will note a See Page, followed by a Number. Turn to the page referenced for a more detailed description of that particular Restaurant, Lodging Facility, or Winery. For more information on the Restaurants & Lodging Facilities; I suggest you read the Travelogs on the Russian River, Route 1, and Highways 29 (Napa Valley), 101 (Golden Gate Bridge to the Oregon Border), and 128 (Cloverdale to the Pacific Coast of Mendocino). Route 1 covers the Coastline from Muir Beach to the town of Leggett where it junctions with Hwy 101. You might also read the Wine Tour Stories. The numbers assigned to the Listings refer to their locations on the Maps which begin on Page 261. An additional Index is provided on Pages 268 & 269.

NUMERICAL SYMBOLS: **1** Winery **①** Restaurant **[1]** Lodging Facility

---

MARIN COUNTY RESTAURANTS

1. CHEZ MADELEINE
French
11102 Sir Francis Drake Blvd.
Point Reyes
(415) 663-8998

2. MANKA'S
Czech & European
56 Argyle, Inverness
(415) 669-1034, Res. advised

3. MARSHALL TAVERN
American & Fresh Seafood
Hwy. 1 N., Pt. Reyes Station,
Marshall (415) 663-1700
See Page 54

4. NICK'S COVE
Seafood
Hwy 1, Marshall
(415) 663-1033
See Page 53

5. STATION HOUSE CAFE
Fresh Seafood & Vegetarian
Hwy, Corner of A & 3rd Street,
Point Reyes (415) 663-1515
See Page 52

6. VILLAGE COFFEE SHOP
American
Downtown Tomales
(707) 878-2863
See Page 51

7. VLADIMIR'S
Czechoslovakian
Sir Francis Drake Blvd., Inverness
(415) 669-1021 Res. advised
See Page 55

SONOMA COUNTY RESTAURANTS

100. A CHEZ NOUS
French
8235 Old Redwood Hwy, Cotati
(707) 795-9860

101. ANGELO'S
Italian Cuisine
1 mile east of Monte Rio on
Russian River Blvd.
(707) 865-2215

102. AU RELAIS RESTAURANT
French
691 Broadway, Sonoma
(707) 996-1031 Res. advised

103. BLACK FOREST INN
Continental
138 Calistoga Rd., Santa Rosa
(707) 539-4334 Res. advised
See Page 17

104. BLUE HERON INN
Gourmet & Vegetarian
No. 1 Steelhead Blvd., Duncans Mills
(707) 865-2269 Res. for parties of 8
See Page 41

105. BODEGA ART GALLERY & REST.
Gourmet Foods
17125 Bodega Ln., Bodega
(707) 876-3257
See Page 37

106. BRASS ASS
Pizza
550 E. Cotati Ave, Cotati
(707) 795-1000
535 Summerfield Rd., Santa Rosa
(707) 539-6320

107. BREAD BOARD
Continental & Vegetarian
344 Coddingtown Center, Santa Rosa
(707) 545-6237
See Page 10

108. BUNNY'S COUNTRY KITCHEN
American
9900 Sonoma Hwy., Kenwood
(707) 833-4001 Res. advised

109. BURDON'S
Continental
15405 River Rd., Guerneville
(707) 869-2615
See Page 38

110. CAMP ROSE INN
Continental Cuisine
2140 S. Fitch Mtn. Rd, Healdsburg
(707) 433-4557

111. THE CAPRI
Continental & Italian
101 E. Napa, Sonoma
(707) 996-3866 Res Necessary
See Page 76

112. CASA de JOANNA
Mexican & Continental
17500 Orchard Ave., Guerneville
(707) 869-3756
See Page 37

113. CASA di GIORGIO'S
Family Style Italian
108 Petaluma Blvd. N., Petaluma
(707) 778-0220

114. CATELLI'S THE REX
Italian
Old Redwood Hwy., Geyserville
(707) 857-9904 Res. advised
See Page 24

115. CATTLEMEN'S RESTAURANT
Steak & Lobster
2400 Midway Dr., Santa Rosa
(707) 546-1446, Res. advised
See Page 12

116. CATTLEMEN'S RESTAURANT
Steak & Lobster
5012 Petaluma Blvd. N., Petaluma
(707) 763-4114 Res. advised
See Page 12

117. CAZANOMA LODGE
German
1000 Kidd Creek Rd., Cazadero
(707) 632-5255
See Page 43

118. CHANSLOR RANCH
Gourmet Dinners
2 miles north of Bodega Bay on Hwy 1
(707) 875-3386 Strictly Reservations

119. CHEZ PEYO
Country French
2295 Gravenstein Hwy. S., Sebastopol
(707) 823-1262
See Page 35

120. CHEZ RENE
(FORMERLY MARK WEST LODGE)
French Cuisine
727 Mendocino Ave., Santa Rosa
(707) 542-1890
See Page 29

121. COURTHOUSE CAFE
Continental Cuisine
535 4th Street, Santa Rosa
(707) 523-1171

122. CRICKLEWOOD
American
4618 Old Redwood Hwy., Santa Rosa
(707) 527-7768
See Page 28

123. D'S AIRPORT INN
Continental Cuisine
Sonoma County Airport, Santa Rosa
(707) 538-3689

124. DEPOT HOTEL
Continental
241 1st St. W., Sonoma
(707) 938-2980 Res. advised
See Page 75

125. DE SCHMIRE
French Cuisine
304 Bodgea Ave., Petaluma
(707) 762-4722 Res. advised

126. DINUCCI'S
Italian
Hwy. 1, Valley Ford
(707) 876-3260
See Page 37

**127. EASTSIDE GROCERY
& OVEN ROOM RESTAURANTS**
Continental & American
133 E. Napa St., Sonoma
(707) 938-4909

128. THE EGGERY GALLERY CAFE
Unique Gourmet Foods
4480 Bodega Ave., Petaluma
(707) 762-7228
See Page 65

129. ELIM GROVE
Continental
5400 Cazadero Hwy, Cazadero
(707) 632-5259

130. ENGLISH ROSE PUB
English Fare
2074 Armory DR., Santa Rosa
(707) 544-7673
See Page 10

131. FARRELL HOUSE
Seafood & Continental Cuisine
222 Weller, Petaluma
(707) 778-6600
See Page 60

132. FIFE'S
Continental Cuisine
16467 River Road, Guerneville
(707) 869-0656
See Page 40

133. FIORI'S ITALIAN RESTAURANT
Italian
3657 Main St., Occidental
(707) 823-8188

134. FIORI & GRACE PUB
Italian
2755 Mendocino Ave., Santa Rosa
(707) 527-7460

135. FLAMINGO RESORT HOTEL
Chinese
4th & Farmers Lane, Santa Rosa
(707) 545-8530
See Page 13

136. FRANCHESCO'S PLUM TREE
French Cuisine
1055 4th St., Santa Rosa
(707) 546-1700 Res. advised

137. GARDEN OF EATIN'
Breakfast & Continental Dinners
1780 Piner Road, Santa Rosa
(707) 528-9878
See Page 17

138. GINO'S OF SONOMA
Italian
420 1st St. E., Sonoma
(707) 996-4466
See Page 77

139. GIORGIO'S
Pizza & Italian
25 Grant Ave, Healdsburg
(707) 433-1106
See Page 28

140. GLEN ELLEN INN
Omelettes & Continental Specials
13670 Arnold Dr., Glen Ellen
(707) 938-3478

141. GOLDEN BEAR LODGE
American
1717 Adobe Canyon Rd., Kenwood
(707) 833-5201

142. GOLD COIN RESTAURANT
Mandorin Chinese & American
2400 Mendocino Ave., Santa Rosa
(707) 544-2622 Res. advised
See Page 16

143. GOLD COIN RESTAURANT
Mandarin Chinese & American
7311 College View Dr., Rohnert Park
(707) 795-7331 Res. advised
See Page 16

144. HEXAGON HOUSE
French & American
16881 Armstrong Woods Rd., Guerneville
(707) 869-3991
See Page 39

145. HIGHLAND HOUSE
Steaks
Sonoma Hwy. & Los Alamos Rd.,
Santa Rosa
(707) 539-0928

146. HOFFMAN HOUSE
Gourmet Deli & Dinners
Canyon Rd. off ramp - Hwy 101,
Geyserville
(707) 857-3818
See Page 27

147. HUNGRY WOLF
Gourmet Delicatessen
13648 Arnold Dr., Glen Ellen
(707) 938-9854

148. IL DESINARE
Catering
20540 Broadway, Sonoma
(707) 938-3760
See Page 78

149. JOE FROGGERS
Farm Fresh Dinners
527 4th Street, Santa Rosa
(707) 526-0539
See Page 6

150. LA CASA MEXICAN RESTAURANT
Mexican
127 E. Spain, Sonoma
(707) 996-3406

151. LA FONTANA
Italian
19 Old Court House Square,
Santa Rosa
(707) 545-4797 Res. advised
See Page 7

152. LA GARE
French Cuisine
208 Wilson, Santa Rosa
(707) 528-4355

153. LA PROVINCE
French Cuisine
521-525 College Ave., Santa Rosa
(707) 526-6233 Res. advised
See Page 9

154. LE CHALET
French Cuisine
16650 River Rd., Guerneville
(707) 869-9908 Res. advised
See Page 39

155. LE POMMIER
French
1015 Gravenstein Hwy South, Sebastopol
(707) 823-9865

156. LE POULAILLER
French Cuisine
122 Washington St., Petaluma
(707) 762-0792

157. L' OMELETTE
French
6685 Front Street, Forestville
(707) 887-9945

158. LONDON LODGE
Continental
13740 Arnold DR., Glen Ellen
(707) 996-6306 Res. advised

159. LOS ROBLES LODGE
Continental
925 Edwards Ave., Santa Rosa
(707) 545-6330

160. MAMA NINA'S
Northern Italian
Hwy 101, 1 mile north of Cloverdale
(707) 894-2609
See Page 23

161. MANDALA CAFE
Natural Foods
620 5th St., Santa Rosa
(707) 527-9797
See Page 9

162. MARIONI'S
Continental
8 West Spain, Sonoma
(707) 996-6866

163. MARSHALL HOUSE
Luncheions
835 2nd St., Santa Rosa
(707) 542-5305 Res. advised
See Page 8

164. MURPHY'S JENNER BY THE SEA
Seafood Continental
Coast Hwy 1, Jenner
(707) 865-2377
See Page 44

165. NORTHWOOD RESTAURANT
Seafood & Steaks
19400 Hwy 116, Monte Rio
(707) 865-2454
See Page 41

166. OMELETTE EXPRESS
Breakfast Omelettes & Specialties
112 Fourth St., Santa Rosa
(707) 525-1690

167. OLD CHICAGO PIZZA
Pizza & Italian Dishes
41 Petalum Blvd. N., Petaluma
(707) 763-3897
See Page 64

168. OLD MEXICO
Mexican & American
4501 Montgomery Dr., Santa Rosa
(707) 539-2599
1484 Petaluma Blvd. N., Petaluma
(707) 762-9690 Res. for 6 or more

170. PETALUMA CAFE
American
23 Petaluma Blvd., Petaluma
(707) 763-9839
See Page 64

171. RIVER'S END RESORT
German & Gourmet Entrees
Hwy. 1, Jenner
(707) 865-2484
See Page 45

172. ROSIE'S CANTINA
Mexican
610 3rd St., Santa Rosa
(707) 523-2110
See Page 6
173. ROSIE'S CANTINA
Mexican
570 Cotati Ave., Cotati
(707) 795-9211
See Page 66

174. RUSSIAN RIVER VINEYARDS
Continental
5700 Gravenstein Hwy. N.,
Forestville
(707) 887-1562 Res. advised

175. SEA RANCH LODGE
Continental & Seafood
Sea Walk Dr., Sea Ranch
(707) 785-2371 Res. advised
See Page 47

176. 610 MAIN
Crepes & Gourmet Specialties
610 Petaluma Blvd., Petaluma
(707) 762-6625 Res. advised
See Page 67

177. SONOMA CHEESE FACTORY
Cheese & Gourmet Foods
2 W. Spain St., Sonoma
(707) 996-2300
See Page 79

178. SOURDOUGH REBO'S
Klondike Seafood
24 4th St., Santa Rosa
(707) 526-6400 Res. advised
See Page 14

179. SOUVERAIN RESTAURANT
Continental
400 Souverain Rd., Geyserville
(707) 857-3789 Res. advised
See Page 210

180. 3rd STREET STATION
German & American
200 Wilson at corner of 3rd Street,
Santa Rosa
(707) 526-4089
See Page 14

181. STEAMER GOLD LANDING
American
No. 1 Water St., Petaluma
(707) 763-6876
See Page 61

182. SWISS HOTEL
Italian, American, & Chinese
18 W. Spain St., Sonoma
(707) 938-9822 Res. advised

183. TACO ED'S
Mexican
8196 Bodega Ave., Sebastopol
(707) 823-9994

184. TAMAULIPECO
Mexican
309 A St., Healdsburg
(707) 433-5202 Res. advised
See Page 25

185. TIDES RESTAURANT
Fresh Seafood & American
Hwy 1, Bodega
(707) 875-3553

186. TIMBER COVE INN
Seafood Continental
3 miles north of Fort Ross
on Coast Hwy 1
(707) 847-3231
See Page 46

187. TOPAZ ROOM
American
96 Old Courthouse Sq., Santa Rosa
(707) 542-7753

188. UNION HOTEL
Italian
Main St., Occidental
(707) 874-3662

189. VAST'S GARDEN DINING
American Farm
Hwy 116, between Cotati & Sebastopol
(707) 795-4747
See Page 35

190. THE VILLA
Italian & Seafood
3901 Montgomery Dr., Santa Rosa
(707) 528-7755
See Page 11

191. VILLAGE INN
International Gourmet
20822 River Blvd., Monte Rio
(707) 865-1180 Res. advised
See Page 42

192. WASHOE HOUSE
American
Stony Point Rd. & Roblar Rd.,
Petaluma
(707) 795-4544
See Pages 62&63

193. WINE COUNTRY
Steaks, Poultry, & Seafood
106 Matheson St., Healdsburg
(707) 433-7203
See Page 26

NAPA COUNTY RESTAURANTS

200. THE ABBEY
American & French
3020 N. St., St Helena Hwy., St. Helena
(707) 963-2706 Res. advised
See Page 92

201. CALISTOGA INN
Continental & Italian
1250 Lincoln Ave., Calistoga
(707) 942-4101
See Page 90

202. CARRIAGE HOUSE
Modified Continental
1775 Clay St., Napa
(707) 255-4744 Res. advised
See Page 100

203. CHUTNEY KITCHEN
American
Vintage 1870, Yountville
(707) 944-2788
See Page 98

204. THE DINER
American
6476 Washington St., Yountville
(707) 944-2626

205. DOMAINE CHANDON
French Cuisine
California Dr., Yountville
(707) 944-2467

206. EL FARO
Mexican
1353 Lincoln Ave., Calistoga
(707) 942-4400
See Page 91

207. FRENCH LAUNDRY
French Cuisine
6640 Washington, Yountville
(707) 944-2380 Res. advised

208. GRAPE VINE
Italian
7331 St. Helena Hwy., Yountville
(707) 944-2225

209. HOOPER CREEK INN
American
6518 Washington St., Yountville
(707) 944-8826

210. LA BELLE HELENE
French
1345 Railroad Ave., St. Helena
(707) 963-9984 Res. advised
See Page 93

211. LA BOUCANE
French Cuisine
1778 Second St., Napa
(707) 253-1177

212. LA GAMELLE
French Cuisine
1010 Lincoln Ave., Napa
(707) 226-2633

213. MAGGIE GINS
Chinese
1234 Main St., St. Helena
(707) 963-9764
See Page 95

214. MAGNOLIA HOTEL
Continental
6529 Yount St., Yountville
(707) 944-2056

215. MAMA NINA'S
Northern Italian
6772 Washington , Yountville
(707) 944-2112 Res advised
See Page 99

216. MIRAMONTE
French Cuisine
1327 Railroad Ave.. St. Helena
(707) 963-3970 Res. advised
See Page 94

217. MOUNT VIEW HOTEL
Classic French
1457 Lincoln Ave, Calistoga
(707) 942-6877
See Page 89

218. OAKVILLE GROCERY CO.
Gourmet Groceries
7856 Saint Helena Hwy, Oakville
(707) 944-2011
See Page 95

219. OLIVE TREE INN
Continental
221 Silverado Trail, Napa
(707) 252-7660 Res. advised

220. OLIVER'S
Classic International
1700 Second St., Napa
(707) 252-4555 Res. advised
See Page 99

221. OPTIMUM FOODS
Natural Foods
132 Soscol Ave., Napa
(707) 224-1514

222. THE PENGUINS
Seafood - Continental
1533 Trancas, Napa
(707) 252-4343

223. RAINBOW BRIDGE
Continental
1335 Pueblo Ave., Napa
(707) 255-2311

224. RUTHERFORD SQUARE
Homemade Specialties
Rutherford Square, Rutherford
(707) 963-2617 Res. advised
See Page 96

**225. SILVERADO RESTAURANT,
TAVERN & WINE SHOP**
Steaks, Seafood, & Daily Specials
1374 Lincoln Ave., Calistoga
(707) 942-6725
See Page 88

**226. WASHINGTON STREET
RESTAURANT & BAR**
Continental Cuisine
6539 Washington St.,   Yountville
(707) 944-2406

**227. YOUNTVILLE RESTAURANT
and COFFEE SALOON**
American
6480 Washington, Yountville
(707) 944-2761 Res. advised
See Page 97

MENDOCINO COUNTY RESTAURANTS

300. BEAR WALLOW RESORT
American
2 miles east of Boonville
on Mtn. View Road
(707) 895-3295 Res. advised
See Page 147

301. MA'S WILDFLOWER INN
Gourmet & Italian Cooking
316 South Main St., Willits
(707) 459-6362
See Page 117

302. BROILER STEAK HOUSE
American
8400 Uva Way, Redwood Valley
(707) 485-7301

303. CAFE BEAUJOLAIS
French
44835 Ukiah St., Mendocino
(707) 937-5614 Res. advised
See Page 107

304. CARINE'S FISH GROTTO
Seafood & Italian
Noyo Harbor, Fort Bragg
(707) 964-2429

305. COACH HOUSE
Continental
131 East Mill St., Ukiah
(707) 462-6342
See Page 116

306. EGGHEAD OMELETTE
Omelets (Breakfast & Lunch)
326 N. Main St., Fort Bragg
(707) 964-5005

307. ELK COVE INN
German & French
Hwy 1 South of Elk
(707) 877-3321

308. GREENWOOD PIER CAFE
Gourmet & Continental Cuisine
South Hwy 1, Elk
(707) 877-9997

309. GREGORY'S RESTAURANT
Continental & German
3000 N. Hwy 1, Albion
(707) 937-0272 Res. advised

310. GUALALA HOTEL
Breakfasts & Italian Dinners
S. Hwy 1, Gualala
(707) 884-3441

311. HOWLING WOLF CAFE
American & Natural Foods
on Hwy 101, 4 miles north of Leggett
(707) 925-6211
Famous Wild Animals

312. LAYTONVILLE INN
American
Downtown Laytonville
(707) 984-9974

313. LEDFORD HOUSE
Country Continental
7051 N. Hwy 1, Little River
(707) 937-0282 Res. necessary
See Page 106

314. THE LIDO
Italian - American
228 E. Perkins, Ukiah
(707) 462-2212   Res. advised
See Page 114

315. LITTLE RIVER CAFE
French Cuisine
7750 N. Hwy 1, Little River
(707) 937-0404 Res. advised

316. LITTLE RIVER INN
Seafood & Steaks
Little River
(707) 937-5942 Res. advised

317. MAD CREEK INN
Gourmet Home Cooking
14 miles north of Laytonville
(707) 984-6206 Res. advised
See Page 117

318. PALACE BAR, GRILL & HOTEL
Seafood & Steaks
272 N. State St., Ukiah
(707) 468-9291 Res. advised
See Page 115

319. PARADISE BAKERY CAFE
Continental Cuisine
647 N. Main, Fort Bragg
(707) 964-7746

320. THE RESTAURANT
Continental
418 Main St., Fort Bragg
(707) 964-9800 Res. advised

321. SCOTTY'S OLD MILL
Continental
9601 Hwy 101 N., Redwood Valley
(707) 485-0665
See Page 116

322. SEA GULL
American & Fresh Seafood
Corner Lansing & Ukiah Sts.,
Mendocino
(707) 937-5204 Res. advised
See Page 107

323. ST ORRES
Continental
2 miles north of Gualala
(707) 884-3303 Res advised

HUMBOLDT COUNTY RESTAURANTS

400. ANGELINA INN
Italian - American
Old Hwy 101 at Fernbridge,
Ferndale
(707) 725-2369 Res. advised

401. BENBOW INN
Continental
Off Hwy 101 south of Garberville
(707) 923-2124 Res advised
See Page 158

402. BENBOW VILLAGE GREEN
Continental
2650 Benbow Dr., Garberville
(707) 923-2411

403. BRASS RAIL
Steaks
Redwood Dr., Redway
(707) 923-3188 Res. advised

404. BRET HARTE'S
Gourmet Delicatessen
and Night Club
791 8th Street, Arcata
(707) 822-4747

405. CAFE ANTILLIES
Continental & West Indies
942 G. St., Arcata
(707) 822-0305
See Page 122

406. COLONIAL INN
American & Seafood
Patrick's Point Dr., 2 miles
north of Trinidad
(707) 677-3340
See Page 124

407. EATERY & GALLERY
American
300 Trinity Rd., Trinidad
(707) 677-3777

408. THE EMBERS
American
4485 Broadway, Eureka
(707) 442-9655

409. EUREKA SEAFOOD GROTTO
Seafood
6th & Broadway, Eureka
(707) 443-2075

410. HARTSOOK INN
Continental
8 miles south of Garberville, Piercy
(707) 247-3305 Res. advised
See Page 156

411. LAZIO'S
Steaks & Fresh Seafood
Foot of C St.. Eureka
(707) 442-2337
See Page 121

412. MAXWELL'S BISTRO
Continental
527 West Wabash Ave., Eureka
(707) 443-9221 Res. advised

413. MERRYMAN'S
American
Moonstone Beach, Trinidad
(707) 677-3111 Res. not accepted
See Page 123

414. MIRANDA MANOR INN
International Cuisine
Downtown Miranda
(707) 943-3559 Res. advised
See Page 119

415. NORTHTOWN PARK
American
752 18th St. Arcata
(707) 822-4619 Res. for 6 or more
See Page 121

416. O-H's TOWNE HOUSE
Steaks, Prime Rib, & Seafood
6th & Summer, Eureka
(707) 443-4652

417. OLD TOWN BAR & GRILL
Continental & Seafood
325 Second St., Eureka
(707) 445-2971

418. PARLATO'S
Fresh Seafood & American
320 Main St., Fortuna
(707) 725-9961 Res. advised
See Page 119

419. PETE'S BELLA VISTA INN
Continental Cuisine
3 miles north of Arcata at
1300 Central Ave., McKinleyville
(707) 839-3395

420. REDWOOD PALACE
American
Avenue of the Giants, Miranda
(707) 943-3174
See Page 118

421. REYES Y CASAS VIEJAS
Mexican
1436 2nd Street, Eureka
(707) 442-5072

422. RIVERWOOD INN
Continental
Downtown Phillipsville
(707) 943-9983 Res. advised

423. SAMOA COOKHOUSE
Family Style Dinners
Samoa
(707) 442-1659

424. SCOTIA INN
American
Scotia
(707) 764-5683 Res. advised

425. SHANGHAI LOW
Chinese
1835 4th St., Eureka
(707) 443-8191

426. SHELTER COVE GROTTO
Fresh Seafood & American
410 Redwood Dr., Redway
(707) 923-3262 Res. advised
See Page 118

427. TOMASO'S TOMATO PIES
Sicilian Style Pizza & Dinners
216 E. St., Eureka
(707) 445-0100 Res. advised
See Page 120

428. VICTORIAN VILLAGE INN
Continental
290 Francis St., Ferndale
(707) 786-9775

429. VOLPI'S
Italian - American
6269 Loma St., S. Hwy 101, Eureka
(707) 442-1376 Res. advised

430. WATERFRONT SANDWICH CO.
Luncheon & Dinner Specialties
102 F St., Eureka
(707) 445-2832
See Page 120

431. WEATHERBY'S
Seafood & American
1906 4th St.,Eureka
(707) 442-0683

432. WILLOW INN
American
1 mile east of Willow Creek on Hwy 299
(916) 629-3331 Res. on weekends

433. WOODROSE CAFE
International & Vegetarian
911 Redwood Dr., Garberville
(707) 923-3191 Res. advised

434. YOUNG'S
Chinese
2020 Main St., Fortuna
(707) 725-3767

435. YOUNGBERG'S
Italian & Seafood
791 8th St., Arcata
(707) 822-1712 Res. advised
See Page 122

DEL NORTE COUNTY RESTAURANTS

500. CRIVELLI'S
American, Seafood, & Italian
Hwy 169, Klamath
(707) 482-3713

**501. JIMMY'S CRESCENT
BEACH RESTAURANT**
Continental
1455 Hwy 101, Crescent City
(707) 464-6000 Res. advised
See Page 124

502. HARBOR VIEW GROTTO
Seafood & Steaks
Citizen's Dock Rd., Crescent City
(707) 464-3815

503. KNOTTICAL INN
Continental
on Hwy 101 overlooking the
Pacific 2 miles south of Oregon
(707) 487-4113

504. PATRICK'S CREEK LODGE
Continental Cuisine
26 miles N.E. of Crescent City on
Hwy 199 & 6½ miles N.E. of Gasquet
Call Crescent City operator & ask
for Toll Stn No. 5 to Patrick's Creek
See Page 161

505. REQUA INN
Bed & Breakfast Inn
British Fare
Requa
(707) 482-5231

506. SHIP ASHORE
American & Seafood
3 miles south of Oregon Border
near the Smith River
(707) 487-3141

MARIN COUNTY LODGING

1. ALTA MIRA HOTEL
Bulkley Avenue, Sausalito
(415) 332-1350

**2. BYRON RANDALL'S FAMOUS
TOMALES GUEST HOUSE**
25 Valley Street, Tomales
(707) 878-9992
See Page 134

3. CASA MADRONA HOTEL
156 Bulkley Avenue, Sausalito
(415) 332-0502
See Page 134

4. HOLLY TREE INN
3 Silver Hills Road, Point Reyes
(415) 663-1554
See Page 135

5. INVERNESS LODGE
Callendar Way & Argyle, Inverness
(415) 669-1034

6. PELICAN INN
10 Pacific Way, Muir Beach
(415) 383-6000
See Page 135

7. SAUSALITO HOTEL
16 El Portal, Sausalito
(415) 332-4155

SONOMA COUNTY LODGING

51. BELLE de JOUR
16276 Healdsburg Ave., Healdsburg
(707) 433-2724/7892

52. BLACKBERRY INN
3657 Church St., Occidental
(707) 874-3023 Res. Necessary
See Page 144

53. BODEGA BAY LODGE
Hwy 1, Bodega
(707) 875-3665 Res. advised
See Page 142

54. CHANSLOR RANCH
2 Miles N. of Bodega Bay on Hwy 1
(707) 875-3386 Strictly Res.

55. CAZANOMA LODGE
1000 Kidd Creek Road, Cazadero
(707) 632-5255
See Page 43

56. FERNGROVE
16650 River Road, Guerneville
(707) 869-9992
See Page 143

57. FIFE'S
16467 River Rd., Guerneville
(707) 869-0656
See Page 40

58. FLAMINGO HOTEL
4th & Farmers Lane, Santa Rosa
(707) 545-8530
See Page 13

59. HEXAGON HOUSE
16881 Armstrong Woods Road
Guerneville
(707) 869-3991 Res. Necessary
See Page 39

60. LOS ROBLES LODGE
925 Edwards Ave., Santa Rosa
(707) 545-6330

61. MOUNTAIN HOME RANCH
3400 Mtn. Home Ranch Rd., Calistoga
(707) 942-6616 Res. Necessary

62. NORTHWOOD LODGE
& GOLF COURSE
Hwy 116, ½ way between Monte
Rio and Guerneville
(707) 865-2126
See Page 41

63. RIDENHOUR RANCH HOUSE INN
12850 River Road, Guerneville
(707) 887-1033
See Page 141

64. RIVERWOOD RESORT
16180 Neely Road, Guerneville
(707) 869-9978
See Page 141

65. RIVERVIEW LODGE
20526 Hwy 116, Monte Rio
(707) 865-1664

66. SALT POINT LODGE
23255 Hwy 1, 17 miles
north of Jenner
(707) 847-3234
See Page 143

67. SEA RANCH
Sea Walk Dr., Sea Ranch
(707) 785-2371 Res. advised
See Page 47

68. SONOMA HOTEL
110 W. Spain St., Sonoma
(707) 996-2996 Res. advised
See Page 140

69. STILLWATER COVE RANCH
16 miles north of Jenner
Cottages, rooms, barn bunks
(707) 847-3227 Res. advised

70. TIMBER COVE INN
North Coast Hwy 1, Jenner
(707) 847-3233 Res. advised
See Page 43

71. VILLAGE INN
20822 River Blvd., Monte Rio
Dining: (707) 865-1180 Res advised
Lodging: (707) 865-2738 Res advised
See Page 42

72. WINEBIBBER'S INN
603 Monte Vista Ave., Healdsburg
(707) 433-3019
See Page 139

NAPA COUNTY LODGING

100. BURGUNDY HOUSE
6711 Washington, Yountville
(707) 944-2711 Res. Necessary
See Page 137

101. CALISTOGA INN
1250 Lincoln Ave., Calistoga
(707) 942-4101 Res. advised
See Page 90

102. CHALET BERNENSIS
225 St. Helena Hwy., St. Helena
(707) 963-4423 Res. advised
See Page 139

103. HARVEST INN
1 Main Street, Saint Helena
(707) 963-WINE
See Page 138

104. INK HOUSE
1575 St. Helena Hwy, Saint Helena
(707) 963-3890

105. LARKMEAD INN
1103 Larkmead Lane, Saint Helena
(707) 942-5360

106. MAGNOLIA HOTEL RESTAURANT
6529 Yount, Yountville
(707) 944-2056 Res. Necessary

107. MEADOWOOD LODGE
& GOLF COURSE
900 Meadowood Lane, Saint Helena
(707) 963-3646

108. MIRAMONTE
1327 Railroad Ave., Saint Helena
(707) 963-3970
See Page 94

109. MOUNT VIEW HOTEL
1457 Lincoln Ave, Calistoga
(707) 942-6877
See Page 89

110. NAPA VALLEY LODGE
Hwy 29 at Madison St., Yountville
(707) 944-2468 Res. advised
See Page 136

111. SILVERADO COUNTRY CLUB
& RESORT
1600 Atlas Peak Rd., Napa
(707) 255-2970 Res. advised
See Page 137

112. WEBBER PLACE
6610 Webber Street, Yountville
(707) 944-8384

113. WINE COUNTRY INN
1152 Lodi Lane, St. Helena
(707) 963-7077 Res. advised

MENDOCINO COUNTY LODGING

150. AME'S LODGE
42287 Little Lake Rd., Mendocino
(707) 937-0811 Res. advised

151. BEAR WALLOW RESORT
2 miles east of Booneville on Mtn View Rd.
(707) 895-3295 Res. required
See Page 147

152. BIG BEND LODGE
3 miles north of Cummings
(707) 984-6321
See Page 156

153. BIG RIVER LODGE
44850 Comptche-Ukiah Rd., Mendocino
(707) 937-5615

154. BLUE ROSE GUEST HOUSE
520 N. Main St., Fort Bragg
(707) 964-3373 Res. required
See Page 154

155. BOONEVILLE HOTEL
Anderson Valley Cuisine
(Home cooked meals using the
freshest Anderson Valley Produce)
14050 Hwy 128, Booneville
(707) 895-3478 Res. advised

156. BROOKTRAILS LODGE
Sherwood Rd., Willits
(707) 459-5311 Res. advised

157. CASA del NOYO
500 Casa Del Noyo Dr., Fort Bragg
(707) 964-9991

158. COBWEB INN
38921 N. Hwy 1, Westport
(707) 964-5588 Res. necessary
See Page 154

159. DEHAVEN VALLEY FARM
39247 N. Hwy 1, Westport
(707) 964-2931

160. ELK COVE INN
Hwy 1 just south of Elk
(country inn in Elk proper)
(707) 877-3321 res. required

161. FOOLS RUSH INN
N. Hwy 1, Little River
(707) 937-5339

162. GLENDEVEN
8221 N. Hwy 1, Little River
(707) 937-0083 Res. advised

163. GREENWOOD PIER
Hwy 1 in downtown Elk
(707) 877-9997

164. GREY WHALE INN
615 N. Main St., Fort Bragg
(707) 964-0640 Res. advised
See Page 152

165. HARBOR HOUSE
5600 S. Hwy 1, downtown Elk
(707) 877-3203 Res advised
See Page 148

166. HEADLANDS INN
44950 Albion St., Mendocino
(707) 937-4431

167. HERITAGE HOUSE
5200 N. Hwy 1, Little River
(707) 937-5885 Res. necessary

168. HILL HOUSE INN
10701 Palette Dr., Mendocino
(707) 937-0554 Res. advised
See Page 152

169. IRISH BEACH
Irish Beach, Manchester
(707) 882-2467 Res. necessary
See Page 155

170. JOSHUA GRINDLE
44800 Little Lake St., Mendocino
(707) 937-5942 Res. advised

171. LITTLE RIVER INN
Little River
(707) 937-5942 Res. necessary

172. MacCALLUM HOUSE
740 Albion St., Mendocino
(707) 937-0289 Res advised
See Page 150

173. 1021 MAIN STREET
GUEST HOUSE
1021 Main St., Mendocino
(707) 937-5150 Res. required
See Page 149

174. MENDOCINO HOTEL
45080 Main St., Mendocino
(707) 937-0511 Res. advised
See Page 151

175. MENDOCINO VILLAGE INN
Main St., Mendocino
(707) 937-0246 Res. advised
See Page 148

176. OLD MILANO HOTEL
1.84 miles north of Gualala on the left
(707) 884-3256 Res. advised
See Page 146

177. PINE BEACH INN
N. Hwy 1, Fort Bragg
(707) 964-5603

178. PALACE HOTEL,
BAR & GRILL
272 N. State St., Ukiah
(707) 468-9291 Res. advised
See Page 115

179. RIDGEWOOD PARK MOTEL
S. Redwood Hwy., Willits
(707) 459-5373

180. ST. ORRES
2 miles north of Gualala on right
(707) 884-3303

181. SEA GULL INN
Corner of Lansing & Ukiah, Mendocino
(707) 937-5204 Res. advised
See Page 107

182. S.S. SEAFOAM LODGE
Little River
(707) 937-5516 Res. advised

183. VICTORIAN FARM HOUSE
7001 N. Hwy 1, Little River
(707) 937-0697
See Page 147

184. VISTA MANOR
1100 N. Main St., Fort Bragg
(707) 964-4776
See Page 153

185. WHALE WATCH
35100 S. Hwy 1, Gualala
(707) 884-3667
See Page 146

HUMBOLDT COUNTY LODGING

200. BENBOW INN
Off Hwy 101 just south of Garberville
(707) 923-2124 Res. necessary
See Page 158

201. BISHOP PINE LODGE
900 Patrick Point Dr., Trinidad
(707) 677-3314 Res. advised
See Page 159

202. EUREKA INN
7th & F Streets, Eureka
(707) 442-6441 Res. advised
See Page 160

203. FORTY WINKS
537 Redwood Dr., Redway
(707) 923-2660 Res. advised

204. HARTSOOK INN
8 miles south of Garberville
at Piercy
(707) 247-3305 Res. necessary
See Page 156

205. HOLIDAY GARDENS
Alliance Ave. & Stewart Ave., Arcata
(707) 822-4651

206. MIRANDA GARDENS
Avenue of the Giants, Miranda
(707) 943-3011 Res for summer
See Page 159

207. RED LION MOTOR INN
1929 4th ST., Eureka
(707) 445-0844

208. SHERWOOD FOREST MOTEL
814 Redwood Dr., Garberville
(707) 923-2721 Res. advised
See Page 157
209. SINGING TREES
6 miles south of Garberville at Piercy
(707) 247-3434 Res. advised
See Page 157

DEL NORTE COUNTY LODGING

250. NORTHWOOD INN
655 Hwy 101 S., Crescent City
(707) 464-9771

251. PATRICK CREEK LODGE
26 miles N.E. of Crescent City on
Hwy 199 & 6½ miles N.E. of Gasquet
Call Crescent City Operator and ask
for Toll Stn. No. 5 to Patrick's Creek
See Page 161

252. REQUA INN
on the Klamath River at Requa
(707) 482-5231 Res. advised
(recently re-opened Bed & Breakfast
Inn with 16 rooms and a restaurant
serving English Fare)

253. SHIP ASHORE
Hwy 101 in Smith River
(707) 487-3141 Res. for summer

254. TREES OF MYSTERY
Klamath
(707) 482-3152 Open seasonal
Restaurant, Motel, Gift Shop, and Park
surrounded by Redwoods.

Continued from page 243

at the end of a private road make them ideal retreats. Camp 1 1980 rates are $2.50 per person per day, winter mimimum 60 people or $150 per day, summer minimum (May 15-Sept 15) is 120 people or $300 per day - maximum occupancy is 200 people. However, by prior arrangement smaller groups can be accommodated. Camp 1 also has a 1800 square foot recreation hall complete with dance floor, a first aid trailor and a cooks cabin" each with plumbing and electricity. Diesel generator electricity is provided to all of the community use buildings, but not to the cabins. Bring battery powered lights and also your own bedding for the link spring cot & mattress you will be sleeping on. For a brochure and reservation information write: Mendocino Woodlands, P.O. Box 267, Mendocino, Calif. 95460 or call (707) 937-5755.

Up the hill from the Mendocino Woodlands is the Old Mill Farm. The trail is clearly marked and is only a 15 to 20 minute hike. An alternative way is to drive in. Most everybody, except senior citizens and nursery school age groups are required to hike in, however.

At the turn of the century people used to travel all day by buckboard from the Old Mill Farm to reach the hardware store in Mendocino. By car it takes 40 minutes of slow driving on six miles of blacktop and on six miles of narrow gravel road that winds through a spectacular redwood forest. To receive instructions and make reservations regarding the Old Mill Farm write: Old Mill Farm, P.O.Box 463, Mendocino, Calif. 95460 (please enclose a self addressed stamped envelope for a quicker response). Reservations are a must.

The proprietors of the Old Mill Farm are Chuck Hinsch and Eva Palm. They believe that a good and full life can be lived in a primitive mountain society which encourages fun, creativity, cooperation and self sufficiency.

The Old Mill Farm is a wonderful opportunity for otherwise "city locked" children and adults to submerge themselves in rural farm skills. "Where else can a tree be pulled out of the forest by a team of Belgium draft horses and be milled into useable lumber right before your eyes," states Chuck. Eva adds, "the garden and animal products can be a final treat to an enjoyable day: eggs, milk, berries and honey combined in a six quart, hand cranked ice cream freezer provides a dessert few will forget." What makes the food we eat extra special is that not only

Continued to page 271

Sonoma County Wineries

1. ALEXANDER VALLEY VINEYARDS
8644 Hwy. 128, Healdsburg
(707) 433-6293
Tours by appt., Retail Sales
See Page 209

2. BUENA VISTA WINERY
18000 Old Winery Rd., Sonoma
(707) 938-8504
Tours, Tasting, Retail Sales
See Page 199

3. BANDIERA WINES
155 Cherry Creek Rd., Cloverdale
(707) 894-2352
Retail sales

4. DAVIS BYNUM WINERY
8075 Westside Rd., Healdsburg
(707) 433-5852
Tours by appt., Retail Sales
See Page 204

5. CAMBIASO WINERY & VINEYARDS
1141 Grant Ave., Healdsburg
(707) 433-5508
Tours by appt., Retail Sales

6. CHATEAU ST. JEAN
8555 Sonoma Hwy., Kenwood
(707) 833-4134
Tasting, Retail Sales
See Page 203

7. DRY CREEK VINEYARDS
Dry Creek & Lambert Bridge Rds.,
Healdsburg
(707) 433-1000
Tours, Tasting, Retail Sales
See Page 205

8. FOPPIANO VINEYARDS
12781 Old Redwood Hwy., Healdsburg
(707) 433-1937
Tours by appt., Tasting, Retail Sales
See Page 206

9. GEYSER PEAK WINERY
Corner Canyon Rd. & U.S. 101
Geyserville
(707) 433-6585
Tours by appt., Tasting, Retail Sales
See Page 208

10. GRAND CRU VINEYARDS
No. 1 Vintage Lane, Glen Ellen
(707) 996-8100
Tours, Tasting, Retail Sales

11. GUNDLACH-BUNDSCHU WINERY
3775 Thornsberry Rd., Sonoma
(707) 938-5277
Tours, Tasting, Retail Sales
Appointments advisable

12. HACIENDA WINE CELLARS
1000 Vineyard Lane, Sonoma
(707) 938-3220
Tours, Tasting, Retail Sales
See Page 201

13. HANZELL VINEYARDS
18596 Lomita Ave., Sonoma
(707) 996-3860
Tours, Retail Sales

14. ITALIAN SWISS COLONY
Hwy. 101, Asti
(707) 894-2541
Tours, Tasting

15. HOP KILN WINERY
6060 Westside Rd., Healdsburg
(707) 433-6491
Tours by appt., Tasting, Retail Sales
See Page 204

16. JOHNSON'S ALEXANDER VALLEY
WINES
8333 Hwy. 128, Healdsburg
(707) 433-2319
Tours, Tasting, Retail Sales
See Page 205

17. KENWOOD VINEYARDS
9592 Sonoma Hwy., Kenwood
(707) 833-5891
Tasting, Retail Sales
See Page 202

18. F. KORBEL & BROS.
13250 River Rd., Guerneville
(707) 887-2294
Tours, Tasting, Retail Sales
See Page 198

19. LANDMARK VINEYARDS
9150 Los Amigos Rd., Windsor
(707) 838-9466
Tours, Tasting, Retail Sales
See Page 198

20. MARTINI & PRATI WINES, INC
2191 Laguna Rd., Santa Rosa
(707) 823-2404
Tasting, Retail Sales

21. MAZZONI WINERY
23645 Redwood Hwy. N., Geyserville
(707) 857-3691
Retail Sales

22. MILL CREEK VINEYARDS
1401 Westside Rd., Healdsburg
(707) 433-5098
Tours by appt., Retail Sales

23. NERVO WINERY
19585 Redwood Hwy. S., Geyserville
(707) 857-3417
Tasting, Retail Sales

24. PASTORI WINERY
23189 Geyserville Ave., Cloverdale
(707) 857-3418
Tours, Tasting, Retail Sales
See Page 209

25. J. PEDRONCELLI WINERY
1220 Canyon Rd., Geyserville
(707) 857-3619
Tasting, Retail Sales
See Page 211

26. RAFANELLI WINERY
4685 W. Dry Creek Rd., Healdsburg
(707) 433-1385
Retail Sales by appt.

27. REGE WINERY
26700 Dutcher Creek Rd., Cloverdale
(707) 894-2953
Tasting, Retail Sales

28. RUSSIAN RIVER VINEYARDS
5700 Gravenstein Hwy. N.,
Forestville
Tours, Tasting, Retail Sales
(707) 887-2956

29. SAUSAL WINERY
7370 Hwy. 128, Healdsburg
(707) 433-2285
Tasting, Retail Sales by appt.

30. SEBASTIANI VINEYARDS
389 4th St. E., Sonoma
(707) 938-5532
Tours, Tasting, Retail Sales
See Page 200

31. SEGHESIO WINERY
14370 Grove St., Healdsburg
(707) 433-3579
Retail Sales

32. SIMI WINERY
16275 Healdsburg Ave., Healdsburg
(707) 433-6981
Tours, Tasting, Retail Sales

33. SONOMA VINEYARDS
11455 Old Redwood Hwy., Windsor
(707) 433-6511
Tours, Tasting, Retail Sales

34. SOTOYOME WINERY
641 Limerick Lane, Healdsburg
(707) 433-2001
Tours, Retail Sales
Appointments advisable

36. SOUVERAIN OF ALEXANDER VALLEY
Independence Lane at Hwy. 101, Geyserville
(707) 857-3531
Tours, Tasting, Retail Sales
See Page 210

37. TRENTADUE
19170 Redwood Hwy., Geyserville
(707) 433-3104
Tasting, Retail Sales
See Page 207

38. VALLEY OF THE MOON
777 Madrone Rd., Glen Ellen
(707) 996-6941
Tasting, Retail Sales
See Page 202

39. VINA VISTA WINERY
24401 Old Redwood Hwy., Geyserville
(707) 875-3722
Tours

46. BEAULIEU VINEYARDS
1960 St. Helena Hwy., Rutherford
(707) 963-3671 or 963-2411
Tours Tasting, Retail Sales

47. BERINGER WINERY
2000 Main St., St. Helena
(707) 963-7115
Tours, Tasting, Retail Sales

48. BURGESS CELLARS
1108 Deer Park Rd., St. Helena
(707) 963-4766
Informal tours, Retail Sales

49. CARNEROS CREEK WINERY
1285 Dealy Lane, Napa
(707) 226-3279
Tours by appt.

50 CAYMUS VINEYARDS
8700 Conn Creek Rd., St. Helena
(707) 963-4204
Tasting
See Page 176

51. CHAPPELLET VINEYARDS
1581 Sage Canyon Rd., Rutherford
(707) 963-7136
Open by appt. only

52. CHATEAU MONTELENA
1429 Tubbs Lane, Calistoga
(707) 942-5105
Tours by appt.
See Page 185

53. CHRISTIAN BROTHERS WINERY
2555 N. Main St., St. Helena
(707) 963-2719
Tours, Tasting, Retail Sales
and
4411 Redwood Rd., Napa
(707) 226-5566
Tours, Tasting, Retail Sales
See Page 173

54. CLOS DU VAL
5330 Silverado Trail, Napa
(707) 252-6711
Tours by appt.
See Page 175

55. CUVAISON CELLARS
4560 Silverado Trail, Napa
(707) 942-6100
Tasting

56. DIAMOND CREEK VINEYARDS
1500 Diamond Mt. Rd., Calistoga
(707) 346-3644
Tours by appt.

57. FRANCISCAN VINEYARDS
1178 Galleron Rd., St. Helena
(707) 963-7111 or 963-7113
Tours, Tasting
See Page 178

58. FREEMARK ABBEY
3022 St. Helena Hwy., St. Helena
(707) 963-7105
Tours
See Page 181

59. HEITZ WINE CELLARS
500 Taplin Rd., St. Helena
(707) 963-3542
Tasting, Retail Sales

60. INGLENOOK VINEYARDS
St. Helena Hwy., Rute   Rutherford
(707) 963-7182 or 963-7184
Tours, Tasting, Retail Sales

61. HANS KORNELL CHAMPAGNE CELLARS
1091 Larkmead Lane, St. Helena
(707) 963-2334
Tours, Tasting, Retail Sales
See Page 183

62. CHARLES KRUG WINERY
St. Helena Hwy., St. Helena
(707) 963-2761
Tours, Tasting, Retail Sales
See Page 182

63. J. MATHEWS NAPA VALLEY WINERY
1711 Main St., Napa
(707) 224-3222
Tasting, Retail Sales

64. LOUIS MARTINI WINERY
St. Helena Hwy., St. Helena
(707) 963-2736
Tours, Tasting, Retail Sales
See Page 179

65. MAYACAMAS VINEYARDS
1155 Lokoya Rd., Napa
(707) 224-4030
Tours & Retail Sales by appt.

66. DOMAINE CHANDON
(MOET-HENNESSEY)
Winery & Restaurant
California Dr., Yountville
(707) 944-8844
Tours, Tasting, Retail Sales

67. ROBERT MONDAVI WINERY
7801 St. Helena Hwy., Oakville
(707) 963-7156
Tours, Tasting, Retail Sales
See Page 177

68. MT. VEEDER WINERY
1999 Mt. Veeder Rd., Napa
(707) 224-4039
Tours by appt.

69. NICHELINI VINEYARDS
Hwy. 128, St. Helena
(707) 963-3357
Informal tours, Tasting, Retail Sales
See Page 176

70. OAKVILLE VINEYARDS
7840 St. Helena Hwy., Oakville
(707) 944-2457
Tasting, Retail Sales by appt.

71. JOSEPH PHELPS VINEYARDS
200 Taplin Rd., St. Helena
(707) 963-2745
Tours by appt., Retail Sales

72. POPE VALLEY WINERY
6613 Pope Valley Rd., Pope Valley
(707) 965-2192
Tours, Tasting, Retail Sales
See Page 185

73. V. SATTUI WINERY
St. Helena Hwy. S., St. Helena
(707) 963-7774
Tasting, Retail Sales
See Page 180

74. SCHRAMSBERG VINEYARD
Schramsberg Rd., Calistoga
(707) 942-4558
Tours, Retail Sales by appt.

75. SPOTTSWOODE CELLARS
1245 Hudson Ave., St. Helena
(707) 963-7433
Open by appt. only

76. SPRING MOUNTAIN VINEYARDS
2805 Spring Mtn. Rd., St. Helena
(707) 963-4341
Open by appt. only
See Page 181

77. STAG'S LEAP WINE CELLARS
5766 Silverado Trail, Napa
(707) 255-4284
Open by appt. only

78. STAG'S LEAP WINERY
Stag's Leap Ranch, Napa
(707) 944-2792

79. STERLING VINEYARDS
1111 Dunaweal Lane, Calistoga
(707) 942-5151
Tours, Tasting, Retail Sales
See Page 184

80. STONEGATE
1183 Dunaweal Lane, Calistoga
(707) 942-6500
Tours by appt.

81. **SUTTER HOME WINERY**
277 St. Helena Hwy., St. Helena
(707) 963-3104
Tasting, Retail Sales

82. **TREFETHEN VINEYARDS**
1160 Oak Knoll Ave., Napa
(707) 255-4477
Tours & Retail Sales by appt.

83. **VEEDERCREST VINEYARDS**
2203 Mt. Veeder Rd., Napa
(707) 652-3103
Tours & Tasting by appt.

84. **VILLA MT. EDEN**
Mt Eden Ranch, Oakville
(707) 944-8431
Open by appt. only

85. **YVERDON VINEYARDS**
3787 Spring Mtn. Rd., St. Helena
(707) 963-4270
Tours by appt., Retail Sales

86. **ZD WINERY**
8383 Silverado Trail, Napa
(707) 963-5188
Tours and tastings by appoint.
See Page 174

MENDOCINO COUNTY WINERIES

100. CRESTA BLANCA WINERY
2399 N. State St., Ukiah
(707) 462-0565
Tours, tastings, retail sales

101. EDMEADES VINEYARDS
5500 Hwy 128, Philo
(707) 895-3232
Tours, tastings, retail sales
See Page 216

102. FETZER VINEYARDS
Hwy 101, Downtown Hopland
(707) 744-1737
Tasting & retail sales
See Page 215

103. HUSCH VINEYARDS
Hwy 128, Philo
(707) 895-3216
Tours & tasting by appointment

104. McDOWELL VALLEY
3811 Hwy 175, Hopland
(707) 744-1774
Tours by appointment only

105. MILANO WINERY
14594 S. Hwy 101, Hopland
(707) 744-1396
Tasting, retail sales, tours by appoint.
See Page 215

106. NAVARRO WINERY
5751 Hwy 128
(between Philo & Navarro)
(707) 895-3686
Tours, tasting, retail sales
See Page 216

107. PARDUCCI WINE CELLARS
501 Parducci Rd., Ukiah
(707) 462-3828
Tours, tasting, retail sales
See Page 217

108. PARSON'S CREEK
3001 South State St., Ukiah
(707) 462-8900
Tours & tasting by appointment

109. TYLAND VINEYARDS
220 McNab Ranch Rd., Ukiah
(707) 462-1810
Tours & tasting by appointment

110. WEIBEL CHAMPAGNE CELLARS
7051 N. State St., Ukiah
(707) 485-0321
Tasting & retail sales

NORTH OF SAN FRANCISCO MAPS

COUNTY:

266.	Del Norte
264. & 266.	Humboldt
261.	Marin
262. & 264.	Mendocino
265.	Napa
262. & 263.	Sonoma

REGION:

264.	Mendocino & Little River
262.	Russian River Resort Area
262.	Ukiah & Redwood Valley

CITY:

266.	Arcata
267.	Eureka
264.	Fort Bragg
265.	Napa
263.	Petaluma
267.	Saint Helena
263.	Santa Rosa
265.	Sonoma
267.	Yountville

NOTE: An enlargement of the Avenue of the Giants in
Humboldt County is on page 129.

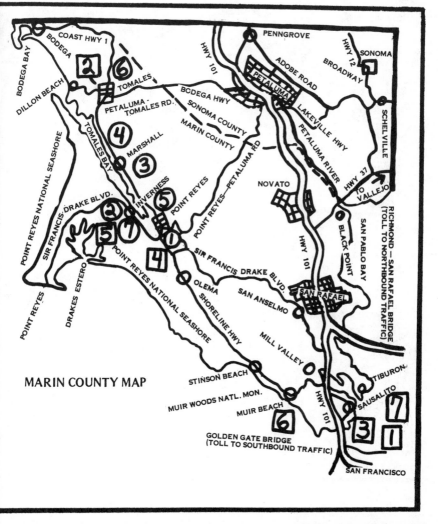

MARIN COUNTY MAP

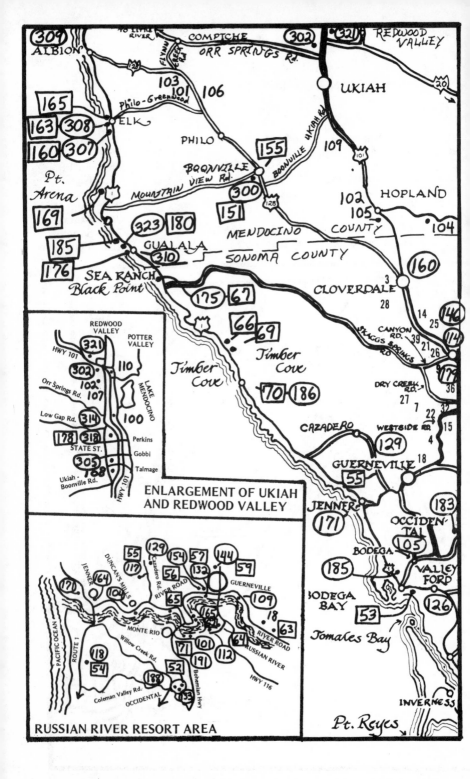

TO HEALDSBURG
INDUSTRIAL DR.
OLD RD. HIGHWAY
PINER RD.
(134)
(142)
TO CALISTOGA
CALISTOGA RD.
(137) BI-CENTENNIAL OVERPASS
FRANKLIN AVE.
(58)
(103)
HWY. 12 E TO SONOMA
STEELE LN.
(135)
(107)
GUERNEVILLE RD.
(130)
MENDOCINO AVE.
(145)
(60) (159)
(120)
(153)
(136)
(190)
MONTGOMERY DR.
(168)
(106)
(115)
COLLEGE AVE.
SONOMA AVE.
OLD TOWN SANTA ROSA
US HWY. 101
5th
(161)
(152) (166)
4th
COURTHOUSE SQUARE
(187) (163)
TO SEBASTOPOL
4th
(151)
3rd
(149) (121)
HWY. 12 W
(178)
(80)
TO PETALUMA
SANTA ROSA AVE.
PETALUMA HILL RD.

Inns, Restaurants & Winery

SANTA ROSA
California

(51) TO COBB
GEYSERVILLE
23 37 30 16
33
(128)
(84)(72)
HEALDSBURG
(175)
(139) 5 35
19
(110)
(122)
CALISTOGA
TO CLEAR LAKE
(116)
RIVER ROAD
(29)
(123)
SANTA ROSA (SEE INSET)
(161)
PETALUMA BLVD. N.
HIGHWAY 101
PETALUMA CITY MAP
FOREST-VILLE
(101)
(5)(20)
(12)
(176)
PETALUMA RIVER
WASHINGTON
HIGHWAY 101
(17)
SEBAS-TOPOL
(116)
(125)
KENTUCKY ST.
WELLER
(131)
(155) (173)
GLEN ELLEN
(156)
(119)
(189)(100)
BODEGA AVE.
YACHT HARBOR
DRAW BRIDGE
COTATI
(192) (143)
(12)
(113)
PETALUMA BLVD. S.
(28)
(116)
WESTERN AVE.
(181)
D STREET (BECOMES PETALUMA ROAD IN MARIN COUNTY)
PETALUMA
(116)
SONOMA
(67)
(170)
B STREET
TO NOVATO
VALLEJO
(121)
MARSHALL
PT. REYES STA.
SIR FRANCIS DRAKE DR. TO MARIN
SOUTH

FOR INFORMATION ON KENWOOD,
NAPA, SONOMA, ST. HELENA, YOUNT-
VILLE, GLEN ELLEN & CALISTOGA,
SEE INSET MAP PAGE

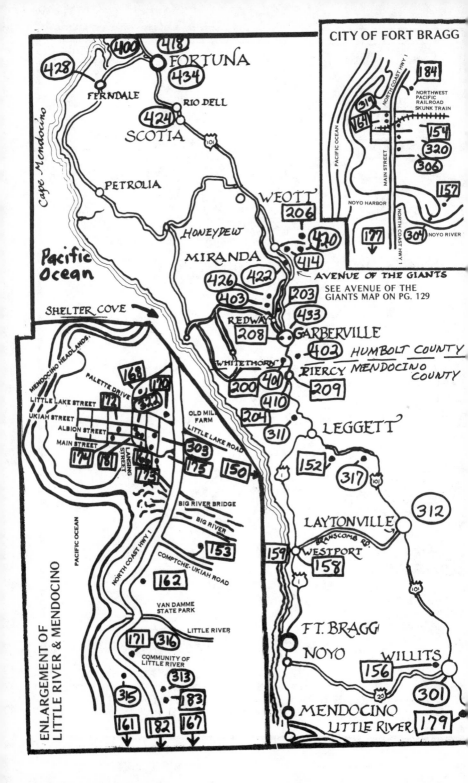

CITY OF FORT BRAGG

NORTHWEST PACIFIC RAILROAD SKUNK TRAIN

184
154
320
306
157
304
177
319
161

North Coast Hwy 1
Main Street
Noyo Harbor
Noyo River
Pacific Ocean
North Coast Hwy 1

FORTUNA
400 418 434
428
FERNDALE
RIO DELL
424
SCOTIA
PETROLIA
Cape Mendocino
Pacific Ocean
101

WEOTT
206
HONEYDEW
470
414
MIRANDA
426 422
403
203
SHELTER COVE
AVENUE OF THE GIANTS

SEE AVENUE OF THE GIANTS MAP ON PG. 129

433
REDWAY
208
GARBERVILLE
403 HUMBOLT COUNTY
WHITETHORN
PIERCY MENDOCINO COUNTY
200 401
209
410
204
311
LEGGETT
152
317
101
312
LAYTONVILLE
159 BRANSCOMB RD.
WESTPORT
158
101
20
FT. BRAGG
NOYO
156
WILLITS
301
MENDOCINO
LITTLE RIVER 179

ENLARGEMENT OF LITTLE RIVER & MENDOCINO

MENDOCINO HEADLANDS
PALETTE DRIVE
168
170
LITTLE LAKE STREET
171 322
UKIAH STREET
OLD MILL FARM
ALBION STREET
LITTLE LAKE ROAD
MAIN STREET
LANSING STREET
174 181
175
303
175 150
BIG RIVER BRIDGE
BIG RIVER
153
PACIFIC OCEAN
NORTH COAST HWY 1
COMPTCHE-UKIAH ROAD
162
VAN DAMME STATE PARK
LITTLE RIVER
171 316
COMMUNITY OF LITTLE RIVER
313
315
183
161 182 167

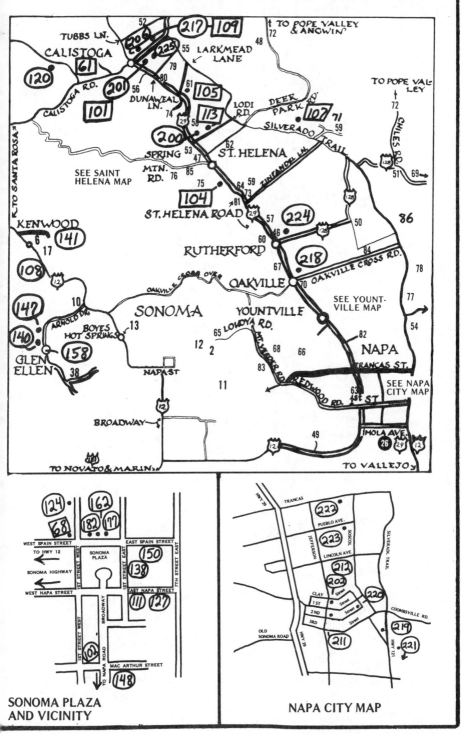

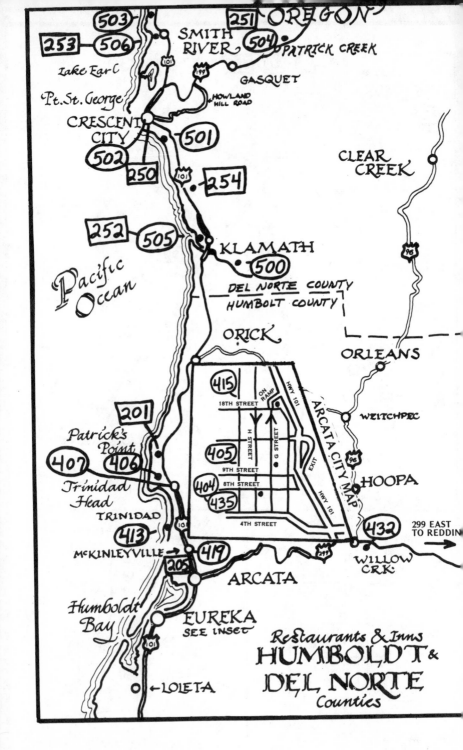

503

253 506

251 OREGON

SMITH RIVER

504 PATRICK CREEK

Lake Earl

GASQUET

Pt. St. George

HOWLAND HILL ROAD

CRESCENT CITY

501

502

250

101

254

252 505

Pacific Ocean

KLAMATH

500

DEL NORTE COUNTY

HUMBOLT COUNTY

CLEAR CREEK

96

ORICK

ORLEANS

415

18TH STREET

ON RAMP

HWY 101

WEITCHPEC

201

H STREET

G STREET

ARCATA CITY MAP

96

Patrick's Point

405

407 406

9TH STREET

EXIT

HOOPA

Trinidad Head

404

8TH STREET

435

TRINIDAD

101

4TH STREET

HWY 101

413

432

299 EAST TO REDDIN

McKINLEYVILLE

419

299

WILLOW CRK.

205

ARCATA

Humboldt Bay

101

EUREKA

SEE INSET

Restaurants & Inns

HUMBOLDT & DEL NORTE Counties

LOLETA

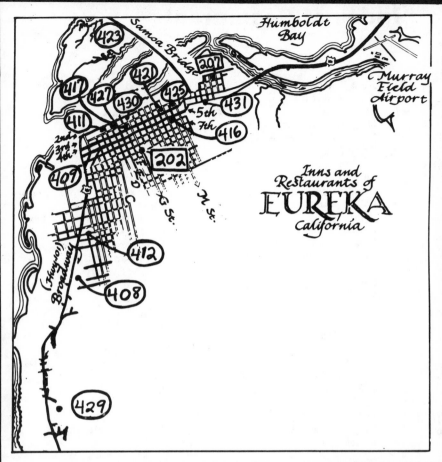

Inns and Restaurants of
EUREKA
California

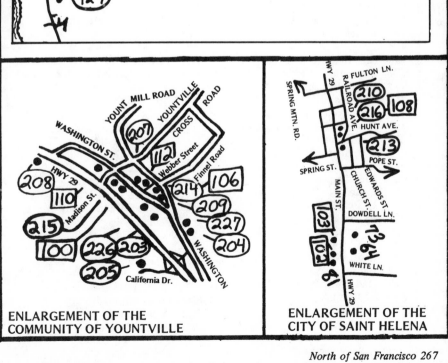

**ENLARGEMENT OF THE
COMMUNITY OF YOUNTVILLE**

**ENLARGEMENT OF THE
CITY OF SAINT HELENA**

Index of Restaurants

Index of Inns

Index of Wineries

FIVE YEAR ANNIVERSARY EDITION: 1975 - 1980
THE NORTH OF SAN FRANCISCO STORY

The following are contributors. . . . . .

Roy Thompson, John Boskovich Jr., Phyllis Boskovich, John Boskovich Sr., Joan Goode, Larry Gibson, Laurie Ehlers, Victoria Henry Hufford, Linda Pederson, Tom Byrne, Jim Dowlan, Harvey Hanson, Betty Niece, Ed Langhart, Rosalie Phillippi, Phil Bray, Dennis Finn, Greg Gessaman, Joe Hix, Gary Pihl, Marilee Pihl, Ed Manion, Maureen Manion, Jack Mason, Mary Littlefield, Laura Serbins, Don Silverek, Rick Cassina, Bruce Delaplaine, Brian Elder, Janon, Diana Towery, Marilyn Anderson, Barbara Dorr Mullen, Harold Erickson, Debbie Erb, Kathy Buller, Kathy Ely, Mark Ricci, Robert Morra, Rob Diegnan, Mike Gray, Harry Lapham, John Schubert, Joe Wherry, Jim Alexander, Russ Kingman, Winnie Kingman, Betty Dopson, Mike Topolos, Steve Serafini, Becky Sheppard, Laurel Shoemaker, Diane Brown, Mary Ann Gilderbloom, Larry Bernheim & Kath Samatha Nelson, John Wieland, Toby Smith, Joe Truzalino, Richard Paryz, Linda Buttons, Olaf Palm, Greg Graziano, Bob Keenan, John Reiley, Earl Thollander, Sebastian Titus, Doreen Dornbush, Andy Genzoli, Hobart Brown, Peter Palmquest, Lynwood Carranco, Ray Raphael, Ron Botier, Terry Dolan, Ste Doty, Hank Garvey, Jan Haraszthy, Jacqueline Lang, Sandi Passalacqua, Barry Squires, Francie Bannister, Art Rogers, Josh Murphy, William A. Porter, Edmond Andre Guiral. Hal Ogle,Walt Rinder, Hal Kramer, Ruth Kramer, Timberline & Sta

Hopefully someday, someone not yet born, a century from now will pull this book from a dusty shelf and begin to read. As these pages are turned the collective spirit of these creative souls will begin to move through you. Our voices, now silent, will once again speak. Whoever you are, I hope you can still see the sunshine, your cupboards are full, and a smile comes to your face.

Photo by Rebecca Sheppard

Robert W. Matson, the author, lives in a secluded retreat in Northern California. He has given up the superficial luxuries of "civilization" and gone back to the land. "It is here that you find the healthy God intended luxuries of life," he states. "Mother Nature pays most of my bills. There are no phones or power lines to my house, yet I live a more comfortable and elegant lifestyle than many. Best of all, I grow my own food and generate my own electricity. This is nothing new to the American Experience and anyone can do the same. The stumbling block is the social conditioning that prevents most from breaking away. Once you get back in touch with your biological heritage your thoughts crystalize. You soon experience a spiritual rebirth and look at land not as a commodity, but as a source for all life. You move yourself into a new world of common sense ethics. In the process you naturally put humanity before profit and thats called evolution."

If you'd like to get in touch with Robert you can write directly to him. Whether it is a personal message or a matter of business, just fill in the information requested on page 272 and mail to: North of San Francisco, *Box G, Santa Rosa, CA 95402.*

Continued from page 256

did we grow it from seed, but we know it is pure and because of this we receive a personal inner feeling of contentment after one of our delicious farm meals."

A farm never stops. Seasonal fresh produce comes daily from a garden utilizing Bio-Dynamic French Intensive Garden Methods. The well tended soil produces lettuce in two weeks, beets in three weeks and Jerusalem artichokes in less than a month. "It's such a shame," says Eva, "sometimes children don't even know the names of the vegetables!" They are more apt to remember the hay ride on the wagon pulled by the pair of draft horses or the fresh apple or pumpkin pie they helped make (delicious meals are only $1 to $5). But no one forgets the experiences they shared at the Old Mill Farm. People who choose the rigor of farm life show by personal example, concern for the lives and futures of young Americans. After a few hours here, people seem to instinctually recall that. "Our purpose is to help secure the future through the adults and children who pass through our gates by teaching them respect for all land and life." Indeed, the wealth of a nation can be judged by it's youth.

This Old Mill Farm has a special charm. The farm house with it's library on farming & rural skills, the precious seed bank proudly tucked in a wood & glass cabinet, and delicious aromas wafting from the country kitchen. A treasury of stained glass windows light up, one by one as they catch the sunbeams of the day. The animals gently foraging over the lush green landscape. The golden wheat waves in the late afternoon breeze. There is the crow of the rooster too early in the morning, and the hoot of the owls too late at night. Deer graze side by side with sheep and goat. Evenings the frogs perform a concert from lilly pads as thousands of plants grow in the nearby garden. And the wind whistles through the evergreens and all sleeps peacefully as the moon silently bathes this magical mountain top setting called the Old Mill Farm. This heritage was the first chapter Americans lived, we cannot allow it to be the last.

OLD MILL FARM
Delicious farm fresh meals $1 - $5
P.O. Box 463. Mendocino, Calif. 95460
(707) 937-4862 for information
Classes in rural farm skill - the fees vary.
Group overnight camping $1.50/person,
Tepee - $15, Cabin - $15. Hayrides $25
with a minimum of 20 people. Reservations
two weeks in advance. Work exchange is
considered (a great way to learn farm skills).
No pets, bring a flashlight, seasonal clothes
(raincoats to swimming suits), sleeping bag.

And if it is right, so shall it be for generations to come.

IS THERE SOMETHING WE LEFT OUT?

A new or favorite restaurant? _____

A new or favorite lodging facility? _____

A new or favorite winery? _____

A point of interest or historical significance? _____

Did you have a bad dining experience or stop-over somewhere North of San Francisco? If so, let me know. _____

_____

What is your name? _____

Address? _____ **Phone Number? (___)** _____

City? _____ **State?** _____ **Zip?** _____

To our readers: If your local bookstore does not carry *North of San Francisco,* write us at Box G, Santa Rosa, CA 95402 for information and and an order form or send $6.95 plus 6% sales tax and $1.00 for postage and handling to the same address. Make checks or money orders payable to Robert W. Matson. Bookstores and wholesale outlets get 40% off on a minimum order of 10 books. Guaranteed sales.

I would also be interested in:

☐ Reprints of the stories _____
   which ones (titles)   _____
   _____

☐ Art Prints and Post Cards _____
   which drawings (page nos.) _____
   _____

☐ Photographs _____
   which pictures _____
   (page nos. and location) _____

☐ I am also interested in purchasing a North of San Francisco Calendar, 13 beautiful pen and ink etchings (suitable for framing, depicting the seasons and events North of San Francisco.

North of San Francisco Newsletter. This year we will be publishing a newsletter called *North of San Francisco.* It will be our way of keeping you informed of the more timely Northern California events, such as the opening of new Inns, Restaurants, and Wineries, and of new wines releases, tours, and other news items of interest to the Northern California traveler or resident. If you are interested in receiving a free copy, fill in the blanks below and mail to Box G, Santa Rosa, CA 95402.

Name: _____
Address: _____
City/State/Zip: _____

DRIVING SAFETY AND EMERGENCY INFORMATION

[G]ASOLINE AVAILABILITY: Call any of the LODGING FACILITIES listed in the back [N]orth of San Francisco. They usually have current information available and are more [than] happy to assist the traveler. I also want to point out that during the last "gas pinch," [serv]ice stations in several locations like Garberville, were closing, not because they didn't [hav]e enough gas - THEY DIDN'T HAVE ENOUGH CUSTOMERS to warrant staying open. [S]don't be mislead by the greedy power barons. GET OUT THERE AND ENJOY [YO]URSELF!!

[WE]ATHER AND NEWS REPORTS: Tune into these Northern California Radio Stations. [Nap]a - KVON (AM - 1440), Petaluma - KTOB (AM - 1490), Santa Rosa - KSRO (AM - 1350), [K]ZST - (FM - 100), or KPLS - (AM - 1460), or KVRE (FM - 101.7 & AM 1460), Ukiah - [K]JKI (AM - 1400), Eureka - KFMI (FM - 96.3) or KINS (AM - 980), or KRED (AM - 1480), [&] Crescent City - KPOD (AM - 1310) or KVXJ (FM - 90.1).

[N]EVER TURN YOUR BACK ON THE OCEAN

[FO]R 24 HOUR ROAD CONDITION REPORTS CALL:

[CO]UNTY	DEPARTMENT	TELEPHONE NUMBER	
[S]AN FRANCISCO	CHP	*(415) 557-3755*	*General Recording*
[M]ARIN	Sheriff	*(415) 479-2311*	*San Rafael Emer.*
[S]ONOMA	CHP	*(707) 585-0326*	*General Recording*
	Sheriff	*(707) 527-2121*	*Santa Rosa Emer.*
[N]APA	CHP	*(707) 643-8421*	*General Recording*
[L]AKE	Sheriff	*(707) 263-5656*	*Lakeport Emer.*
	CHP	*(707) 263-5314*	*Dispatcher 24 hrs.*
[M]ENDOCINO	CHP	*(707) 937-0808*	*Dispatcher 24 hrs.*
	Sheriff	*(707) 462-2951*	*Ukiah Emer.*
[H]UMBOLDT	CHP	*(707) 822-7214*	*General Recording*
[D]EL NORTE	Sheriff & CHP	*(707) 464-4191*	*Dispatcher 24 hrs.*
[C]ALIFORNIA SIERRA'S		*(916) 445-7623*	*General Recording*
[O]REGON STATE PATROL		*(503) 776-6200*	*Medford Info.*

[C]ALIFORNIA HIGHWAY PATROL (C.H.P.) EMERGENCY NUMBER:
[D]ial 0 and ask the operator for ZEINTH 1-2000.
[T]his is also the best number to call to report a fire, accident of any kind,
[o]r emergency situation. The C.H.P. can be in radio contact with the approp-
[r]iate agency or emergency services within seconds of your call.

A WORD TO THE WISE: It is impossible for the Road Condition Reports to be kept [c]urrent of whats happening along every mile of highway in Northern California. There [a]re a few very common hazards which I will briefly mention. Along Route 1 (Coast Highway One), there are periodically high winds, fog (night time and early morning [u]ntil the sun burns it off), grazing sheep, deer, cattle, and goats. After the first rain [s]torm and during winter & spring the roads are slick and there are numerous rock and mud slides. Huge waves sweep the beaches clean. Heavy timber may fall across the road during high winds accompanied with rain or snow. Ice slicks are common during winter along shaded stretches of road that wind through valleys and canyons. Flooding is common along the Russian River, Eel, Klamath, Smith Rivers and their tributaries. Along the Redwood Highway (Hwy 101) in Mendocino, Humboldt, and Del Norte Counties be especially cautious of rock and mud slides during rain storms. Deer and elk can be a hazard too. You may find yourself debating road rights with a log or chip truck. If one gets on your tail and is impatient then just pull over and let em by. If you notice traffic build- ing up then pull over and let'em by. These precautions will make your vacation or drive through the Redwood Empire much safer and fulfilling. Happy Trails!

This edition of North of San Francisco is dedicated in memory of Phyllis O'Neil Boskovich who was born November 4, 1927 in Eureka and passed on Thanksgiving morning 1979 in Santa Rosa. Her dedication to the production of this book during the hard times will long be remembered by the artists, writers, and photographers she delt with. The above drawing was rendered by her son John. It depicts the rugged coastline near Trinidad, a spectacular region North of San Francisco which has inspired countless visitors.

Epilog

"The God who gave us life, gave us liberty
at the same time: the hand of force may
destroy but cannot disjoin them. This, Sire,
is our last, our determined resolution."

-Thomas Jefferson, 1774

The days begin early North of San Francisco. The same way they begin elsewhere in the country; the same way they began 200 years ago - men and women awake carrying dreams and hopes for the day in their hearts. Only the names and events have changed, but the people are still the same - they love, cry, hate, laugh and still search for what brings meaning into their daily lives.

We've always been a land of restless people - searching, creating, leading, teaching others, freedom loving and living a relatively free life. Some of us have paid for it the hard way; others have paid nothing. We've become too self serving in our age - seems like we're almost never happy with what we have; someone finds something else to be had and the rush is on . . .

"To see men without clothes to cover their
nakedness, without blankets to lie on, without
shoes, for want of which their marches might
be traced by the blood from their feet, and
almost as often without provisions . . . is proof
of the patience and obedience which in my
opinion can scarce be paralleled."

- George Washington, 1778

We live in an age of troubles. Doubt envelopes our highest institutions. Our material demands press upon the limits of our natural environment It seems that what we cherish the most we quite often destroy.

Eventually we'll come to terms with the land - or we'll starve. We'll come to terms with polution - or we'll choke. We'll come to terms with our neighbor - or we'll war. We'll come to terms with our loved one's - or we'll seperate. We'll come to terms with our children - or they'll suffer· in their innocence. And we'll come to terms with our God - or We'll cease to exist . . .

"These are the times that try men's souls.
The summer soldier and the sunshine patriot
will in this crisis, shriek from the service of
his country; but he that stands it now, deserves
the love and thanks of man and woman."

- Thomas Paine, 1776

America's experience has never been a tranquil one. Americans go on making the same mistakes; but God Bless us; we're usually one of the first ones there when someone else is in trouble. Of that we can be proud, that is, unless we were the cause.

It's all so simple - but why do we let history repeat itself over and over? We have failed to learn from the past mistakes of our leaders., our neighbors, our loved ones, and ourselves. When will we apply the lessons we have learned in our daily lives?

In 1776 the United States of America was officially born and the "Spirit of 76" was burning in the hearts of men and women everywhere. A driving gale had swept this country and the fires of liberty blazed. With it, our founding fathers asked for a blessing and sought the will of God.

In the early days Americans were closer to seeking Divine Guidance. The dreams they had for this land were realized for the blessings they received were many. The lack of reverence today has caused the Spirit of 76 to wane and the fires of liberty have become the coals of despair. In some of us the Spirit still dwells, and we see a spark leap occasionally from the cooling embers, but the collective Spirit of the United States our forefathers knew is all but gone. Like a neglected child our country waits for we the people, by the people, for the people to bring the Spirit back into our lives. And the Spirit is there simply for the asking.

> *"They knew they were pilgrims... So they committed themselves to the will of God and resolved to proceed... Thus out of small beginnings greater things have been produced."*
>
> William Bradford, 1620

As you travel north of San Francisco, be thankful for what we have been blessed with. And with the 200th birthday of our country behind us - ask yourself in what Spirit do I walk? And if it is right, so shall it be for generations to come.